Unfathomable Depths

UNFATHOMABLE DEPTHS

Drawing Wisdom for Today
from a Classical Zen Poem

Sekkei Harada

TRANSLATED BY
Daigaku Rummé
and Heiko Narrog

WISDOM PUBLICATIONS • BOSTON

Wisdom Publications
199 Elm Street
Somerville, MA 02144 USA
www.wisdompubs.org

Library of Congress Cataloging-in-Publication Data
Harada, Sekkei, 1926– author.
  Unfathomable depths : drawing wisdom for today from a classical Zen poem / Sekkei
Harada ; Translated by Daigaku Rummé and Heiko Narrog.
    pages cm
  Includes bibliographical references and index.
  ISBN 978-1-61429-083-4 (pbk. : alk. paper) — ISBN 1-61429-083-0 (pbk. : alk.
paper) — ISBN 978-1-61429-103-9 (ebook)
  1. Meditation—Zen Buddhism. 2. Tongan Changcha, active 10th century. Shi xuan
tan. I. Rummé, Daigaku, 1950– translator. II. Narrog, Heiko, translator. III. Tongan
Changcha, active 10th century. Shi xuan tan. English. IV. Title.
  BQ9288.H347 2014
  294.3'4435—dc23
                              2014012684

ISBN 978-1-61429-083-4   ebook ISBN 978-1-61429-103-9

18 17 16 15 14
5   4   3   2   1

Cover and interior design by Gopa&Ted2, Inc. Set in Sabon LT Pro 10.125/14.5.

Wisdom Publications' books are printed on acid-free paper and meet the guidelines
for permanence and durability of the Production Guidelines for Book Longevity of the
Council on Library Resources.

This book was produced with environmental mindfulness. We have elected to print this
title on 30% PCW recycled paper. As a result, we have saved the following resources:
10 trees, 5 million BTUs of energy, 890 lbs. of greenhouse gases, 4,826 gallons of water,
and 323 lbs. of solid waste. For more information, please visit our website, www.
wisdompubs.org.

MIX
Paper from
responsible sources
FSC® C011935
www.fsc.org
FSC

Printed in the United States of America.

Please visit www.fscus.org.

Contents

For the first time in English, this book presents—in tandem with a modern-day exposition offered by the Japanese Zen master Sekkei Harada—the *Ten Verses of Unfathomable Depth*, a tenth-century Chinese poem composed by the Zen master Tong'an Changcha. Readers seeking background information on the poem itself and its relationship to the modern Dharma talks will find these matters discussed in detail in the accompanying commentary. The remainder of this preface, however, will focus on Sekkei Harada's exposition and its significance for contemporary Zen practitioners worldwide.

Master Harada's Dharma talks (*teishō*) were offered during *sesshin* (periods of intensive sitting practice) between 1998 and 1999 at the temple Hosshinji, an official training monastery of the Sōtō school of Zen Buddhism in Obama, Japan. They were transcribed from tape recordings and edited by Keiko Kando for publication in Japanese in 2002. This English edition is translated from the Japanese book written by Daigaku Rummé and Heiko Narrog. Hongliang Gu of East China Normal University helped greatly when it came to translating the original Chinese poems as well as the Chinese source materials cited in the commentary.

Dharma talks, such as those from which this book is drawn, are usually based on a classic text and serve to illuminate matters of practice and teaching related to the present circumstances of the listeners. Although they involve preparation, they represent essentially spontaneous speech and are attuned to the audience present at the occasion. In this case, the addressees were chiefly monks and nuns practicing at the monastery where Master Harada is abbot. The lectures were conducted either in the Zen hall (*zendō*) with the audience in zazen position facing the wall and continuing their zazen during the talk or in the main hall of the monastery where sesshin participants had assembled with the express purpose of listening to the lecture. The Dharma talks were not followed by a public question-and-answer period, but listeners were instead encouraged to visit the master and to ask about the Dharma in one-on-one encounters (*dokusan*).

Despite the intimate setting of these talks, there has been a long tradition in Zen of recording and publicizing a master's lectures and sayings in order to make teachings available beyond the immediate setting of the monastery or temple and to preserve those teachings for posterity. Massive amounts of such records (Chin. *yulu*; Jap. *goroku*) have been produced in China and Japan, exceeding the textual output of any other denomination of Mahāyāna Buddhism. To date, only a tiny fraction of this output has been translated into English or into other Western languages.

Although on the one hand "transmission outside of the teaching" and "independence from anything written"[1] are important tenets of Zen, both the written and the spoken word have been amply used as tools for propagating the teaching and stimulating and guiding students. A metaphor frequently cited in connection with this phenomenon is the "finger pointing at the moon." Sekkei Harada himself puts the ambiguous relationship between verbal communication and Zen as follows: "All of the 84,000 Dharma teachings, as well as the words of the ancestors, are fingers pointing at the moon. If we do not act in accord with them, it will not be possible to see the moon. However, when you have seen the moon, then they are no longer necessary, and this is to have returned to your original, essential Self."[2]

Besides trying to convey timeless truth, every new record also appeals to, and thus reflects, the sensitivities of the time and the social and religious landscape within which it is situated. In Zen Buddhism, doctrines are essentially viewed as an expedient, or "skillful means," to be used flexibly and to be constantly transformed in ways that correspond to the needs of one's audience. Thus, every new record is also a window to the circumstances under which it originated. This metaphor also applies to the talks preserved in this book.

Sekkei Harada is one of the best-known and most widely acknowledged masters of contemporary Sōtō Zen in Japan. He was born in 1926 in Aichi prefecture and ordained in 1951 at Hosshinji in Obama, Fukui prefecture, by the abbot Harada Sessui. From 1953, he practiced with Master Inoue Gien at the temple Ryūsenji in Hamamatsu, and he received Dharma transmission (*inka shōmei*) in 1957. In 1974, he was selected as abbot of Hosshinji, one of twenty-five current training monasteries of the Sōtō sect. He became vice chairman of the Sōtō Sect Conference of Zen Teachers in 1996, acted as senior teacher (*seidō*) at the sect's main monastery Sōjiji from 1998 to 2002, and he then served as Director of the Sōtō sect in Europe from 2002 to 2004. Seven records of his talks have been published in Japanese. One of them, *The Essence of Zen*, has appeared in English, French, German, Indonesian, and Italian translation.

Hosshinji, Sekkei Harada's monastery, has a unique history. It was founded in the sixteenth century by the local feudal lord Takeda Moto-mitsu (1494–1551), a figure who used the temple as a residence from where he would conduct political affairs as a monk. Undergoing several cycles of decline and restoration, Hosshinji gained religious importance especially in the twentieth century under the guidance of its twenty-seventh abbot, Harada Sogaku (1871–1961). Harada Sogaku was one of the most influential and prolific Japanese Sōtō Zen masters of the twentieth century, a fact borne out by the vast number of prominent disciples to whom he laid claim and by the steady production of books based on his lectures. In addition to a revival of kōan practices in Sōtō Zen, he opened monastery doors to lay men and women alike, allowing foreigners as well as locals to participate in monastery training. Hosshinji is therefore renowned as a place where pioneering Westerners went to study Zen Buddhism throughout the post-war era.

When Sekkei Harada became the thirtieth abbot, he likewise encour-aged the attendance of laymen and laywomen, foreign and local alike—a phenomenon that remains even now an exception in training monaster-ies in Japan. Since the 1980s he has regularly traveled abroad to lead sesshin in India and throughout the West, particularly in Europe, but also in the U.S. He speaks with a critical voice on the current state of Zen Buddhism in Japan, particularly epitomized by the rote formal-ization of Dharma transmission. He expresses this concern about the current state of Zen Buddhism in Japan, combined with strong appeals to his audience to preserve what he understands to be genuine Dharma transmission, throughout his talks.

In addition to Harada Roshi's commentary, Heiko Narrog has created a series of tables that provide information about the people, texts, places, and quotations to which he refers throughout the book. We are fully aware that alternative translations of various terms and, in some cases, entire verses are possible. We have aimed, however, to be consistent and to make the most appropriate choices in light of the particular contexts of these poems and talks.

Finally, but most importantly, we wish to express our deep gratitude to Sekkei Harada Roshi and to the editor of the Japanese edition, Keiko Kando, who enabled us to work with these wonderful texts. We also wish to thank Josh Bartok for generously giving this book a place within Wisdom Publications and Andy Francis for his marvelous work editing this book.

Acknowledgments by Daigaku Rummé

I would like to thank Rev. Shinjō Yamagishi, Brian Morren, and Rev. Kōnin Cardenas for their help and friendship during the time that I worked on this translation. I would also like to thank Heiko Narrog for his diligent work in preparing the introductory material as well as his help in translating the text.

Acknowledgments by Heiko Narrog and Hongliang Gu

We would like to thank the Harvard-Yenching Institute that provided the opportunity for us to cooperate on these translations at Harvard during the 2010–2011 academic year. Heiko Narrog would further like to thank James Robson and Francis X. Clooney (both Harvard University) and James Robson's 2011 graduate seminar for their valuable support and suggestions to this project.

Unfathomable Depths

十玄談

原田雪溪 普説

PUBLISHER'S ACKNOWLEDGMENT

The publisher gratefully acknowledges the generous contribution of the Hershey Family Foundation toward the publication of this book.

Ten Verses of Unfathomable Depth

1. *The Mind Seal*

I ask you, "What does the Mind Seal look like?"
And "What sort of person dares to transmit it?"
Throughout the ages, it has remained firm and unshaken.
As soon as you call something the Mind Seal, it is already
  meaningless.
You must know that in essence all things originate from
  infinite emptiness.
You can compare it to a lotus flower in a red-hot kiln.
Don't say that a free and empty mind is the Way;
A free and empty mind is still separated from it by a great
  barrier.

2. *The Mind of the Enlightened Ones*

This mind is like emptiness, but it isn't empty.
How could the unfathomable function ever degenerate to
  being the result of achievement?
The bodhisattvas at the three stages of wisdom have still not
  clarified this.
And how can the higher ranks of bodhisattvas ever reach it?
The golden carp that has passed through the net remains
  trapped in the water.
But the stone horse still on the way leaves its sand cage
  suddenly.
Why have the meaning of Bodhidharma coming from the
  West explained in every detail?
Don't ask about the coming from the West, nor about
  the East.

3. *The Unfathomable Function*

You cannot rely on looking far ahead to the end of the universe.
And why would you tie yourself down to tainted worldliness?
Essentially, the miraculous body is not bound anywhere.
It is already throughout the whole body, so what other traces
     could there be?
A single efficacious word transcends the multitudes.
It is far beyond the Three Vehicles and does not require
     cultivation.
Shake off your hands and get away from the sages of all ages.
Then your path of return will resemble an ox in the midst
     of fire.

4. *The Transcendent within Dust and Dirt*

That which is impure is impure by itself; that which is pure is
     pure by itself.
Highest wisdom and delusion are likewise empty and even.
Who could say that nobody can appreciate Bianhe's jade?
I say that the jewel of the black dragon shines everywhere.
Only when the myriad dharmas disappear does the whole thing
     appear.
The Three Vehicles split up and assumed only provisional
     names.
Truly outstanding people have determination that knows no
     bounds.
Do not try to go where the buddhas have already gone.

5. *The Buddhist Teaching*

The Three Vehicles spoke golden words one after another.
But the buddhas of the past, present, and future only declared the
     same thing.
In the beginning, when they expounded the reality of skandhas
     and then complete emptiness, everyone grew attached to it.

Later, when they negated both reality and emptiness, everyone
discarded it again.
The complete treasury of sutras in the Dragon Palace is meant to
be prescriptions.
Even the Buddha's last teaching does not reach the
unfathomable.
If even one deluded thought arises in the world of true purity,
This already means spending eight thousand years in the world
of human beings.

6. *The Song of Returning Home*

Don't be distracted by the King of Emptiness when you are
still on the Way.
You must drive your staff forward, moving on until you
reach home.
If you travel for a long time like clouds and water, don't get
attached to it.
Even in the deep recesses of snowy mountains, don't forget
your mission.
Ah! I regretted that in past days my face was like jade.
And I lamented that at the time of my return my hair had
turned white.
Returning to my old home with dangling arms, there was
no one who recognized me.
Also, I had nothing to offer my parents.

7. *The Song of Not Returning Home*

Having the intention of going to the source, of returning
to the origin, is already a mistake.
Essentially, there is nowhere to settle down, no place to call
one's home.
The ancient path through the pines is covered with deep snow.
The long range of mountain peaks is furthermore blocked
by clouds.

When host and guest are tranquil and serene, everything is
  incongruous.
When lord and vassal are united, there is wrong in the midst of
  right.
How will you sing the song of returning home?
In bright moonlight, the dead tree is blooming in front of
  the hall.

8. *The Revolving Function*

It is still dangerous even inside the castle of nirvana.
Strangers come across each other without appointment.
People call someone who provisionally puts on a dirty robe
  "a buddha."
But if someone wears precious clothes, what should you
  call him?
In the middle of the night, the wooden man puts on shoes and
  leaves.
At dawn, the stone woman puts on a hat and goes home.
An ancient emerald pool, the moon in the empty sky.
Screening and filtering over and over to catch the moon, for
  the first time you will really know.

9. *Changing Ranks*

Growing hair and horns, you enter town,
Resembling a blue lotus flower blooming in the midst of fire.
All afflictions become like rain and dew in the vast sea.
All ignorance becomes like clouds and thunder on a mountain.
You completely blow out the furnace below the cauldron
  of hell,
Smashing to pieces a forest of swords and a mountain of
  daggers with a single shout.
Even golden chains cannot hold you back at the entrance.
Going into the realm of other beings, you transmigrate
  for a while.

10. *Before the Rank of the Absolute*

> In front of many dead trees and steep boulders, there are many wrong tracks heading off course.
> Those travelers who have reached this place all trip and stumble.
> A crane stands in the snow but does not have the same color.
> The bright moon and the flower of reeds do not really resemble each other.
> "I'm finished, I'm finished, I'm finished!" When you think so, you cannot really be finished.
> If you say, "This is it! This is the ultimate source!" you also need a good shout.
> From the bottom of your heart, you play a melody on the harp with no strings.
> How would it be possible to grasp the moonlight shining in the empty sky?

I. Introduction

HEIKO NARROG & HONGLIANG GU

The Text

THE *Ten Verses of Unfathomable Depth* were a highly regarded text in premodern China, Korea, and Japan, but they are not part of the small canon of poems still regularly employed in Zen teaching and practice in Japan and abroad. They are therefore unfamiliar to all but specialists. This introduction will, therefore, serve to provide basic information on the poem for those curious about its historical, religious, and philosophical background and its relationship to the following commentary given by the modern Japanese master Sekkei Harada.

The Ten Verses are themselves undated. But if the attribution of their authorship to Tong'an Changcha is correct, they must have been written in the first half of the tenth century, no later than about 960. They were first published posthumously in the twenty-ninth volume of the *Jingde Era Record of the Transmission of the Lamp*, which is a collection of texts foundational for the self-understanding and history of Chan/Zen Buddhism.

Although the earliest Chan records stem from the sixth century, the tradition of composing texts with the purpose of establishing Dharma transmission lineages and a history of schools only began in the ninth century with the text called *Transmission of the Treasure Grove*. Such records were not based on a concept of precise historiography as modern Western scholarship imagines it but were rather tools created to establish legitimacy and orthodoxy in an age where these became increasingly precious commodities. As Buddhism flourished, numerous Buddhist sects and groups within sects across China competed for authority, followers, and official recognition. The Dharma lineages of prominent Zen masters were often the subject of serious controversy. Consequently, the lineages claimed in the *Jingde Era Record* sometimes differ from those claimed in earlier records.

While the *Transmission of the Treasure Grove* was only temporarily canonized, and the *Collection from the Ancestors' Hall*, an important successor dated 952, failed to be included in the Chinese Buddhist canon, the *Jingde Era Record*, completed in 1004, was admitted to the imperial Buddhist canon in 1011 and has been included in the Buddhist canons ever since. Despite the canonization of numerous other transmission records compiled at the same time or later than it, the *Jingde Era Record* gained the status of authority and orthodoxy due to its historical position and has since been regarded as the most representative transmission record. The *Jingde Era Record* is the ultimate source known to us for many of the stories contained in more popular Chan records, such as the *Blue Cliff Record*. Yet the Record has never been fully translated into a modern language. The volume containing the Ten Verses has not been translated, to our knowledge, either.

Transmission records also served to collect extant material for the purpose of preserving them against being scattered and lost. Of course, these texts were also important tools for teaching. This is especially true of the twenty-ninth volume of the *Jingde Era Record*, which contains the Ten Verses. Unlike the preceding twenty-eight volumes, it is not concerned with establishing lineage history but contains a collection of writings that the editors found worthy of preservation as teachings for students of Chan.

We do not know the original form of the *Jingde Era Record*. In fact, the textual history of this work stands out for its complexity even among ancient Chinese Buddhist texts. The original edition is lost, and the earliest extant version of the text is an abridgment edited under a different title: *Precious Flowers of the Lamp Transmission*. At least twenty major editions of the work itself are known, but the content of many of these vary. According to Nishiguchi, the editions can be roughly divided into two lineages, the Sibu-Yanyou text lineage and the Dongchansi-Ming text lineage.[3] Although the Dongchansi-Ming text lineage claims the oldest known extant complete edition, being dated to 1080, the Sibu-Yanyou lineage may actually represent an older and more reliable stage of the text. However, even the older extant editions of the *Jingde Era Record* lack some material and seem considerably sloppy in their execution. This is especially true of the Ten Verses, which appear in the early Song edition in an abridged form of only eight verses and are represented in the *Precious Flowers of the Lamp Transmission* in only one verse. It is furthermore not clear whether the original edition of the *Jingde Era Record* even contained a faithful rendering of the poems. We know for example that the text of the *Jingde Era Record* as a whole was subject to censorship and interfered with for various purposes even prior to its first publication.[4] Therefore, we may never know the original version of either the poems or of the record as a whole, and it is difficult to even establish an earliest or most accurate version of the work.

The abridgment of the Ten Verses in the Song edition of the *Jingde Era Record* was criticized. The monk Mu'an Shanqing, editor of the Buddhist encyclopedia called *Chrestomathy from the Ancestors' Hall* (1108), may have played the decisive role in the eventual restoration of the full version. In the Chrestomathy he reports that he visited Tong'an temple, the monastery where Master Changcha had resided, where he retrieved from the memorial hall of the temple the previously ignored preface and a version of the text itself, to which he added comments. Shanqing's account has been widely accepted as truthful.[5] The preface retrieved, as well as the title of the poems, are generally ascribed to Fayan Wenyi, the Dharma lineage grandfather of Ying'an Daoyuan, the primary editor of the *Jingde Era Record*. The preface reads as follows:

These Verses of Unfathomable Depth are marvelous. They far surpass the three vehicles. No longer are they entangled in origination through circumstance, nor are they independent.

When put into practice they resemble the bright moon and illuminate the sky. But if times change and the opportunity is lost, they resemble a bright jewel hidden in the depths of the sea.

Moreover, while students of the Way have different levels of ability, the wondrous truth is infinite. Very few have reached it and many are confused about its source.

These verses are an exceptionally bright light on all phenomena and things. This means that both principles and phenomena recede with them, and names and words are defeated. Thus, they kindheartedly point at the moon, without missing the tiniest things.

If you don't get lost searching for the needle in the water, the treasure already held in your fist waiting to be opened will be bestowed on you.

I have given these small words, in brief, as a preface to demonstrate the gist of the poems.

Since this preface, cited in the *Chrestomathy from the Ancestors' Hall*, is found practically unaltered in later editions of the *Jingde Era Record*, we may assume that the manuscript as found by Shanqing influenced these later editions as well. Nevertheless, we do not know which edition would most faithfully reflect possible amendments to the verses, so we also do not know the shape of the poems in which Shanqing found them.

These problems with the text are somewhat mitigated by the fact that the differences in wording in the various editions do not significantly alter the meaning of the text but remain variations of expression. The most salient variations can be found in the titles given to the individual poems, which are believed to have been given by the author himself but later revised by the editors of the various editions of the *Jingde Era Record*. These variations were of considerable concern to contemporary monks and scholars of the Chan tradition, but from a modern perspective few of them lead to significantly different interpretations of the poems. Among all premodern editions of the Ten Verses which we have access to, the edition in the Korean canon version has clearly been the most carefully edited. It contains no apparent inconsistencies or misspellings, and no abridgments, which is quite remarkable for an ancient manuscript. The Ming edition seems to contain the most errors of any edition.

After the *Jingde Era Record*, the second major classical record containing the Ten Verses was the *Essentials of the United [Records of the Transmission of the] Lamps of Our School* (*Zongmen liandeng huiyao*), produced about 180 years later. The inclusion of the Ten Verses in this compilation demonstrates the status of the text during the Song period, since the fourteen poems published therein were chosen by the editors as a selection of the most important poems of the Chan tradition going back to its beginning. The collection also includes most of the few poems from that era that are still part of Zen teaching and practice nowadays.

The Author

THE TEN POEMS are attributed to a Chan master active in the first half of the tenth century with the Dharma name "Changcha of Tong'an Temple." The dates of his birth and death are unknown. We are not aware of any writing within the Buddhist tradition or any research that contests the attribution of the Ten Verses to Master Changcha. As will be seen below, sectarians would gain little by attributing the poems to Changcha as opposed to somebody else. If the editors of the *Jingde Era Record* had intended to further aggrandize the figure of Changcha's contemporary, Fayan Wenyi, whose Dharma heir, Daoyuan, was the central editor of the Record, they could have done so. But they did not. In any case, it is safe to assume that Tong'an Changcha was the actual author of the poems.

Not much is known about the life of Tong'an Changcha, as the biographical information available on him in extant Chan records is sparse. The minimum that such records preserve is a master's Dharma name, lineage, and the temple where he resided. Beyond this, they may provide his birthplace, secular name, and those dialogues and sayings attributed to him that demonstrate his spiritual achievement. Many of such dialogues may also be taken up as kōans. The number and degree of detail exhibited in dialogues will vary greatly depending on the master and the importance assigned to him. Finally, records may also preserve further biographical or hagiographical elements, which show such things as the master's devotion to Buddhist practice from an early age or his first encounter with Buddhist teaching, for example. Modern scholarship unaffiliated with the Buddhist sects generally disputes the historicity of the records because of the presence of sometimes quite egregious inconsistencies between various records, and because records may contain what are clearly nonhistorical elements, such as descriptions of supernatural phenomena or the appearance of bodhisattvas as actors in a master's life, alongside elements that are likely historical, such as verifiable personal and place names.

We have found mention of Tong'an Changcha in at least twenty-two records of the Buddhist canon, in addition to the records that exist in the historically important but noncanonical *Collection from the Ancestors' Hall*. Not all of these twenty-two incidences are equally relevant. First of all, earlier sources contain more original material, whereas subsequent sources largely repeat material that exists in the earlier ones. Secondly, there are some records that are simply considered more authoritative and influential within the Chan/Zen tradition than others. Given that the *Collection from the Ancestors' Hall* and the *Jingde Era Record* have historically been the most significant records, and that the *Record of Equanimity*, the *Assembled Essentials of the Five [Records of the] Lamp*, and the *Empty Hall Anthology* have been records of particular importance and authority within the tradition, we thus choose to focus our examination of the person of Tong'an Changcha on the entries preserved in these texts. We will mention other records only where relevant.

We present below translations of the relevant portions of each of these records in chronological order. It is not always clear in the dialogues if one person is asking the master on one occasion or if different people are asking on different occasions. The same question-and-answer sequence that appears to indicate a single questioning monk on a single occasion in one record sometimes seems to indicate multiple questioners on multiple occasions in another. We have chosen to end our translations where there seems to be a natural break in the flow of represented conversation.

Collection from the Ancestors' Hall, *vol. 12 (952)*

The *Collection from the Ancestors' Hall* was composed during the time of Tong'an Changcha and is therefore most likely to contain historically accurate information. The editors of the *Jingde Era Record* either did not know of its existence or intentionally ignored it.[6] Subsequent Chinese and Japanese Chan records, beginning with the *Jingde Era Record*, have basically been composed independent from the *Collection from the Ancestors' Hall* since the latter was eventually lost in China and only survived in Korea. The passage regarding Master Changcha in the *Collection from the Ancestors' Hall* runs as follows:

> The priest of Tong'an inherited the Dharma from Jiufeng. He lived in the Jianchang county in the Hong region. His master title was Changcha. He was a person from Changxi county in the Fuzhou region. His family name was Peng. He took the precepts when he came of age, then left Fujian province to study with Jiufeng. He received transmission, reaching the final gate, and then settled at the Phoenix mountain range.
>
> A monk asked: "How is the condition at the Phoenix mountain range?"
> The master replied, "In what place are you right now?"
> The monk asked, "How is what has been passed down from above?"
> The master answered, "What has been passed down does not work."
> The monk said, "So what should I do from now?"
> The master replied, "Even ten thousand people won't be able to tell you." (1)

Jingde Era Record of the Transmission of the Lamp, *vol. 17 (1004)*

The *Jingde Era Record*, written fifty years later, preserves an account similar to but more lengthy than the one from the *Collection from the Ancestors' Hall*:

> Master Changcha of Tong'an temple at the Phoenix mountain of Hong region.
>
> A monk asked, "Although this is the home of the phoenix, why is there no house style?"[7]

The master replied, "We don't welcome visitors, and we don't treat anyone as a guest."

The monk asked, "Then, for what purpose do we visit all places between the four seas?"

The master replied, "If there is a plate for sacrifice, there will always be someone who gives." (2)

A monk asked, "How is the condition at Phoenix mountain range?"

The master replied, "The thousand mountain peaks line up beautifully. The ten thousand cliffs do not know when spring comes."

The monk asked, "How about the person under these conditions?"

The master replied, "He sits on lonely cliffs and high boulders, his mind being as high as the white clouds." (3)

The "house style" mentioned in the first dialogue refers to differences in the style of Chan/Zen that depend on particular masters or their lineages. The question of house style in relation to Tong'an temple is raised in a frequently quoted dialogue from the first abbot of the temple, Tong'an Daopi (?–905), recorded in the sixteenth volume of the *Jingde Era Record*. The dialogue runs as follows:

A monk asked, "What is your house style?"

The master said, "The golden hen carries its son and returns to heaven. The pregnant jade rabbit enters the heavenly palace."

The monk asked, "If I suddenly encounter a guest coming, how should I treat this guest respectfully?"

The master replied, "The golden fruit—early in the morning the ape plucks it and takes it away. The jade flower—after dusk the phoenix comes holding it in its mouth."

The core biographical information on Master Changcha given in the *Jingde Era Record* is identical to the information given in *Collection from the Ancestors' Hall.* Given that the *Jingde Era Record* is presumably independent of the Collection, the fact that the two concur would seem to support the information that these records provide. The twenty-third volume of the *Jingde Era Record* and the eighth volume of the *Record of the Correct Lineage of the Dharma Transmission* both note a single Dharma heir for Changcha by the name Lianggong. No further information is provided on this figure, except that he settled at Mt. Yangshan in what is now Jiangxi province and had no Dharma heir of his own.

Record of Equanimity *(1223)*

The *Record of Equanimity* is about three centuries removed from the time of Master Changcha, yet it has a special status in the Sōtō Zen tradition as its most prominent kōan collection, comparable to the *Blue Cliff Record* or the *Gateless Barrier* in the Rinzai Zen tradition. The key dialogue with Master Changcha found in this collection runs as follows:

COMMENTARY ON CASE 80

A monk asked Tong'an Changcha, "How is it if there are no weapons?"

Changcha said, "You cannot hang a sword into an empty space. The jade hare in the moon cannot wear body armor." (4)

Besides this short dialogue, the *Record of Equanimity* also quotes the first line of the tenth verse of Changcha's Ten Verses when commenting on case 35 and quotes the third and fourth lines of the third verse when commenting on case 68.

Assembled Essentials of the Five [Records of the] Lamp, *vol. 6 (1252)*

Lineage histories proliferated after the successful canonization of the *Jingde Era Record*. The composition of lineage histories provided sectarian scholars a welcome opportunity to record their version of religious history, even while the Chinese state retained control and authority over Buddhism through the system of canonization. The proliferation of records led to the need for compendia that would systematize the information contained in the various versions. The *Assembled Essentials of the Five [Records of the] Lamp* is probably the best recognized and authoritative of these compendia. It mainly brings together material from five preceding canonical lineage histories: namely the *Jingde Era Record* (1004), the *Record of the Extensive [Transmission of] the Lamp* (1036), the *Jianzhong Jingguo Era Continued Record of the [Transmission of the] Lamp* (1101), the *Essentials of the United [Records of the Transmission of the] Lamps of Our School* (1183), and the *Jiatai Era Comprehensive Record of [the Transmission of] the Lamp* (1204).

The first incident of material on Master Changcha in the Assembled Essentials was faithfully adopted from the *Jingde Era Record* and we will therefore not repeat it here. The remaining material can be traced back to the *Essentials of the United [Records of the Transmission of the] Lamps of Our School*, while the rest cannot be identified in any other texts available to us. We translate each of the passages here in order of their appearance in the Assembled Essentials and indicate allusion to the Ten Verses in boldface type:

A DIALOGUE OF UNCLEAR PROVENANCE

A monk asked, "What is the difference between **Zen mind**[8] and the general Buddhist teaching?"

The master said, "The iron dog barks at the stone cow. The magician watches the moonlight."

The monk asked, "How about the person who has **grown hair and put on horns?**"[9]

The master replied, "With a woven rush raincoat and a bamboo hat you sell gold. How many don't greet each other when they meet?" (5)

DIALOGUES PRESERVED FROM *ESSENTIALS OF THE UNITED
[RECORDS OF THE TRANSMISSION OF THE] LAMPS OF OUR
SCHOOL*

A monk asked, "I am not yet clear about the right opportunity for enlightenment. Please give me instruction."

The master replied, "In the uneven pine and bamboo grove,
the fog is thin; because of the many layers of mountains,
the moon comes out late."

The monk intended to say something else, but the master
said, "Before using your sword and armor, your body has
already been exposed."

The monk asked, "What do you mean?"

The master replied, "The good knife does not cut the bamboo
before the frost comes. The ink painting can only praise
the dragon on the sea."

The monk circled the master's seat and then left.

The master said, "If you close your eyes and eat a snail, it will
at once be sour, tart, and bitter." (6)

A SECOND DIALOGUE OF UNCLEAR PROVENANCE

The monk asked, "**Returning to the origin, returning to the
source,** how is it?"[10]

The master replied, "Even if the cicada has broken out of
its shell, it still cannot avoid clinging to the cold branch."

The monk asked, "What about a very **strong-willed and powerful person?**"[11]

The master answered, "The **stone ox**[12] step by step goes into
the **deep pool.**[13] The paper **horse** shout by shout cries out
in the fire." (7)

FIVE DIALOGUES PRESERVED FROM THE *ESSENTIALS OF THE UNITED [RECORDS OF THE TRANSMISSION OF THE] LAMPS OF OUR SCHOOL*

A newly arrived monk held a tin staff and circled the master three times, he shook the staff once and asked, "Master, please tell me the place that neither the ordinary **nor the saints reach.**"[14]

The master snapped his fingers three times.

The monk said, "Today you are scared, so you are at a loss for words."

The master replied, "Where is your point of departure?"

The monk bowed and walked out.

The master said, "The monk who has already traveled a lot of places; the Zen monk with the staff. If you don't really reach up to me, you won't be able to cast off your doubts."

The monk turned around and said, "Hearing from afar is not as good as seeing with your own eyes."

The master said, "Because you are eager for one cup of wine, you loose a whole ship full of fish."

The monk asked, "How is the person who has eliminated all regrets?"

The master answered, "I have already seen this sort of business."

The monk asked, "What is the **meaning of Bodhidharma coming from the West?**"[15]

The master replied, "The rhinoceros grows a horn because it plays with the moon's arc. The shine enters the elephant's tusk because it is scared by the thunder."

The monk asked, "How is the person that always looks into the future?"

The master replied, "The cicada in fall clings to the **barren tree**[16] without leaves and keeps chirping without turning its head."

The monk asked, "How is the person who has **returned?**"[17]

The master replied, "He is outstanding like a **reed flower** in the fire.[18] You meet him in spring but it looks like fall."

The monk asked, "How is the person who has neither come nor gone?"

The master answered, "The **stone** sheep meets the **stone** tiger. They look at each other and sooner or later they stop fighting." (8)

The head monk asked, "The **three vehicles**[19] and twelve teachings, I know them roughly. But I don't know which Dharma you are teaching."

The master replied, "I teach the **one vehicle**."[20]

He asked, "So how is the one vehicle?"

The master replied, "Several clouds appeared from the top of the mountain; the spring water resounds when it hits the stone."

The monk said, "I didn't ask about that. I asked what the one vehicle teaching is."

The master replied, "You would better be a little smarter."[21] (9)

The master, after looking at the night sky, said to a monk, "How strange, how strange! The stars and the **moon** are both so **bright**,[22] and they can still both be seen. Why does it deviate from the Way like this?"

The monk said, "How is the Way?"

The master answered, "If you try it out you will see."

The monk said, "If someone has no wound, don't injure him!"

The master replied, "If you carry book bags and tackle study, don't rest your bow and arrows." (10)

The master asked a monk, "Where did you go recently?"

The monk replied, "To Jiangxi province."

The master asked, "How does the Dharma of Jiangxi resemble the one here?"

The monk replied, "Luckily you asked me. If you asked somebody else, misfortune would come of it."

The master said, "I see I was rash right now."

The monk said, "I'm not an infant, but you only use candy to stop me from crying."

The master replied, "Hurting the turtle or releasing it, killing it or letting it live, is in my power." (11)

Changcha asked a monk, "Where have you come from?"

The monk replied, "From Mt. Wutai."

The master asked, "Did you also see the Bodhisattva Mañjuśrī?"

The monk spread out his arms.

The master asked, "You are spreading out your arms so much. So who has really seen the Bodhisattva?"

The monk replied, "If you're out of breath, it kills you."

Changcha asked: "If you don't see the wild goose in the clouds, how can you know the coldness of the desert?"

The monk said, "Please let us go quickly to the master's room, and tell me there!"

Changcha replied, "The disciples of Sunbin[23] only talked about divinations."[24]

The monk said, "Yet his reputation was not wasted."

Changcha replied, "Go away and have some tea!"

The monk bowed goodbye.

The master said, "Even if you have earned victory in one battle, you still get your legs cut off." (12)

Two Dialogues of Unclear Provenance

As the master read a sutra, there came a monk who asked something.

The master replied, "The buddhas of the past and present have all taught the same thing."[25]

The monk asked, "So how about you?"

The master slapped him.

The monk said, "That's it! That's it!"

The master said, "This idiot!"

The monk said, "The present and past buddhas are all like this."

The master said, "I wanted to slay a dragon, but I met a dead tiger."

The monk said, "You really radiate."

The master replied, "Standing by a tree stump and holding your breath waiting for hares to clash against it, who would do this if not you?"

The monk said, "You are deaf!"

The master said, "The barbarian sheep went to Chu. Feeling wronged they returned home." (13)

The master asked a monk. "When it is all dark around your eyes, how can you see?"

The monk replied, "The Northern star turns to the East, and the Southern Star moves to the West."

The master said, "Master, you can enter the big ancestor temple."

The monk said, "Like this, in the school of Tong'an the Way dies out and the disciples get dispersed."

The master said, "Carrying the baby horizontally,[26] I wanted to show you the Buddhist teaching." (14)

A DIALOGUE FROM THE ESSENTIALS OF THE UNITED [RECORDS OF THE TRANSMISSION OF THE] LAMPS OF OUR SCHOOL

The master heard the sound of a magpie and said to the assembly, "If a magpie [auspicious bird in Ancient China] cries on the cold juniper [auspicious tree],[27] it means that the **Mind Seal** is going to be **transmitted**."[28]

A monk came forward and asked, "What difference does it make?"

The master said, "Among the monks there is a certain person."

The monk said, "In the school of Tong'an, the Way will cease to exist and the disciples will be dispersed."

> The master said, "The barbarians of Hu drank the milk but they blamed the good doctor."[29]
> The monk said, "Just take a break!"
> The master said, "The old crane entered the dry pond but could not see the traces of fish." (15)

Empty Hall Anthology, *vol. 4 (1295)*

The last dialogue translated here is furthest removed from Master Changcha's lifetime, but it became the most popular of the dialogues and was repeatedly quoted in subsequent records. The passage reads as follows:

CASE 64

A monk asked Master Tong'an Changcha: "How is the teacher of gods and men?"[30]
Changcha replied, "His head is bald, and his body is hairless."[31] (16)

We may note a few things about the dialogues presented here. First of all, those that appear in records that are historically closest in proximity to Master Changcha himself are quite terse. These, namely the *Collection from the Ancestors' Hall*, likely compiled during his own lifetime, and the *Jingde Era Record*, compiled a few decades after his death, we may consider most likely to reflect actual biographical facts. We may also note that the further removed records become from his lifetime, the lengthier and more detailed they become. It is also of interest that the most famous Chan dialogue that involves Master Changcha was recorded more than three hundred years after his death. This pattern is not terribly surprising, as we see very similar patterns surrounding other well-known figures in Chan history as well—most famously with Bodhidharma and the sixth ancestor, Huineng. We know practically nothing for sure regarding the historicity of these two figures, but a vast body of stories and lore has grown up around them over time.

For critically minded scholars, such patterns of increasing elaboration of records in subsequent generations are almost certainly evidence of the nonhistorical nature of such records. However, defenders of the Chan records as historically valuable argue that there are valid reasons that historical material might only have appeared decades or centuries after the fact. First, ancient societies relied on oral transmission much more than have modern societies, where the capacity for printing is cheap and widespread. Second, we know that sects in China and Japan have historically kept important material secret, only choosing to record such material when it becomes threatened with loss or becomes otherwise obscure. Third, records that may have been written down earlier might simply have been lost.

In the end, however, the question of historicity is of little relevance for the tradition itself when compared to the question of whether a story or dialogue truthfully conveys the mind of Chan and effectively transmits its Dharma message. For the Chan tradition, the biographical information preserved in records establishes claims of lineage, and stories and dialogue raise problem consciousness in students and communicate points of practice—that is, they function as kōans. In fact, we do find later masters taking up such dialogues as teaching points in their own lectures.

The twelfth-century master Mi'an Xianjie, for example, comments on two of the above presented dialogues. With regard to the sequence that begins, "Changcha asked a monk, 'Where have you come from?'" Mi'an comments:

> Punch for punch, kick for kick, punching and kicking by turns. Who loses, who wins? Nodding his head and wagging his tail, the monk passes the prison gate. Who would really believe the master's word of cutting off his legs? But still, if there is just a small error, everyone will pick it up and examine it.

He later takes up the dialogue that begins, "The master heard the sound of a magpie," commenting:

They are moving the strings and singing a different tune. One sings and the other responds. The one who sings the tune sings increasingly high, and the one who responds is increasingly harsh. When they perform, they emulate the cacophony of Zhen and Wei. Although it looks chaotic, the five tones, the six rhythms, and their beat are in order.

On the surface these dialogues may seem to indicate that the master defeated the monk, but Mi'an reads them as Dharma battles between equals. Mi'an's reason for choosing these dialogues was clearly to encourage his audience to have no fear of embarrassment or defeat, but to boldly challenge even their master, without consideration of their own inferior position. In this sense, the enigmatic dialogues became a rich source of Dharma instruction for the teachers who took them up.

It is also of interest to note that only the two oldest records refer to Master Changcha's monastery and the places associated with the master, whereas many of those recorded subsequent to them do not speak of location but refer instead to the Ten Verses, the work most closely associated with the master. This likely reflects the fact that prior to publication of the Ten Verses in the *Jingde Era Record*, Master Changcha's most prominent feature as a figure of the Chan pantheon was his association with Tong'an temple. The temple was renowned because of the spectacular natural landscape in which it was situated and because of its first abbot, Daopi.

Two of the above dialogues (numbered 14 and 15) allude to the fact that Changcha's lineage died out quickly. These dialogues must have been composed by writers of later generations who knew that Changcha's lineage actually died out quickly. In these and in the dialogue numbered 13, Master Changcha receives a somewhat unkind treatment. Another salient feature of most dialogues in the Assembled Essentials is that even if the questioning monks use ordinary language, Master Changcha speaks only in rich literary metaphors. On the one hand, these metaphors are less likely to have been produced in spontaneous speech than in premeditated writing, which points again to the fact that the dialogues were probably the product of creative writing.

(Of course, this observation does not apply only to dialogues involving Tong'an Changcha.) On the other hand, the dialogues stress the master's erudition, and he projects a certain aloofness.

Overall, then, we may say that many of the later dialogues, especially those in the Assembled Essentials, seem to represent a reconstructed image of Master Changcha as he might have been imagined based on the sparse biographical information available in the *Jingde Era Record* and based on what character might be gleaned from the Ten Verses. Namely, he appears to be an eminently erudite and enlightened person but not particularly successful as a teacher. At least part of the dialogues, especially those in the Assembled Essentials, may thus be seen as playful inventions by later writers who were catering to the curiosity and imagination of a community of Chan students who only knew Changcha's famous poems and were eager for further stories about his life.

In contrast, the historically accurate core of information about the master—to the extent that we can say that there is any—is most likely limited to what is found in the *Collection from the Ancestors' Hall*. The dialogue here represents a relatively innocent and straightforward question-and-answer session between a Way-seeking monk and a master, rather than a highly stylized and sophisticated Dharma battle, such as those we find in the Assembled Essentials. The two dialogues from the *Record of Equanimity* and the *Empty Hall Anthology* are, again, quite different in their succinctness.

In conclusion, the biographical information available to us regarding Master Changcha that we might consider reliable is quite sparse. The many dialogues involving the master that emerged in later Chan records are likely of little value in terms of the image of the master that they provide. However, they do indirectly tell us something about the high esteem afforded to Master Changcha's Ten Verses by subsequent generations in the Chan community. What we may reliably say about Master Changcha is that he was a very modest figure, the head of an apparently minor temple, that his lineage ended in the generation following his own with a practically anonymous Dharma heir, and he thus had very little impact on the history of Chan lineages. Those entries related to the master in contemporary records were brief and rather stiff. Under normal circumstances, he would have ended up as a historical footnote in later records. We have no other plausible explanation for the later proliferation of stories about Master Changcha than the fame afforded him by the Ten Verses, the content of which we will now explore.

The Title and an Overview of the Text

THE TITLE *Ten Verses of Unfathomable Depth* is not attributed to Tong'an Changcha himself. It would hardly have been appropriate for an author to title his work in such a self-congratulatory way. The title was most likely added to the verses by Fayan Wenyi, the presumptive author of their accompanying preface. In some editions of the *Jingde Era Record*, the poems are simply labeled as "Ten poems by Chan master Tong'an [Chang]cha," or in the abridged Song versions as "Eight poems by Chan master Tong'an." It is common for sets of poems by specific masters to be given simple titles like this in the Chinese Chan records.

The title that is of most interest to us here will be the title by which the work is most well known: *Ten Verses of Unfathomable Depth* (*Shixuantan* 十玄談). Despite the fact that this title was a later addition to the work, it provides some interpretation of the contents of the poems. In Chinese the title consists of the three characters: *shi* 十, meaning "ten," *xuan* 玄, meaning "dark" or "deep," and *tan* 談, meaning "talk," "discussion," or "conversation." The sequence of characters that comprise the Chinese title may be analyzed in three ways: namely as *shixuan-tan*, as *shi-xuantan*, or as *shi-xuan-tan*.

When analyzed in the first way, the compound *shixuan*—comprised of the characters for "ten" and "dark; deep; mysterious"—can be read as an abbreviation of *shixuanmen* 十玄門—comprised of the characters for "ten," "dark; deep; mysterious," and the character *men* 門, meaning "gate." A natural English translation of *shixuanmen* would be "ten gates to deep mystery" or "ten mysterious (or profound) gates." If we expand the title of the Ten Verses in this way, it reads *shixuan-men-tan*—"a talk on the ten gates to deep mystery" or "a talk on the ten mysterious (or profound) gates." "The ten gates" are a concept developed in Huayan Buddhism—a philosophically oriented Buddhist sect that flourished in Tang and Song period China and is generally considered to have been the pinnacle of Chinese intellectual or academic Buddhism.

The Huayan tradition began following the translation of the Flower Garland Sutra into Chinese in the fifth century CE and is associated with a line of original Buddhist philosophers and thinkers that culminates in the early ninth-century figure of Guifeng Zongmi. The tradition originally emphasized theory and doctrine over practice or dhyāna and was thus opposed to Chan. Zongmi, who was also a recognized Chan master, worked to resolve the opposition between Huayan and Chan by establishing a lineage of patriarchs in parallel to Chan practices and by advocating a more equitable balance between theory and practice. Huayan Buddhism is generally perceived to have declined after Zongmi, as it never produced a figure of the same renown again. However, it did survive as an institution, at least in name, throughout the Song period, and it continued to compete with the Chan tradition for the right to administer temples and monasteries. The classical writings of Huayan Buddhism also continued to influence Chan and other schools of Buddhism.

The term "ten gates" is used with both a general and a specific technical sense in Huayan Buddhism. In its technical sense, the term refers to the "ten profound gates" enumerated in Huayan doctrine. The enumeration of these gates, as presented by Yongming Yanshou, a contemporary of Tong'an Changcha, is as follows:[32]

1. The gate of simultaneous completion and response
2. The gate of the mutual inclusion, and yet difference, of the one and many
3. The gate of revelation and concealment in secrecy
4. The gate of Indra's net
5. The gate of the endowment of all qualities
6. The gate of the mastery
7. The gate of the concordance
8. The gate of ten lifetimes
9. The gate of the reliance on phenomena
10. The gate of the excellent creation through the transformation of the mind only

These ten gates are said to analytically represent the interpenetration of all phenomena and their correlation to the mind. When used in a more general sense, however, the term "ten gates" refers simply to the ten entrances to understanding Buddhist teaching and practice. Given that the *Ten Verses of Unfathomable Depth* do not refer at all to anything like the ten gates in their technical sense, we must understand their inclusion in the title of the poem as a more general reference to penetrative understanding of the Buddhadharma.

If we read the Chinese title of the Ten Verses in the second way described above, analyzing *shixuantan* as *shi-xuantan*, that is, as comprised of "ten" and "profound talks," the title then reads "ten profound talks." Reading the title in this way is justified by the fact that the originally Taoist term *xuantan*, or "profound talk," had already been adopted for use in Chinese commentaries on Buddhist sutras by Master Changcha's time. The Profound Discourse on the Flower Garland Sutra (*Huayan Xuantan* or *Huayan Shuchao Xuantan*) by Chengguan, a central figure of Tang period Buddhism, was one such well-known commentary. Whoever titled Master Changcha's poems would almost certainly have been aware of this work. *Xuantan* went on to be used in later Buddhist texts as an independent noun meaning "profound discourse." So if we parse the title in this way, we understand it to be a eulogizing title in praise of the great depth of the poems. This is the most straightforward reading of the Chinese title, which we have chosen to follow in this book. Finally, if we parse the Chinese title as *shi-xuantan*, the title then means "ten talks on the profound."

While in Buddhism the numbers three, five, and seven are often treated as particularly auspicious numbers, the number ten was of greater importance in Huayan doctrine. The core text of the Huayan school, the Flower Garland Sutra, is famous for its explanation of the ten bodhisattva stages, and a large number of Huayan texts and doctrines were organized around the number ten.[33] Since the ten poems contain numerous references to Huayan concepts, it is quite likely that Tong'an Changcha purposefully composed ten verses in keeping with the significance of the number, even if he himself did not title the work. Fayan Wenyi, who composed the preface for and probably coined the title for the Ten Verses, also composed a major work called the *Ten*

Normative Treatises on the Chan School. Wenyi's book is also arranged in ten parts. Thus, given that the number ten was of great importance in the Huayan tradition, and that "ten gates" was both a fundamental concept used in Huayan doctrine and a general term used repeatedly throughout the literature that school produced, it is safe to say that the title given to Master Changcha's poem would have immediately invoked associations with Huayan thought, especially among erudite readers.

After all, at the time of Master Changcha, less than a century after Zongmi, the Huayan tradition was still a formidable presence on the Chinese religious landscape. It is only natural to imagine that it would have presented both a challenge to and a stimulating influence on the Chan that existed during Master Changcha's life. We may even speculate, based on the numerous allusions to Huayan concepts in the poems, that there existed some connection between Master Changcha or his students and Huayan tradition that has escaped the scant biographical records that come down to us from his immediate era.

Apart from Huayan Buddhism, Chinese Chan also drew terms and concepts from Taoist traditions. As Sekkei Harada indicates in his own comments on the title of this work, the term "depth" (*xuan*) can be ultimately traced back to Taoist literature. The Tao Te Ching, for example, ends its first poem with the famous line, "Deep and again deep: the gateway to all mystery."[34] Since both Chan and Huayan Buddhism appropriated Taoist concepts and terminology, the term *xuan* (depth/mystery) could have found its way into the title either via Huayan or as a direct appropriation from Taoist works.

So the title given to Master Changcha's poems resonates with both Huayan and Taoist ideas, although in their contents they resonate more deeply with Huayan alone. The fact that the poem is structured around the number ten further indicates the influence of Huayan Buddhism on the work. Fayan Wenyi's title, therefore, ambiguously evokes associations with both Huayan doctrine and Taoism, a choice that highlights important aspects of the poem and would have attracted the curiosity of contemporary readers. Read in the most straightforward way, the title further elevates the poems and cements their place among Chan literature as "Ten Verses of Unfathomable Depth."

A Synopsis of the Verses

All of the ten verses, in turn, have titles of their own. The verses that comprise the work are each composed of eight lines, and each of these lines are comprised of seven Chinese characters. The composition of each verse is subject to rules of tone and rhyme. This style of verse is known as *qi-lü*, or "seven-character, eight-line regulated verse," and was a metrical pattern created in the Tang period.[35] As a rule one or two Classical Chinese characters correspond to one word in English. However, in the translation given in this book we have not made any attempt to render either the symmetry in length nor the rhyme, which would have been a daunting task—nearly impossible if one privileges accuracy of content over formal rendering. Thus it will be difficult for those who do not read Chinese to fully appreciate the ingenuity of the poetic composition, in which everything seems to fall naturally into the tight constraints of the formal structure.

The following paragraphs are intended to give a short summary of the set of poems, breaking it up into its component parts. Issues that are explained in some detail in the main body of this book will not be repeated here. The first five verses are concerned with doctrine and have the following titles:

1. The Mind Seal
2. The Mind of the Enlightened Ones
3. The Unfathomable Function
4. The Transcendent within Dust and Dirt
5. The Buddhist Teaching; variant: Expounding the Teaching

"The Mind Seal" (*xinyin*) presents the central issue of Dharma transmission as a starting point for the work as a whole. The "seal" refers to a master's confirmation of his or her disciple as Dharma heir. The Dharma, however, cannot be grasped by words and Dharma transmission is difficult to accomplish. All things, including the Dharma, originate in emptiness. But this does not mean that one can attain the Dharma by having an empty mind (*wuxin*; sometimes translated as "no-mind"). This verse and Sekkei Harada's comments on it emphasize that in the

Chan/Zen tradition the ultimate goal of practice is the transmission of the Dharma from one generation to the next, and the ultimate vocation of master and disciple is to continue the lineage of transmission rather than to gain realization or achievement purely for oneself.

The title of the second verse, "The Mind of the Enlightened Ones" (*zuyi*), bears a number of allusions. Read literally, it means the "mind of the ancestors." Sometimes this is interpreted to specifically mean the "mind or spirit of Bodhidharma coming from the West." Interpreted more broadly, it can mean "Buddhist practices of the Chan tradition as opposed to those of other schools of Buddhism." It is given as the title of this verse in apparent contrast to the concept of "empty mind" or "no-mind" touched upon in the previous verse. Having denied that an empty mind is the goal of Buddhist practice, the author next denies that the enlightened mind is the result of achievement. The verse specifically denies the validity of step-by-step, gradual progress toward awakening represented by the forty-two ranks from bodhisattva to buddha. Since these intermediate ranks have not yet reached real insight they have no real value. Instead, the Dharma is realized instantaneously in a manner incomprehensible to ordinary human thought. The central contrast in this verse is between the golden carp, a metaphor for a brilliant figure with excessive abilities, and the stone horse, a metaphor for a figure of utmost simplicity who lacks ambition. Counterintuitively, it is the stone horse that manages to make the ultimate leap. The last two lines of the verse criticize teachings that attempt to explain the Dharma in every detail. In summary, "The Mind of the Enlightened Ones" is thus a rejection of approaches to Buddhism that are based on concepts of empty mind, on stepwise achievement, and on detailed textual exegeses.

The concept of numerous bodhisattva stages toward enlightenment, ranging from four to fifty-seven, was popular in Chinese Mahāyāna Buddhism.[36] The thirty lower bodhisattva stages and the ten higher mentioned in the third and fourth lines of "The Mind of the Enlightened Ones" correspond to the forty-two-stage system laid out in the Flower Garland Sutra, the foundation on which the Huayan tradition based its doctrines. Aside from practices of the Huayan tradition, Master Changcha may also have been referring to contemporary Chan practices. Although the "sudden" approach associated with the Southern

School of Chan had prevailed over the allegedly "gradualist" approach of the Northern School and gradualism was discredited long before Master Changcha's time, the dichotomy between the two approaches was probably much less pronounced in reality, and practices may in general have been rather gradualist.[37] Prominent figures, such as Yongmin Yangshou, even openly advocated a gradual bodhisattva path to enlightenment. It is not a stretch to imagine the last two lines, if aimed at a specific group, as referring to the Huayan School, given its philosophical orientation and principal concern with detailed discussion and analysis of doctrine. Interestingly, "The Mind of the Enlightened Ones" is one of the two verses that were removed from early Song editions of the *Jingde Era Record of the Transmission of the Lamp*. It may be nothing but coincidence, but considering that this is the verse that most explicitly criticizes other approaches to Buddhism, it is conceivable that editors made a conscious decision to remove it.

The verse entitled "The Unfathomable Function" features the same originally Taoist term "unfathomable" (*xuan*) that appears prominently in the title of the overall work. Its appearance in the title to this verse may have been Fayan Wenyi's inspiration for titling the work. "The Unfathomable Function" begins again with admonitions against end of the world beliefs and secular thought. The first clearly refers to the millenarianism and Maitreya worship that had been historically popular movements in Chinese Buddhism, and the second likely refers to Confucianism or popular religious practices. In contrast to such beliefs and practices, true buddha nature is held to be ubiquitous and to transcend all bounds, even those of the Buddhist teaching. Buddha nature, to recapitulate the previous verse, exists independent of gradual practice and cultivation. As a culmination of this discourse on the unbounded nature of the Dharma, Master Changcha advises us to avoid trying to emulate the example of the ancestors and instead to realize our own Dharma. The independent path to this realization is metaphorically represented by two Buddhist symbols of purity, namely the ox and fire. Combined as they are into a single metaphor, they represent the courage and determination required on such an independent path.

The verse entitled "The Transcendent within Dust and Dirt" begins by stating that defilements and delusion on the one hand and enlightenment or highest wisdom on the other are each simply what they are and share the same empty nature. The following lines draw on traditional Chinese cultural knowledge: the story of Bianhe's jade revolves around a jewel in the guise of an ordinary stone that is recognized by no one but a humble peasant and comes from Legalist and Confucian literature; and the metaphor of the jewel of the black dragon comes from Taoist lore. Taken together they illustrate the point that buddha nature, the most precious object, is already ubiquitously present and need only be recognized and appreciated for what it is. The verse goes on to suggest that it is in fact the myriad Buddhist teachings that obscure the presence of the buddha nature, and that the buddha nature will clearly appear once the teachings have been discarded. The closing lines of the verse mirror "The Unfathomable Function," urging us not to imitate the paths of past buddhas and ancestors, and praising the determination of those that proceed on paths independent of previous teachings.

The final verse in this opening series of five "doctrinal" verses is entitled "The Buddhist Teaching." It delves in some detail into the status of the three vehicles and of the Buddhist teachings alluded to in the previous two verses. Master Changcha puts forward the view that although Buddha sometimes taught contradictory teachings, they are nevertheless all fundamentally one. This position is known as the doctrine of "one vehicle" and was especially propagated in Huayan and Tiantai Buddhism. The verse goes on to say that all Buddhist scriptures, even the most advanced teachings of the Mahāyāna schools, are merely temporary expedients. "The treasury of sutras in the Dragon Palace" may refer either to all Buddhist sutras or specifically to the Flower Garland Sutra, which according to legend was retrieved from the Dragon Palace. "Buddha's last teaching" refers specifically to the Nirvana Sutra. Here, the point is that the Buddhist teachings resemble a prescription or medicine—that is, they are only a means to an end. Consequently, even total immersion into the teaching will not lead to true realization. A single dualistic thought is enough to cause a person, who is otherwise living in total purity according to the teachings, to be lost in the cycle of life and death for eternity.

We may see this verse as a final rebuke of philosophically oriented forms of Buddhism, such as Huayan, that place doctrine above practice.

Likewise, if the Buddhist teachings are only a temporary expedient, and even the most profound sutras cannot reach the ultimate, then the *Ten Verses of Unfathomable Depth* must only be an expedient as well, and should not be imagined to represent the Dharma itself. No matter how much we study Buddhist teachings and immerse ourselves in them, we will never actually attain the Mind Seal by doing so. When we have arrived at a good understanding of the teaching as encapsulated in the first five verses, we must then begin to practice. Thus, the second group of five verses principally discusses the practice of Chan. The verses are given the following titles:

6. The Song of Returning Home (Returning to the Root)
7. The Song of Not Returning Home (Returning to the Source)
8. The Revolving Function (Changing Ranks and Returning)
9. Changing Ranks [and Returning] (The Revolving Function)
10. Before the Rank of the Absolute ([After Passing] One Color)[38]

The titles of the second set of five poems vary much more than those of the first set. We have given preference to the titles as recorded in the Chrestomathy and have placed variant titles in parentheses after these. If Mu'an Shanqing actually retrieved the poems from Master Chang-cha's temple, as he claimed, then the titles given in the Chrestomathy should be the most reliable ones. The greatest variance in titling may be that of the seventh verse. The more provocative Chrestomathy title corresponds better to the contents of that verse than does the variant. The Chrestomathy also presents a clearly more accurate choice of titles for the eighth and ninth verses, where the variants have reversed the titles. Given that verse nine refers directly to changing ranks, the Chrestomathy titling seems more apt there. Concerning the titles given to the tenth verse, both "Before the Rank of the Absolute" and "After Passing One Color" render the poem's purport faithfully, provided that the "before" here actually refers to a stage "transcending absoluteness," as the *Zengaku Daijiten* suggests.[39]

One can divide the five "practical" verses roughly into three parts—namely, verses that deal with practice toward enlightenment (six and seven), verses that deal with post-enlightenment practice (eight and nine), and a verse that deals with the stage beyond post-enlightenment practice (ten).

The verses entitled "The Song of Returning Home" and "The Song of Not Returning Home" form a pair. The first urges us to move constantly toward the metaphorical home, toward our original nature, and not to get stuck along the way. The second reverses the perspective of the first, exposing the inherent contradiction between the concept of a journey home and the concept of ultimate nonexistence of a Way or a goal in Chan teaching and practice. The "King of Emptiness" is an epithet for the historical Buddha, but it also refers to the buddha of the coming "age of emptiness" and may echo the warning against millenarianism delivered in the fourth verse. The third and the fourth line admonish us to neither to get comfortable in an unbound and carefree life as mendicants nor to get stuck in enlightenment or enlightenment-like experiences, since neither are the ultimate goal. Master Changcha reports from his own experience how he regrets wasting time stuck in various conditions of practice. Though the final lines of the verse seem desolate, they positively indicate that the return home is only possible when one has lost and given up everything. The first two lines of the seventh verse immediately contradict the previous verse by stating that there actually is no "home" to return to. The four middling lines of the seventh verse again warn against getting stuck, this time in meditational practices or in a superficially peaceful state. The final lines of the verse express the insoluble contradiction, the paradox, laid out in the two verses.

The eighth and ninth verses, entitled "The Revolving Function" and "Changing Ranks," also form a pair. This pair picks up where the previous verses left off. While the previous verses warned of the danger of growing attached to the mendicant's life and to certain states of experience, this verse warns of the danger of getting stuck in the comfort of temple life as a monk and being spoiled by the veneration that ordinary people have for one wearing a monk's robes. The "castle of nirvana" may be taken to refer to a physical place, such as a temple or monastery, or to a psychological state, such as the condition of total peace of mind or enlightenment. The third and the fourth lines criticize any gap between appearance and substance in monks. Master Changcha's indignation for monks wearing precious robes is apparently even greater than his indignation toward monks who work to deliberately appear poor. Monks who take on the superficial appearance of buddhas are contrasted with "wooden men" and "stone women," symbols for real freedom and true enlightenment. The eighth verse also ends in paradox, urging the reader to realize the impossible through continuous effort.

Verse nine presents the logical consequence of the dilemma represented in verse eight. Instead of retaining the superficial appearance of a buddha in monk's clothing and choosing the misleading peace and safety of life as a monk, we are urged to renounce the comfort of the monastery for a certain time and enter secular life, or the world of constant rebirth, as a way to transcend absoluteness or enlightenment. This verse was also deleted from early editions of the poem. If the deletion occurred as an editorial decision, rather than as an accidental scribal omission, we must ask why editors would have chosen to delete this verse. If the editors had to sacrifice a verse in parallel to the controversial second verse, this one may just have been the one most easily removed without seriously impairing the overall work. The theme of constantly moving on and not becoming stuck in comfortable physical or psychological conditions has already been expressed in the previous verses, and so the ninth verse may have been seen as merely elaborating on those. Another possibility may be that the explicit suggestion to renounce monastic life and reenter the secular world may have been perceived as provocative or threatening by those interested in maintaining a strict monastic order and presenting Buddhist practice as moving along a stepwise ascent up a monastic career ladder. It may be that in this case the two most provocative verses were deleted.

While we may expect the last verse to express highest praise of those who have finally proceeded beyond enlightenment and completely transcended both delusion and enlightenment, or the relative and the absolute, in fact, it states almost the opposite. The final verse, entitled "Before the Rank of the Absolute," hands us the strongest warning of all, cautioning of the pitfalls that await us even at this advanced stage. Even those who come this far "trip and stumble." The third and the fourth lines of this verse again warn of deceptive appearances. What may superficially appear to be enlightenment or buddhahood may in fact be something else. The fifth and the sixth lines say those who are convinced of their own buddhahood are inevitably mistaken. The ultimate truth cannot be captured or pinned down with words but is beyond recognition and perception. The overall gist of the tenth verse echoes that of the first: it is difficult to realize the Mind Seal, and Dharma transmission is a rare event to be handled with caution. The tenth verse tells us that even a student who has progressed through practice and enlightenment, as explained in verses six through eight, and who has transcended enlightenment, as explained in verse nine, does not qualify for transmission if even a trace of self-consciousness or consciousness of those achievements remains.

Overall, the ten verses are mostly a series of cautions and warnings to students of Chan. Instead of setting up some fixed doctrine, Way, method, or end point of practice, the verses constantly deny them. The poems continually pull the rug out from under us, urging us to move ever onward, never to be satisfied with our current condition and achievements, however wonderful they may seem. The first five verses urge us to study. They emphasize teaching (jiao) rather than practice (chan), not so as to rely solely on the study of scripture, but as the ground for future practice. The second five verses urge us to practice. We must not be satisfied with any condition, however harmonious and gratifying it may be, and must transcend even the comfort of religious status or the condition of enlightenment. In the end we must transcend both the absolute and the relative, and then transcend transcendence itself.

The fame that the Ten Verses earned its author may be due to the beauty of its composition and its formal perfection, which are difficult to capture in English. Moreover, its strict and uncompromising attitude toward teaching, practice, and Dharma transmission must have struck a chord with teachers and students of Chan, a tradition in which the standard for the ultimate goal of transmission has always been elusive and the line between master and imposter has always been subtle. As the following section shows, the Ten Verses also resonated very well with Sekkei Harada's concerns about contemporary Zen practice.

Tong'an Changcha's Verses and
Sekkei Harada's Dharma Lectures

A DETAILED ANALYSIS of Harada Roshi's discourse and his intentions therein would be superfluous here, as his comments are generally clear and accessible to even a general readership. Despite his frequent references to classical Zen literature, his lectures are not academic in nature and invite all readers to directly engage with Master Changcha's poem and to arouse awareness of problems through that engagement. Nevertheless, it will likely be useful to indicate where the Chinese poem and Harada Roshi's interpersonal reading of it correspond or diverge, especially where they refer to the broader religious environment. An examination of this kind will help us understand the relationship between the poem and the talks inspired by it, as well as the relevance of the talks in their immediate religious context.

The Ten Verses are not well known in contemporary Zen Buddhist circles. At the outset of his talks, Harada Roshi explains his reasons for choosing this work as the basis for his Dharma lectures. In his opinion Zen Buddhism is in a state of general decline, and an important element of this decline is the waning emphasis on the study of classical Zen texts among contemporary Zen institutions. Bemoaning this fact, Harada provides us with a list of classical texts that must be studied to lay a proper foundation for practice. He laments the fact that important texts are not only practically forgotten, but the ability to read them is also practically lost even among Zen priests. He remarks that "hardly anyone involved in contemporary Zen Buddhism knows these records, and the day is approaching when nobody will even be able to read them." This remark extends to the Ten Verses as well, which were held in high esteem by contemporary Buddhists of Song China, and which were later respected in Korea and Japan up until the premodern Edo period, but which are no longer a part of the small body of texts employed in Zen training. In sum, Harada Roshi's choice to lecture on the Ten Verses was partly motivated by his desire to put the spotlight on high quality classical texts that are being increasingly forgotten.

With regard to the contents of Master Changcha's poem and Harada Roshi's lectures, one cannot help but be struck by the wide range of references to concepts, stories, metaphors, allegories, and other materials drawn from far beyond the bounds of Zen Buddhism. Clearly, neither author intends to propagate a purely sectarian doctrine, but instead both draw on any material, whether it is Buddhist or not, as long as it is helpful in communicating the message at hand.

However, it is also noteworthy that the references to Huayan Buddhism, which were such a formidable presence in the Chinese poem, are entirely absent from Harada's comments. Their absence likely stems from the fact that the Huayan school is practically irrelevant to present-day Japanese Buddhism. Although the tradition has survived in Japan, nowadays it is only a small denomination that can boast no major religious or institutional impact, and it is practically only of interest to historical and philosophical scholars. There is no school or sect in contemporary Buddhism that holds a position comparable to that of the Huayan Buddhism during the Tang and Song dynasties with regard to sharing teachings that overlap with the Zen tradition and which provoke the intellectual stimulation that the Huayan tradition once did. The greatest intellectual and doctrinal provocateurs of contemporary Zen are the various internal sects of the Zen tradition itself. Harada Roshi makes ample reference to these sects and the contentious issues they debate. There are specifically three major issues that appear as recurrent topics throughout the lectures: (1) the problem of Dharma transmission, (2) the problem of kōan Zen, and (3) the problem of doctrine and practice in contemporary Sōtō Zen.

The Problem of Dharma Transmission

The first major problem addressed by Sekkei Harada concerns not only individual practitioners of Zen but the entire tradition and its sects. Since Tong'an Changcha opens his poem with the topic of Dharma transmission, an indication of its key role in Zen, so too does Sekkei Harada begin his Dharma lectures. The poem expresses Dharma transmission as transcendent and elusive in nature. The rhetorical question "What sort of person dares to transmit it?" posed in the second line of the first verse, indicates that for Master Changcha Dharma transmission was no trivial matter but presupposed a special ability.

Aside from the general "inheritance of Dharma" (shihō), in contemporary Zen the certificate that confirms Dharma transmission (inka shōmei)[40] certifies one's ability to teach and have disciples. The concept of Dharma transmission is unique and originates within the Chan/Zen tradition itself. Dharma transmission means that a master confirms that his or her disciple has fully realized his or her own Dharma. "The term 'Dharma transmission' means the inheritance of the Dharma from one's master," as Sekkei Harada puts it. One awakens to the fact that oneself is the Dharma. According to tradition, the first Dharma transmission took place between the historical Buddha and his disciple Mahākāśyapa. This first transmission is commonly described as a "transmission from mind to mind,"[41] without verbal communication, "as if moving water from one vessel to another without losing a single drop."[42]

Dharma transmission and its confirmation were intended to function as a guarantee that only awakened people could exercise religious authority among the Zen sects. The great importance of Dharma transmission is also captured in its epithet as the "lifeline of the Dharma." This lifeline sustains Zen and ensures the survival of its unique tradition. Dōgen, the founder of the Sōtō school in Japan, described it as follows:

> All buddhas surely transmit the Dharma to one another; all the ancestors have transmitted the Dharma to each other. This mutual pledge of enlightenment is the right transmission from master to disciple. Therefore, we have supreme enlightenment. If you are not a buddha, you cannot receive the seal of enlightenment; if you do not possess the seal of enlightenment, you cannot be a Buddha. Who else besides Buddha can give the seal of enlightenment? (from Shōbōgenzō: Shisho as translated by K. Nishiyama and J. Stevens, 1978)

However, Dharma transmission in Chan/Zen has never been without controversy. On the one hand, transmission from mind to mind, beyond words, is elusive, and on the other, it is highly coveted as the key to religious authority. So it is no surprise that conflicts over authentic transmission erupted from very early on. Dharma transmission was not the only source of controversy. Transmission of Dharma lineages also became a source of conflict for early Chan Buddhists. We find, for example, the assignment of the same important masters to various lineages of transmission in competing records of the line of transmission. The variant assignments likely reflect the agenda of the editors of such works, who themselves belonged to or favored a particular lineage. As mentioned above, Tong'an Changcha himself was the subject of such a controversy when an unsuccessful attempt was made to "integrate" him into a different Dharma lineage than the one with which he has been commonly associated.

While Harada Roshi acknowledges the existence of prior problems with Dharma transmission, he is principally concerned with the degenerate state of Dharma transmission in contemporary Zen. "If true transmission were taken seriously," he says, there would be "no priests to fill the temples." In order to preserve the tradition and institutions, Dharma transmission in contemporary Zen has been reduced to a mere formality and the certificate that confirms Dharma transmission has been discarded as worthless. In Harada's assessment, transmission and practice have so disconnected from one another in the Sōtō sect that it is possible to receive transmission without practicing. "This is the worst possible situation," he laments.

While this bleak assessment may surprise Western readers, it merely states the obvious for those familiar with the situation in Japan. The biggest reason for this state of affairs has been the pressure that religious organizations feel to churn out temple priests capable of providing necessary services at the large number of temples spread across the country. The most important social task that temples in Japan perform is the maintenance of graveyards and the performance of funerary rites for families in the temple congregation. Legislation enacted during the Edo period bound families to the temples that maintained family graves, and the secularization of Buddhism during the Meiji reforms of the nineteenth century allowed the priesthood in Japan to become hereditary. As a result of these various factors, Dharma transmission within the

Zen sects has become an automatic formality, undertaken to ensure smooth and continuous temple management.

Apart from social and institutional factors that led to the decline of Dharma transmission in the Zen tradition, the trivialization of the concept of "awakening" or "enlightenment," particularly in the Sōtō sect, has added to the problem. The belief that all beings are endowed with buddha nature, combined with the sloganization of lines written by Master Dōgen, such as "practice and enlightenment are one," have helped to cultivate the impression among modern adherents of Zen that we are all already awakened, and that our ordinary daily lives are automatically expressions of enlightenment. The failure to distinguish between the person (*nin*) and Dharma (*hō*) lays at the root of this "serious mistake." Harada Sensei explains that while "Everything just as it is" and "Nothing to attain; nothing to relinquish" represent the truth from the absolute perspective of Dharma or enlightenment, they become gravely deceitful if spoken from the perspective of one who has not yet truly realized one's own Dharma. Furthermore, the statement that "practice and realization are one" expresses the state wherein the person and Dharma have truly become one and not a statement applicable at just any time.

In general, as a result of the degeneration of Dharma transmission into an automatic formality, it has become impossible to know whether priests are truly awakened in the tradition based solely on the religious title they bear. Even the title Rōshi, which traditionally indicated a person of outstanding spiritual achievement, has come to simply designate a senior temple priest. This state of affairs concerns Harada Roshi, and his mind turns to the topic again and again throughout the lectures.

The Problem of Kōan Zen

The second major issue to which Sekkei Harada turns in his lectures is the problem of kōan Zen. Harada Sensei bases his comments on the second of the Ten Verses, which rejects the idea of a gradual path toward buddhahood and the overly analytical approach to teaching that were characteristic of Huayan Buddhism. This verse instead advocates a sudden realization of buddha nature. Taking an entirely contemporary perspective, Harada Roshi identifies the stepwise path to realization with contemporary kōan practices primarily associated with the Rinzai school of Zen. Students in this school in modern Japan commonly find themselves confronted with a hierarchy of hundreds of kōans. They may, for example, be expected to proceed from practice with kōans from the *Gateless Barrier* to those in the *Blue Cliff Record*, and then on to those in the Ten Major Precepts. Sekkei Harada considers this to simply be a mistake. If a student has resolved a kōan but nevertheless needs to move on to a different kōan, it is an indication that the first kōan has in fact not been resolved. Regarding this, he argues:

> It is not possible, for example, for the eyes to be liberated but not the ears. It is also strange to say, "I have passed Mu, but not the Sound of One Hand Clapping." However, there are some people who do not find anything strange about this and continue to practice in this way until they die. Such people should really ... apply themselves to a kōan in such a way that they completely become one with it. Otherwise, they will not really be practicing the Buddha Way.

Harada Roshi advises students to focus on just one kōan and to work thoroughly on it until everything is resolved. He furthermore rejects the approach in which the same kōan curriculum is administered indiscriminately to all students. From his point of view there is no such thing as a good or bad kōan. Rather, the quality of a kōan depends on the person dealing with it. It is quite possible, Harada says, that someone who has been practicing wholeheartedly may become worse off upon being given a kōan.

Practice with kōans has become highly formalized in modern Rinzai Zen. It is a well-known fact that collections of answers to most kōans are available for purchase in print even in English, and are widely used by students. Practitioners are often passed through the kōan curriculum in a systematized manner on the basis of such answer collections. But we should not think that Sekkei Harada rejects kōan practice out of some sectarian Sōtō loathing of kōans. On the contrary, he has advocated the use of kōans in the Sōtō school and has spent more years lecturing on the kōan collection called *Record of Equanimity* than on any other single text. Here he criticizes what he sees as a fundamental misunderstanding and as excesses in contemporary kōan practice.

Harada generally avoids mention of the Rinzai sect by name, apparently intending not to engage in a debate with the Rinzai sect in Japan, but rather to clarify matters with those among his students who have been influenced by contemporary kōan practice. In this, Harada Sensei may share some affinity with Tong'an Changcha, whose allusions to Huayan doctrine were not necessarily part of an active debate with the Huayan school but may have simply been intended to address individual Chan students influenced by Huayan doctrine.

The Problem of Doctrine and Practice in Contemporary Sōtō Zen

While mainstream Rinzai Zen has undergone a process of formalization in terms of movement through the kōan curriculum, mainstream Sōtō Zen has undergone a process in the opposite direction. Instead of Zen practice being pressed into a stepwise procedure, its ritualized performance as such has become the ultimate goal. This is epitomized by slogans such as "just sit" and "everyday mind is the Way."[43] This style of Zen is not only prevalent in the Sōtō School in Japan but has been spread to Europe and North America by prominent teachers in the West. Unfortunately this approach to practice has come to represent modern Sōtō Zen in Japan and abroad.

Being himself a representative of the Sōtō lineage, this kind of formalization deeply concerns Sekkei Harada, and to a much greater degree than does the formalization of contemporary Rinzai kōan curricula. Pointing out problems with this style of Zen has been a thread running throughout his works published in Japan. We find the most substantive comments on this issue in his lectures on the Ten Verses in his preliminary remarks and his lectures on verses eight and nine.

It is true that one can find quotations among the works of Dōgen, founder of the sect, with which to justify the use of slogans that have become popular in contemporary Zen, such as "everything just as it is" or "practice and enlightenment are one." But Harada points out that these slogans present a one-sided view of classical Sōtō doctrine as laid out by Dōgen. In the *Bendōwa* chapter of the *Shōbōgenzō*, for example, Dōgen does state that the Dharma is "amply endowed in each person," but he also says that "it isn't manifested without practice and is useless if unverified." And while the *Bendōhō* chapter of Dōgen's *Pure Standards* contains the famous line "Be one with the community in activity and stillness; there is no benefit in standing out,"[44] in the same work Dōgen urges relentless sitting, without even lying down at night.

So how are we to reconcile such contradictory elements in the works of Dōgen? Harada's understanding is that sayings such as "practice and enlightenment are one" and "subtle practice within original enlightenment"[45] were uttered from the perspective of one who has actually become one with Dharma—that is, they are stated from the perspective of the Dharma itself. If someone still practicing seated meditation bound by "the self" takes such statements literally, any further progress will be hindered. In the lectures on the Ten Verses recorded below, Sekkei Harada identifies the "everything just as it is" dogma prevalent in current Sōtō Zen with the one-sided condition of "sameness" or "absoluteness" that verses seven through nine of the Ten Verses repudiate.

When commenting on verse nine, for example, he says:

> "When rice is served, eat rice" means that we eat when meals are served. Certainly, it is this way: what is hot is hot, what is cold is cold. Truly, there is nothing else. At this point, however, we come to an impasse at "this is all there is." We let our understanding end at "There are no things," regardless of the fact that the dharma is boundless and without limit. Since we think of the fact of nothingness as a fact, and therefore acknowledge it as existent, we easily fall into the trap of "nothingness." If we don't overcome this trap of nothingness, then things that do exist will not truly disappear for you.
>
> I would like you to be aware that since concepts like "everything just as it is right now," "everyday mind is the Way," "Dharma," or "Zen" are quite easy to understand, we are apt to fall into a one-sided sameness and stop there. It's easy to fall into thinking "I do zazen. I practice my method.

Isn't this condition now all there is?" We call this "the wisdom of sameness" or "the rank of the absolute." We must go one step beyond this rank to a world of boundless flexibility.

In short, Sekkei Harada views the form of practice common to contemporary Sōtō Zen as paralyzed in a condition of "just doing," "nothingness," and "everyday mind is the Way." The clinging to these one-sided forms of practice is a product of ego. Such forms of understanding and practice prevent those who maintain them from transcending the perspective of the self to realize the unity of self and Dharma.

So although Sekkei Harada faces a completely different religious and social environment than those encountered by Master Changcha more than a millennium ago, the Ten Verses provide him with a perfect vehicle with which to address matters of individual practice and to express concerns about the state of contemporary Zen practice. While Tong'an Changcha apparently felt compelled to explain his Zen teachings and practice in relationship to other forms of Buddhism, Sekkei Harada feels compelled to address the present situation within Zen Buddhism. Master Changcha's response to Huayan doctrine is primarily articulated in the first five doctrinal verses of the poem, whereas Harada's view of the situation within contemporary Sōtō Zen is primarily articulated in his comments on the last five practical verses. The first five verses lend themselves to associations with problematic aspects of contemporary kōan Zen. Despite the fact that critique is an element of both authors' work, neither Tong'an Changcha nor Sekkei Harada refer to specific persons or schools. Instead, comments regarding contemporaneous religious contexts are expressed as personal spiritual advice given to an audience comprised of those who live within and are affected by it.

The audience for Master Harada's lectures consisted largely of Japanese monks and nuns. Yet the three major problems of contemporary Zen doctrine and practice focused on in the talks are certainly relevant and applicable outside of Japan. The deterioration of Zen and other traditional forms of Japanese Buddhism into so-called "funerary Buddhism" is a situation historically and socially unique to Japan. But the rote formalization of Dharma transmission and the ritualization of practice in both Rinzai and Sōtō schools are problems in the global Zen community. The Zen teachings and practices that have been transmitted to and are currently being taught in the West have their ultimate source in East Asia, including Japan. However, while present-day Japanese are generally aware of the erosion of these traditions, particularly of Dharma transmission and the concomitant loss of the validity of formal qualifications and titles, people in the West are often not aware of it. The same can be said about the ritualization of practice in contemporary Rinzai and Sōtō Zen. For example, there has evolved in the West a form of Sōtō Zen practice wherein realization of the Dharma is equated with the performance of seated meditation wearing monastic robes while sitting in the correct posture and accompanied by precise rituals, or wherein spiritual accomplishment is measured by the length of time spent seated in the meditation posture. From this perspective, the precautions spelled out by Tong'an Changcha in his *Ten Verses of Unfathomable Depth* and elaborated on by Sekkei Harada in his lectures seem eminently applicable to modern Zen as it is practiced throughout the world.

II. *Commentary on the* Ten Verses of Unfathomable Depth

SEKKEI HARADA

Prologue: Master Tong'an and the Verses of Unfathomable Depth

T HESE *Ten Verses of Unfathomable Depth* are found in a book
called the *Jingde Era Record of the Transmission of the Lamp*
(*Jingde chuandenglu*), compiled by Master Ying'an Daoyuan. They
were written by Master Tong'an Changcha and represent a work of
pure Sōtō Zen. The first five verses set forth the principles of Sōtō Zen,
while the second five are concerned with matters of practice. Thus,
taken together, these verses encapsulate the whole teaching of Sōtō Zen.
However, most people—even those who have been practicing Zen for
a long time—may not be familiar with them.

The name Tong'an Changcha means "Master Changcha from Tong'an
temple." We know that Tong'an Changcha was an outstanding master
by the fact that he is mentioned in many important kōan collections,
such as *Assembled Essentials of the Five [Records of the] Lamp* and
Jingde Era Record of the Transmission of the Lamp, as well as in many
biographical writings. He was the fortieth in the line of Zen patriarchs
that began with Śākyamuni Buddha's disciple Mahākāśyapa. Having
lived approximately 980 years ago, Master Tong'an represents pure
Sōtō Zen. Generations before him, Bodhidharma, the twenty-eighth
great master in the lineage descended from Mahākāśyapa, brought the
Buddha's Dharma to China from India. Through Bodhidharma's suc-
cessors, the teachings were passed down to the sixth master, Dajian
Huineng. Thereafter, Zen split into the precursors of today's Sōtō and
Rinzai sects. The Sōtō lineage began with Master Qingyuan Xingsi,
whose tradition Master Changcha would eventually inherit.

The term "Dharma transmission" means the inheritance of the
Dharma from one's master. This must mean that someone has awakened to the fact that he or she him- or herself *is* the Dharma. However,
if true transmission were taken seriously and practiced only in this way,

we would have no priests to fill the temples. The religious organization of Zen as such would disappear. These days Buddhist priests in Japan are primarily regarded as funeral directors. Most of their efforts are spent bestowing precepts on the deceased at funerals so that they might in turn give the deceased a posthumous Dharma name. Only someone who has been ordained and has received the precepts himself can do this. Thus, it is the duty of someone who has received transmission to bestow precepts and confer Dharma names upon the living and upon the dead. In order to continue this tradition, Dharma transmission has become an almost automatic formality.

In contrast to masters nowadays, for the great masters of the past, Dharma transmission wasn't something done only on paper. They really inherited the Dharma that is transmitted from mind to mind. Master Tong'an was such a person, but since he did not have a big temple where one hundred or two hundred monks practiced, his splendid work was unfortunately scattered and lost. Although Zen is known for "special transmission outside the teaching"[46] and "no dependence on words and letters," numerous records of the old masters were preserved. Rinzai Zen, in particular, has historically collected many such records because it places great emphasis on the study of kōans, which are preserved in them. Thus, later, when people were concerned about the fate of Master Tong'an's work, it was put together again in the form of the *Ten Verses of Unfathomable Depth*.

Many of the works that were collected and preserved by previous generations of students of Zen have become core texts of our tradition today. Central to the Rinzai Zen tradition are, first of all, the so-called "books of the front side":

- *Records of Master Xutang*
- *Blue Cliff Record*
- *Records of Master Linji*
- *Gateless Barrier*
- *Letters of Master Dahui Pujue*
- *Poem Collection of All Schools of Zen*
- *Collection of Texts for Ceremonial Purposes in Zen*

There are also the "books of the reverse side":

- *Miscellaneous Records by Master Kuya*
- *Record of Anecdotes from Lake Luo*
- *Record from the (Chan) Groves*
- *Mixed Records from the Mountain Hermitage*
- *Master Dahui Pujue's Chan Arsenal*
- *Glorious Matters from the Chan Monasteries*
- *Anecdotes from a Hermitage Resting on the Clouds*
- *General Discussions from the Chan Monasteries*

And central to the Sōtō lineage there are:

- *Shōbōgenzō (Eye and Treasury of the True Dharma)*
- *Record of Equanimity*
- *Clarification of the Five Ranks*
- *Comments on the Clarification of the Five Ranks*
- *Records of the Masters Sōzan and Tōzan*

Hardly anyone involved in contemporary Zen Buddhism knows these records, and the day is approaching when nobody will even be able to read them. Anyone who plans to pursue a serious Zen practice should get hold of and study these important books. It is truly difficult to imagine Dharma transmission in the absence of any real awareness of these important teachings that have been handed down to us.

The *Ten Verses of Unfathomable Depth* is comprised, as its title suggests, of ten verses. The first five verses—called "The Mind Seal," "The Mind of the Enlightened Ones," "The Unfathomable Function," "The Transcendent within Dust and Dirt," and "The Buddhist Teaching," respectively—deal with theoretical aspects of Sōtō Zen. The second five—called "Returning Home," "The Song of Not Returning Home," "The Revolving Function," "Changing Ranks," and "Before the Rank of the Absolute," respectively—are concerned with practical matters.

The word "depth" (*xuan*) in the title, which is also found in Laozi's *Daodejing* in the phrase "deepest depth, the gate to all wonders,"[47] signifies something very profound: a bottomless depth. This is not a depth that we can imagine. It is so deep that it can contain everything in the world and yet have room to spare. That is, each and every line of this text is immeasurably profound and perfectly expresses the tenets of Zen. We can say that all of the teachings of all enlightened people, beginning with Śākyamuni Buddha over two thousand years ago, are included within the depths of this "depth."

If, for example, we scoop up in our hands some water from Wakasa Bay, we can taste that it is the same ocean water as anywhere else in the world. Likewise, to the extent that we make the message of these ten verses our own, the full depth of the Dharma will reveal itself to us. Yet their depth is so great that I can only describe a tiny part of it, a portion no bigger than the tip of a needle, no matter in how much detail I explain the verses here. Therefore, if you really want to study the message of this text, you must actually sit, and you must also ask your teacher about the Dharma.

In Zen, we have a saying: "Old pines expound wisdom; birds in the forest whisper truth."[48] In the same way, with regard to the Verses of Unfathomable Depth, their constitution is not a matter of who composed them or where and when they were written. Rather, wherever we are and whatever we see and hear comprises them. It is necessary for us to really accept and to agree with this here and now. As I've been known to say at tea before the beginning of *sesshin*, "Sesshin does not involve doing something special." Rather, it involves simply accepting for oneself that "When tea is served, drink tea. When rice is served, eat rice."[49] That is all there is. That is all there is, and yet there is a depth to it that cannot be limited to "that is all there is." This is what the Verses of Unfathomable Depth express.

The same is true for the famous saying "Everyday mind is the Way." Most people acknowledge this point superficially by saying, "Everything is just as it is," and letting it end at that. The important thing here is that if a clear distinction is not made between the Dharma on the one hand and the person or human thought on the other hand, a serious mistake will be made. And such a mistake is actually being made. Some people say that when it comes to *shikantaza* nothing must be sought for and nothing attained. It is fine just to sit. But that is only true from the perspective of the Dharma. From the perspective of the person, it can never be accepted that someone has realized his or her true nature by just sitting in the proper position, however much they do that. Nevertheless, if someone with a big title or a well-known name tells us that it is fine just to sit, we accept that and do it. We think that this is the final point of the Buddha's Way. Then, without understanding anything at all, we receive Dharma transmission. As more and more people who do not understand the Dharma inherit the Dharma, it becomes more and more difficult to find someone who can truly and immediately testify to what the Dharma actually is.

These days, when Zen monks open their mouths they say, "Everyday mind is the Way." When you ask them about their zazen they will tell you that they get up at four o'clock every morning, sit, and do many periods of zazen until nighttime. The distinction between the Dharma and person is completely lost! To the contrary, all the things that the successive great masters have said are from the vantage point of a person who has actually attained the Dharma.

Whether one refers to a stone lantern in the garden or to a pillar, or to mountains, rivers, grasses, or trees, none of these things use words. Why, then, can it be said that old pines expound wisdom and birds in the forest whisper truth? If someone has not truly attained the Dharma and therefore cannot distinguish between the person and the Dharma, they can only give answers like a parrot repeating words. Their responses are simply repetitive statements of what they know, but such answers are fundamentally useless.

When asked why it can be said that old pines expound wisdom and birds in the forest whisper truth, a person who has actually attained the Dharma must unavoidably speak. But even then some will say, "It's better to speak quietly about that." They will instead talk about shikantaza as "just sitting," wherein there is "nothing to realize and nothing to attain,"[50] and will say "Everything just as it is," as if everybody should already know about and understand these things.

The problem is that both parties—those who know absolutely nothing and those who know something—say "just," "just." So what are we to do? What is ultimately the truth? By "ultimately" I refer to this moment, right now: our sitting right now, our delusion, the thought "I've got to do something"—all of this is already the ultimate. When you can assent to this deeply, this means that "practice and realization are one"—that the person and the Dharma have become one—as we say in the Sōtō sect. Practice and realization are, in short, inseparable. Until that point, even if you understand the Dharma, as a person you are still not in accord with it. So even if you say you have experienced enlightenment or have understood the Dharma, because you as a person are still there as the basis, an immense gap between yourself and the truth remains. Therefore, people who seek Zen must not approve of themselves easily and settle at some halfway point.

This also applies to the unfathomable depth. To put it simply, the "unfathomable depth" and "just" are the same thing. However, to actually reach that point is truly difficult. You must realize that there is no ultimate thing other than your condition right now. The emotions that arise and disappear, along with all those conflicts that play themselves out in your mind, are part of that condition. This means you must practice zazen in such a way that when you are conflicted, you totally become one with this conflict.

But because you cannot endure this state of being, we have you hold on to something that seems like "the Way of the Buddha" or like "practice." These are the various methods of zazen such as shikantaza and kōan practice, including following and counting the breath. With your mind in a scattered condition, you must take up one of these methods as a way to concentrate.

In particular, sesshin is the practice of grinding up zazen by means of zazen. When I say, "Sit single-mindedly," that means there must not be any zazen. One must completely grind up zazen and the method so that no trace remains. This is what it means to "sit single-mindedly." If you are mistaken about this, you will acknowledge the existence of something like zazen and think that since your present condition isn't satisfactory, you must increase your attempts to become one with it. Your practice will forever be one in which you end up judging your method in terms of good and bad, and you will go on thinking of zazen in these terms.

That's definitely not how it should be. We must practice and do zazen in order to forget zazen, to forget practice, to forget the method, and to forget watching the breath. Why? You say that you are doing zazen following the breath, but actually nobody is conscious of his or her breath right now, and you still breathe perfectly. As long as we are not trying to manipulate things with our ideas, everything is already perfectly in order.

Therefore, if you think that your present condition isn't good, don't make the mistake of trying to improve your condition through zazen. If you speculate that this or that condition is *samādhi*, and that you will eventually be able to forget yourself if you continue on in this condition, then you will always be seeking outside your present self for some better condition. I would like you to understand that if you think in these terms, all of your efforts will be in vain no matter how long you continue. In order for that not to happen, you must clearly understand the principles involved here as you continue with sesshin.

1: The Mind Seal

THE FIRST VERSE of *Ten Verses of Unfathomable Depth* is referred to as "The Mind Seal." The "mind" is the mind of all truly realized people of the past and the present, and it is described as "incomparable." The word for heart and mind in Japanese, *kokoro*, refers to something that is constantly shifting and changing without stopping anywhere. We may call this "being distracted" or "being scattered." Thoughts and feelings arise one after another and never come to rest. That is how you perceive the mind because you think of yourself as something separate from it. But that's not the way it actually is. It is the very nature of the mind to be constantly moving without standing still. Therefore, as a precaution in your Zen practice, it is necessary to give up any thought of trying to control the mind by not having it move or by trying to make it settle.

The words "If you compare the whole universe to great enlightenment, it is only like a bubble in a vast ocean,"[51] have been used to describe the minds of the buddhas and ancestors. These words, rather than referring to someone or something out there, refer explicitly to the present state of our own minds, which we think to be deluded. The condition of our minds does not change because of awakening, nor does it lack something prior to awakening. Everything is already there from the very beginning; we are already endowed with awakening. If you understand this point, you no longer need to seek something special.

The Tendai sect[52] teaches that "the three causes are buddha nature." All people are endowed with three types of causes—namely, correct causes, complete causes, and good conditional causes. If you are clear about this alone, then wherever you are, whatever you do, and whenever it is, you can have the mind of the buddhas and ancestors. This is the "mind" of "The Mind Seal."

Let us now turn to the matter of the "seal." Seals are indispensable in East Asian culture as a means of assuring the authenticity of a document. No matter how splendid a document may appear, if it does not have a seal on it, it is worthless. This fact is especially relevant in Buddhism with regard to the certificate that confirms Dharma transmission (*inka shōmei*). As I said earlier, the ancestors and great masters of old, from Dajian Huineng to Tong'an Changcha, all had certified Dharma transmission, verifying that they were genuine. These days, however, "Dharma transmission" has lost its true meaning and become an empty phrase. Regrettably, people dismiss the idea of Dharma transmission, saying, "What's the use of having that?!" As a consequence of this attitude, the guarantee of authenticity that has been passed down from Śākyamuni Buddha all the way through the successive ancestors and great masters of old has been discarded as worthless, and so only very few people really know about it. These *Ten Verses of Unfathomable Depth* have shared a similar fate, too. Even in Zen, which has historically been particularly concerned with "special transmission outside the teaching," people now seem embarrassed to speak about it.

People consider themselves to be "alive" if they can see, hear, and think. However, these merely explain living. Something precedes this explanation, something that *cannot* be explained. Śākyamuni Buddha taught the Dharma for forty-nine years. In all that time he only explained it. Thus it is said that "in forty-nine years he spoke not a single word." When the time came to pass the Dharma on to his disciples, Śākyamuni Buddha held up a golden lotus flower in front of his followers. Only one person in the crowd, the monk Mahākāśyapa, responded by breaking into a smile, and so his mind met with the Buddha's. This was a case of mind-to-mind transmission without verbal communication. From then on we have used the expression in Zen, "As if moving water from one vessel to another without losing a single drop." Realizing that Mahākāśyapa had completely cast off body and mind, the Buddha declared, "I have the eye and treasury of the true Dharma, the marvelous mind of nirvana, and the subtle teaching of the true nature of things, which is without form. Now, I entrust it all to Mahākāśyapa." This was the Mind Seal of the buddhas and ancestors, and it was the first instance of bestowing and receiving the Dharma within the Buddhist lineage.

The Mind Seal of the enlightened ones had previously been transmitted in this way, but nowadays in Japan only a glowing ember remains of what was once a great fire. Nevertheless, the ember remains. If that ember is extinguished, however, everything will be lost. If we don't blow on this ember in order to prevent it from dying, there can never be a blazing fire again. This is why people who have the aspiration to keep it alive come together in earnest to do sesshin.

The historical Buddha as well as the ancestors and great masters were initially all ordinary people who had lived their lives amid dualistic thinking. But at some point, through some circumstance, they came to seek the Way. They carried out a religious practice, and each finally awakened to their true self. You may think that "awakening" means that they changed in some special way, but this is not the case. Rather, awakening is a matter of an ordinary person truly becoming an ordinary person. When an ordinary person has truly become an ordinary person, we call that person a "buddha." This is the case for you as well, for right now, you yourself are merely obscuring your own true nature. Through sesshin there is no doubt that you can also come suddenly to realization. Therefore you must really make every effort when you sit.

Since the beginning of Zen the Mind Seal has also been referred to as "your face before your parents were born."[53] This highlights the fact that delusions arise because we perceive various names. As I have often said, all the things that we see, hear, and think have no substance. We are deceived by names with regard to everything. If you take away all names, there is no need whatsoever to discriminate or to deliberate. Phrases like "the word before anything is said" or "all of the enlightened ones had nothing to transmit" express this.

At Hosshinji we can often hear crows cawing when we sit morning zazen. They remind me of the following poem by Master Hakuin Ekaku.

> In the dark of night,
> when I hear the sound of the crow that does not caw,
> I miss my father before he was born.

The words spoken by the head monk at the Dharma Battle Ceremony[54] are likewise an expression of the Mind Seal:

This staff is a three-foot-long black poisonous snake. It became a golden lotus flower at Vulture Peak, and when it was passed to Shaolin, it turned into the five petals.[55] At other times, it has turned into a dragon that swallowed up heaven and earth...

Upon being asked what Buddha was, a Zen master answered, "a dry shit stick." Others have replied "three pounds of flax," or "drink tea and eat rice." There is also Master Zhaozhou's Mu and Master Hakuin's Sound of One Hand Clapping. These, too, are all different names for the Mind Seal.

If you trace this Mind Seal back through the past and think about it, you will clearly understand its depth. Śākyamuni Buddha, as well as the lineage of great masters, went through considerable suffering and hardship in order to transmit the Mind Seal. For a human being, it is only natural to aspire to be of use to a great number of people and to the world as a whole. There is none who has been of more help than the Buddha, who 2,600 years ago abandoned his palace, his family, and his parents, and dedicated himself to expounding the Dharma for the rest of his life. Even now, Śākyamuni Buddha is doing the greatest work.

Bodhidharma also experienced great hardship when making the voyage from India to China. When he met Emperor Wu of Liang, since there was no "verification and accordance between master and disciple," Bodhidharma went on to sit facing a wall for nine years. In some records it is written that the emperor later realized his mistake and asked that Bodhidharma be brought back to the court once again. However, his advisor Zhigong told him: "That person will never return. He looks like an ordinary human being, but he is actually Guanyin, the bodhisattva of compassion, and the twenty-eighth ancestor in the lineage beginning with the Buddha, who has come from far away in order to transmit the Buddha's Mind Seal to this country."

Bodhidharma indeed never again met with the emperor. Instead, he sat for nine years facing a wall. He personally had nothing to gain from doing this. His sole purpose in doing so was to transmit the Mind Seal. So if you want to do something really great, something that would really benefit people, you should first of all firmly grasp hold of this Mind Seal.

Don't think of fame or profit, not even a little bit. Just do it! Simply working for others—that is the Mind Seal.

I ask you, "What does the Mind Seal look like?"

By writing "I ask you," the author is asking his readers—we ourselves. He is also asking all people in the world about the Mind Seal. Please don't think of his question as something intended only for the people of his era. When Master Changcha asks, "What does the Mind Seal look like?"—or literally, "What sort of face does the Mind Seal have?"—he is posing this question, here and now, directly to us.

Twenty-six hundred years ago, Śākyamuni Buddha proclaimed that all sentient beings have buddha nature—that we ourselves are buddhas. Consequently, there is no need to seek buddhahood outside of ourselves. Instead, we are asked to grind up zazen completely by being one with it. In doing so, we are asked to look closely and to say what all the thoughts and emotions that are constantly arising in and disappearing from our minds are.

The *Song of Realization* begins with the words: "Don't you see that person who has gone beyond all learning and has nothing to do? He neither tries to get rid of delusion nor seeks the truth." Whether you call it "the Way," "the Dharma," or "the Mind Seal," each of these terms refer to you alone, and so it is only possible to see them by looking at yourself. As I often say, it is only a matter of the thing itself knowing the thing itself. You cannot see your own eyeball, but if you cannot remove it and display it in front of yourself, you won't be able to convey the Mind Seal to others. As long as you try to see, consciousness accompanies your perception. That is why I say, "Leave it as it is!" By doing so, you can transcend seeing and not seeing, understanding and not understanding, and only then can you become the thing itself. "The Mind Seal" and "the True Face" are just different expressions for the same thing. Consider the following line:

The mind: when did I start—without really knowing it—to think of it as *my* mind?[56]

This is exactly the way it is. Without really knowing it, at some point, we have come to call something our heart or our mind. But what is it after all? This is the nature of thought. And this is why we must be one with zazen. Zazen does not mean simply to calm the mind, nor is it a means to get rid of all sorts of anguish or random, delusive thoughts. When a thought arises, zazen has disappeared. Thought is everything. During zazen, different states of consciousness invariably arise. As you do zazen, you will come to understand that very well.

When you knew nothing about zazen, those thoughts and feelings didn't bother you. You felt that they were only natural, and they surely flew by without interruption. But as you began sitting, they became a problem for you. Now you constantly label them as random or delusive, or you think you have to do something about them. Yet there is no substance to them. There is neither understanding or not-understanding. There is only the thing itself, the thoughts themselves.

Not realizing this and believing that there is some substance to this consciousness—this state is called ignorance. In order to understand this ignorance, you need to die completely once. When you think, your whole body from your head to your toes is thinking, and that is all. But we have the idea that there is some "mind" inside of us that is operating and creating thought. For that reason, we believe that "I" and the thoughts that arise in "me" are something separate. But it is not like that.

And "What sort of person dares to transmit it?"

In his *Song of Zazen* (*Zazen wasan*), Master Hakuin Zenji likened the condition of searching around for the Mind Seal while being right in the midst of it to "crying out in thirst while in the midst of water." In fact, there are numerous allegories for this situation. For example, we often see people seeking out medicine even though they are not actually ill. In this case, illness stands for delusion. So someone may say, "I'm unclear and confused about myself, and a mess." If we give their predicament a name, we call it "delusion." However, this is only labeling things, and no one is actually burdened with "delusion." And yet, we desperately want this medicine called zazen, we desperately want a method. But we have to realize that delusion and anguish are themselves the very medicines that can immediately cure our so-called delusion. That is a fact, isn't it?

The place where delusion arises and the place where you find that delusion has disappeared are exactly the same place. If we think about it from this perspective, our condition of confusion and our desperate search for a good method to get rid of that confusion are already the method. That is why I advise, "When you are feeling distressed or uneasy, be totally one with that! Don't look elsewhere! Just be distressed or uneasy, be one with your delusion! Be one with your afflictions!" In truth, there is no better medicine.

However, because that medicine works so well, I cannot get you to really believe it. Instead you keep looking for the supposedly best medicine. You wonder, "Should I do kōans, or shikantaza?" Or you think, "If I go to this temple or that master, maybe they will give me such and such a medicine." Should you go around like this, checking out different medicines, you must really take care not to get poisoned by the medicine. So please bear in mind that delusion itself is the medicine to cure delusion. If you feel like your life is a mess, then becoming one with this condition is the only medicine that can really help you.

There is the story of a man who, after practicing zazen for a long time with his master, was able to give outstanding answers to kōans like Mu or the sound of one hand clapping. The master, however, would not approve of him. No matter what the man said, his master would not certify him. Finally at his wit's end, the man gave up. This was not a matter of doubting his master; it was just that he had tried everything. As he let go of seeking, he gradually became peaceful. Yet this "giving up" is not a matter of becoming indifferent. Rather, the man's seeking and his urge to understand had finally reached maturity. Thus he was able to let go of it without resistance. This is the effect of the medicine about which I have just been speaking. This is the way it works. As a result, the man was able to receive certification from his master. The story itself is well-known. If you simply stop seeking, everything becomes the Dharma gate of comfort and ease.

When Linji, the founder of the Rinzai sect, received certification from his master, Huangbo, Huangbo asked an attendant to bring him the sitting board of his own master, Baizhang. But Linji intervened and said, "No. Attendant, bring us some fire." When Huangbo asked Linji why he wanted fire, Linji answered, "Such a thing is of no use to me. I am going to burn that sitting board here." He was saying that whether or not he had the sitting board was just the same. That is, such symbols are not necessary. Reportedly, Huangbo was delighted to hear Linji's high-spirited reply, but he still asked him to accept the sitting board anyway since it would not unduly burden him either.

In fact, in our world, if someone has received a symbol of transmission in the same way that Linji received the sitting board of his master, this means that other people should be able to trust him or her and come to practice Zen with that person. These days, however, everyone receives certification, and thus we are led to believe that there are no longer any Zen priests whose zazen is mistaken. If everything is said to be correct, then we are faced with the question of what is really correct. For this reason, the present state of Zen Buddhism causes a real headache.

There is a saying: "Everyone is fully endowed. Each individual is perfect."[57] The question then remains: If we really are perfect as we are, since when are we deluded? Earlier, I said that there is not even one deluded person. And so there is no need to receive medicine from another person. The greatest doctor is one who can guide people by saying, "Take delusion as your medicine. You don't need to come back to my hospital." My advice is to just keep on working. Do what has to be done without expecting anything from it. Aren't we doing zazen in order to become people who can work steadily and quietly like a fool at the task that has been given to us? It is necessary to do zazen with that goal in mind. If not, you will always think that there is a "Zen" outside of what you are doing right now. Hearing a sound, you will always feel compelled to find something behind the sound that you are hearing. This process is called "putting another head on top of the one you already have."

All of us are surely doing something right, but as it is said, "Merely the slightest difference, and you are separated from it by a thousand miles."⁵⁸ Sometimes, the further ahead we progress, the wider the gap becomes. That is why we must thoroughly sit and sit, until sitting itself disappears.

So the verse says:

Throughout the ages, it has remained firm and unshaken.

The following is a dialogue that occurred between masters Dongshan Lianjie and his disciple, Caoshan, both of whom hail from the Sōtō sect. First you must know that in monasteries, when practice periods come to an end, many monks and nuns ask for leave in order to practice freely. If asked where they intend to go, some will say that they don't even know yet themselves:

> One day Caoshan came to his master to request permission to go on a pilgrimage.
> "Where are you going?" asked Master Dongshan.
> "I am going to a place that neither changes nor is different," Caoshan replied. [In other words, he was saying that he was not going anywhere.]
> Master Dongshan then asked, "If you're going to some place that isn't any different, then why are you leaving?" [In other words, Master Dongshan was suggesting that Caoshan stay.]
> Caoshan, being an outstanding disciple, replied, "Even if I go, nothing changes, and nothing is different"⁵⁹ [That is to say, all the places on a pilgrimage are no different.]

The line "Throughout the ages, it has remained firm and unshaken" also captures the spirit with which Caoshan freely expressed his feelings.

These days I am often telling my students to make more effort at zazen when not sitting. This is what we call "Zen within movement." Master Hakuin taught that "Zen within movement is millions of times superior to Zen within stillness."⁶⁰ I have some experience with this myself. There was a time when I became attached to sitting and was very conscious of sitting as something separate from myself. When you sit in such a way, you really start to understand that "zazen teaches zazen." Not caring what people around me would think, I made every effort, always trying to be one with my sitting. I sat so single-mindedly that even in the midst of winter I would be bathed in sweat, clenching my teeth. But I gradually realized that even though I had been told that I must be one with zazen, because of trying to do my best and exerting myself and always thinking that I *had* to do it, there was actually a gap between zazen and my method of sitting.

What could I do? "To be one with" are the words of someone who has become one, but that was still not the case for me. At this point, it was not good to hesitate. By any means possible, I was going to become one. I knew clearly that because of my seeking mind, I perceived things and then tried to become them. I knew it and yet I just had to do something to become one. There was no other choice for me. This was not because someone else told me to do it. It had to be. And this was something that zazen taught me without words, so it was not painful at all. And that is how I endeavored at zazen.

I do not tell you this in order to hurry things up. There is no point in wanting to get a result too quickly or too hastily. Practice will then become unpleasant. I am sure you will find a way not to be in a rush and yet still become the thing itself, quietly and steadily. Master Dōgen wrote in "The Real Form of All Things" chapter of his *Shōbōgenzō*:

Life and death come and go, but your body itself is the truth.

Whether alive or dead, it is you. People haven't gone anywhere because they have died. Nor can you say that you are here because you are alive. Whether alive or dead, we are always a true person. "Throughout the ages, it has remained firm and unshaken" also captures this sentiment.

If you seek elsewhere and constantly try to change yourself, you should consider the saying, "It won't even happen in the year of the donkey." There is no year of the donkey in the Chinese calendar. So this is to say that no matter how long you wait, there will never be a moment of fruition for you. You must realize that seeking such change is only to go round and round in circles.

As soon as you call something the Mind Seal, it is already
meaningless.

Long ago, Nāgārjuna wrote:

To think and to discriminate is like being caught up in a fish-
ing net that the devil has cast over you: you cannot move.
This is so because you think, because you discriminate. Yet,
being unable to move, having nothing to rely on, that is in
fact the true Dharma Seal, the Mind Seal.

He also compared trying to attain enlightenment by speculating on
what enlightenment might be like to trying to burn to cinders a huge
mountain with the light of a firefly: it is totally impossible.

When we say the word "fire," it does not burn our lips. This is
because we only attach the name "fire" to the thing itself. So even if
we say "fire" over and over, it will not cause our lips to burn. So why
don't we try not to label things with such names? But what should we
do instead? "Know hot and cold for yourself."[61] This expression means
that hot and cold are something that only we can know. Experience
everything for ourselves, just as it is. Fire is not "hot," nor is water
"cold." Knowing cold and hot for yourself does not mean putting your
hand into a fire in order to discover that it is hot. Knowing cold and hot
for oneself means to become the thing itself. If we do not really clarify
the true nature of things, don't we violate the precept not to tell lies,
even if we may have no intention of doing so?

You must know that in essence all things originate from infinite
emptiness.

"Infinite emptiness" is of a size and scale greater than anything you
have ever encountered before. We tend to think, since we live on the
Earth, that Earth is the only world. But there are countless worlds in
infinite emptiness. The author wants us to know that the Mind Seal is
just such an infinity.

You can compare it to a lotus flower in a red-hot kiln.

The word "fire" often appears in Buddhist texts. In the context of Zen, we should understand fire to mean something totally pure. The Mind Seal is something that cannot be defiled or stained by anything else. All the buddhas and enlightened ones of the past have protected and maintained it. The lotus flower in the fire of a red-hot kiln is something that essentially cannot exist, but this image expresses the mode of life of one who has attained the Mind Seal.

There is a short poem by Master Dōgen that goes like this:

> If someone asks you, "What sort of person is a Buddha?"
> One could say, "An icicle hanging in the midst of a
>   fire house."[62]

A "fire house" is a small hut that people formerly built out in the wilderness where they wanted to cultivate a field, and they would maintain a fire in it to keep animals away. Master Dōgen replaces the lotus flower with ice in his poem. Both similes express something that is completely impossible to understand by means of rational thought.

Another saying goes:

> Last night, the mouth of vast space opened and laughed.
> A great fire swallowed up Lake Dongting.[63]

What does this mean? This is something we can easily understand and does not describe something far away. We might open our mouths to chant sutras every day. We always eat three times a day. Just these activities are described with this imagery. Infinite emptiness always opens its mouth in this way. We think of vast, empty space as being something different from ourselves, and we also do not identify ourselves with blazing fire. To associate ourselves with the water of Lake Dongting seems absurd. We are in the habit of imagining things as being outside of us. But Zen is not this way. We must understand that all Zen expressions refer to us right now.

Don't say that a free and empty mind is the Way;

Many people say, "Give up all your discriminating thoughts and intentions! A buddha is someone who is in such a state of no-mind." But here, Master Tong'an tells us that we must not say things like "No-mind is the Way." If we acknowledge the existence of something labeled "no-mind" or "infinite emptiness," then to that extent we leave a mark on everything, and freedom is obstructed. We may often say things like, "Give up all your discriminative thinking!" or "You still have an ego!" or "Be intimate with the Way!" and let it end at that. This line means that it is not really appropriate to say such things.

A free and empty mind is still separated from it by a great barrier.

Whether or not you understand this, just let go of it quickly. Why? Because there really is no need to attain a mind free of discriminating thoughts and intentions. As I said earlier regarding delusion, you must not think that you will eventually attain a liberated mind by means of practice and zazen. If you constantly think of becoming or attaining something, your thoughts become a great barrier.

Long ago, someone said:

> Far more virtuous than making an offering to millions of buddhas is to make an offering to one person of the Way with a liberated mind.[64]

Any who single-mindedly sit sesshin are in fact "people of the Way with liberated minds." The only problem is that we deny this by saying, "No, I am not such a person." So quickly cast away all that is good and all that is bad, let go of it all, release it—this is true practice. Work at not being attached to anything.

2: The Mind of the Enlightened Ones

EVERYTHING IS IMPERMANENT. Morning becomes noon, and with the passing of time, a baby grows up and becomes a young person. Likewise, over time, delusions become enlightenment. Surely we notice that all of these things take place unaided by human agency. They all occur due to the continual flow of impermanence. The Diamond Sutra says:

> So you should view all of the fleeting worlds:
> A star at dawn, a bubble in the stream;
> A flash of lightning in a summer cloud;
> A flickering lamp, a phantom, and a dream.[65]

There can be no mistake. This is our condition right now, just as we are. There is nothing wrong with how we are and so there is also nothing right about it. Since there is no delusion, there is also no enlightenment. This condition of things is what we refer to as "suchness" or being "as it is." It is not a matter of understanding our condition as it is, but rather of simply assenting to it.

However, as one becomes familiar with Zen, one begins to learn terminology. The worst terms one could learn are "everything is empty," "all is nothing," and "everything is just what it is, as it is." Yet we learn these words for emptiness and nothingness and begin to play with them. The most that could happen to us under these circumstances is that time just passes by and nothing will be left. Since nothing remains, we think this absence is what is called "Zen." We may not even recognize that we have become bound up in the comfortable position that "everything is just what it is." We may begin to think it acceptable to just sit quietly, telling ourselves that there is nothing to let go of and nothing to throw away, things are just as they are. Many in the past and many today cling to words like "emptiness" and "nothingness" and are unable to discard them.

It was precisely for this reason that Master Changcha felt compelled to write the *Ten Verses of Unfathomable Depth* and leave them behind for our benefit. "Ten Verses of Unfathomable Depth" does not mean that there are ten things. Rather, the author has divided one thing into ten parts and has then spoken about it in detail. It is only natural, then, that to understand "The Mind of the Enlightened Ones" we must be able to understand the other nine parts as well. "One thing" refers to the infinite. When we say, "Be one," we mean, "Be one with everything." The nature of forgetting the self is to be one. Please, make no mistake about this point.

The infinite has no limits. "No limits" means that all objects disappear. Since all objects disappear, there exists nothing to be limited. In contrast, if we are bound by human thought, no matter how successful we might be, there will come a time when we reach our limit. There is no telling when our time will come. But when it does, we will feel abandoned by everything, and then we will feel lonely. This is because we are bound by the word "lonely." It is the same with birth and death. We simply do not recognize that we are bound up by words like "birth" and "death."

If we really make the Mind Seal of the first verse our own, then we must also understand the mind of the enlightened ones of the second verse. "The Mind of the Enlightened Ones" refers to the spirit or heart of the ancestors. During the Tang dynasty there was a Zen priest named Mazu Daoyi who was said to have had eighty-four disciples, each of whom had true knowledge of Zen. It has also been said that only two among the eighty-four, namely the great masters Baizhang Huaihai and Huangbo Xiyuan, were truly outstanding monks. We can see from this example just how difficult it is to truly understand, and thereby pass on, the Mind of the Enlightened Ones.

The Tang era was the golden age of Zen in China. But it did not last very long and the wind of Zen died down during the Southern Song dynasty. Later, Master Dōgen was able—just barely—to transmit the Zen tradition to Japan. However, in Japan Zen once again fell into decline during the Tokugawa Era, and there was even a movement to destroy Buddhism during the subsequent Meiji era. Luckily, through the enthusiastic and zealous efforts of a handful of people, Japanese Buddhism escaped destruction. Zen Buddhism has been revived, albeit not completely, and its pulse now beats faintly. It is up to us now to make every effort to not let it die off completely.

In bygone ages disciples were beaten again and again with the *kyō-saku* (the warning stick) during sesshin. There is the well-known poem by Master Tengan Sogyō:

Hit so much my body was black and blue.
When I look back, it makes my hair stand on end.
True joy must be gained through pain.
Looking at my condition now, I resent that the tip of the stick
    was too lenient.
Hit so much my body was black and blue.

He was beaten so much that his arms and shoulders were covered with bruises. He was constantly showered with blows. He says that a true sense of satisfaction arises because of the hardships one must go through. Looking back, Master Sogyō laments that had he been hit even harder while training, he would have accomplished an even deeper understanding. When I was younger, I often heard this account when sitting zazen. We resented listening to it because the person wielding the stick didn't strike us in the place where we really needed to be struck. At other times, we felt antipathy toward the person wielding the stick because it was impossible to sit quietly when we were constantly being hit. Consider acupuncture. The acupuncturist must use his needles skillfully in order to really pierce the root of sickness. Similarly, when it comes to use of the kyōsaku during sesshin, the stick must be used skillfully in order to touch the sickness that is the extremely tenacious desire of attachment to the ego. If the kyōsaku is not used skillfully and the stick misses the right point, there can be no cure.

This mind is like emptiness, but it isn't empty.

Here the word "like" demonstrates that nothing is fixed, that we should not get stuck in one place. Put simply, we should be free to change. At the very end of his *Lancet of Zazen* (*Zazenshin*), Master Dōgen leaves us with a truly wonderful expression:

Fish swim like fish, birds fly like birds.[66]

To say "like" birds and "like" fish suggests that the actors in question—the fish and the birds—are undecided, unfixed, unsettled. They have not made themselves comfortable in some place. They have not become stuck. So using the term "like" to qualify the actions of animals is to consider what it means to become truly free, unfixed. It is also possible to think of what the word "like" suggests about sameness and difference, the absolute and the relative. So the line "This mind is like emptiness, but it isn't empty" expresses that sameness is difference, that emptiness is form.

As I have said many times, "difference" or "form" is the endless variety of things that come together due to causes and conditions. There are rich people, poor people, people who are suffering, and those who are comfortable and at ease. Their various states are all the nature of difference. Different as they are, none can be compared to any other.

We might be suffering now. We might feel confused and entirely backed up against a wall. Yet even though such differences exist, there is no reason whatsoever for conflict. We will never clearly understand real sameness and difference so long as true sameness means something other than to become truly one with suffering or with delusion. It has been said since long ago that the wisdom of sameness is relatively easy to realize, but the wisdom of difference is exceedingly difficult.

The point is that we must forget the self and be one with each thing. This is the significance of the first line of the second verse. If we examine our present condition right now, I think we can easily understand this. If there is suffering, then be suffering itself. If there is difficulty, then abandon yourself to difficulty, as it is. That is all. From there it is a matter of transcending things, even transcending "not suffering" or being "like." We must transcend transcendence and really become empty. Such is the condition expressed in this line.

How could the unfathomable function ever degenerate to being
the result of achievement?

The "enlightened mind," the mind of the ancestors, transcends being
empty or not empty, existent or nonexistent. It never degenerates into
something limited. It does not get stuck or settle into just one place. This
is tantamount to saying that all things are independent.

In autumn, the leaves on the trees change color. When leaves on the
various trees turn different shades of color, and begin to look different
from one another, that is when we first say that they look like brocade.
It seems as if the mottled color of the leaves form a single pattern. But
it is only because the various colors of the leaves on ten, twenty, or
thirty trees are interwoven with one another that we can say that they
look like a single brocade pattern. At sesshin many people with different
thoughts gather together to sit, but no one pushes himself or herself
forward. We all follow the rules so that a sesshin can flow smoothly.
Isn't this an expression of a condition of No-Self? It is a splendid thing
to dwell within cause and conditions as they are. If there were only one
thing and no difference, how could there ever be something called true
sameness?

There is nothing else to seek and there is nothing else to let go of.
This is conveyed in the expression "Be the master wherever you go;
be in harmony with every condition."[67] Zen sayings like this perfectly
express our immediate condition in just a few words. We have each lived
lives in which there is no separation between self and others. If we take
a moment to notice it, we will see that the condition expressed in this
saying is a fact appearing right now in front of you.

The bodhisattvas at the three stages of wisdom[68] have still not
clarified this.

The "three stages of wisdom" refer to ranks in practice. These are like
the ranks of bodhisattvas who are on their respective ways to becoming buddhas. Some will wonder if in fact there are such ranks, but it
is actually we ourselves who create various ranks by thinking that we
are still at this or that stage. There are different levels of achievement

such as the ten ranks of faith, the ten ranks of stability, the ten ranks of practice,[69] and the ten ranks of devotion. Yet it is abundantly clear that people who situate themselves within these ranking systems spend a great deal of time thinking about where they and others fit within such vertical hierarchies. They are completely unable to see the horizontal nature of equality or the absolute. These people say things like, "I used to practice Mu, but now I'm working with the *Gateless Barrier*," or "I'm working with the *Blue Cliff Record*," or "I'm working with the *Ten Major Precepts*." In this way, practitioners define ranks, thinking that someone looking at the *Gateless Barrier* is not as advanced as someone looking at the *Blue Cliff Record*, or that someone looking at the *Blue Cliff Record* is less advanced than someone looking at the *Ten Major Precepts*. This is a mistake. One does not gradually improve until one reaches the end.

For those who practice counting the breath (*sūsokkan*), the breaths are counted from one to ten and then the counting starts over again from one. But when we count "one, two, three...," "two" is not a number between "one" and "three." Rather, "two" is everything, "three" is everything, and so on. When we really become one with any individual number, all the rest must disappear. Yet many are mistakenly told, "If you carefully count from one to ten, your mind will become quiet and settled. So you must continue to do this on and on, carefully and conscientiously." Taking such advice to heart, people will continue to do this for ten or twenty years, simply repeating the series from one to ten over and over and over. And then, after having done this for ten or twenty years, they'll ask, "Is it really Zen to do only this?"

This is not to say that it is bad to count breaths, nor is it to say that kōans themselves are either good or bad. Many people in the past have cast off body and mind by means of kōan practice. The problem lies rather with the teachers who have not reached the final destination but still instruct students in sūsokkan or kōan practice.

And how can the higher ranks of bodhisattvas ever reach it?

This line continues the sentiment of the previous line. It is said that if a person does not progress through all forty-two of the bodhisattva ranks, they will not become a true buddha. But it is fine to understand these ranks as referring to a process that is still underway, one in which the goal has not yet been reached. Consider the saying "Still on the way, without having left one's house." True practice is to forget the self by being difference itself, so that even when we say, "I always seem to be stuck in the same place," we continue being at a standstill until it disappears. It would be a mistake to look elsewhere. Delusion is the medicine for delusion. We fail to practice the Buddha Way if we use something else to become free of delusion.

This is called "No Dharma outside the mind." Our mental activity right now is Buddhadharma. Since Śākyamuni Buddha was the first person to realize this, we call it *Buddha*dharma. But if someone named Albert had realized it, we would call it *Albert*dharma. We cannot compare Albert's Dharma with the Buddha's Dharma. Dharma does not belong to anyone other than the one who has grasped it. We will not reach the Dharma unless we follow the Dharma of the Buddha or the teachings of the ancestors. When we do reach it, it becomes our own. The Dharma that is reached in the end isn't the Buddha's Dharma. It is the Dharma of each person who reaches it. So it is only natural that there exist a Sōtō, Rinzai, Unmon, Igyō, and Hōgen sect.[70] Whatever the case may be, we must not seek outside of our current condition.

As Master Dōgen said:

To study the Way is to study the Self.
To study the Self is to forget the ego-self.[71]

This means that we will not understand the objective of practice until we have followed the teachings of the ancestors for some time. As soon as we are able to walk on our own, however, all we must do is keep walking in our own way. I have often said that the teachings are a finger pointing at the moon. The teachings are necessary in order to see the moon, but once we have seen the moon, then neither the finger nor the moon are necessary any longer. That is the Buddhadharma. I would like you to be freed from anything that you think you cannot let go of. To the extent that there is "No Dharma outside the mind," there is no Buddhadharma outside of your own present mental activity.

There are those who, upon hearing this, will, without really understanding the meaning, come and say, "I am my Dharma. You are your

Dharma. There is no Buddhadharma outside the mind, right? That is fine with me. Please verify my realization of this." This is precisely why I say it is no good to learn and then simply play around with words. We must be careful about this. If we start out with words as our point of departure, we are apt to fall into the trap of words. You must be careful about this as you practice the Way of Buddha.

> The golden carp that has passed through the net remains
> trapped in the water.

This line refers to Case 49 of the *Blue Cliff Record*, which reads:

Introduction
Making holes in the enemy's defenses, seizing his drums, and capturing his banners; surrounding him a hundred times with a thousand checkpoints, watching the front, and guarding the rear. Even if you can hold the tiger's head and secure its tail—this is not yet true mastery. The ox head disappears, the horse head appears—that also is not yet a great wonder. Now, what happens when someone with excessive abilities comes. See the following:

The Case
Sansheng asked Xuefeng, "What shall the golden carp that has passed through the net feed on?"

Xuefeng replied, "When you have gotten out of the net, I will tell you."

Sansheng said, "Although you are the renowned teacher of fifteen hundred monks, you don't even recognize what I am talking about."

Xuefeng said, "I am the chief abbot, and have much to attend to."

Xuedou's Verse
The golden carp that has passed through the net
Don't say it is stuck in the water.

It shakes the heavens and moves the earth,
Swinging its fins, lashing its tail.
Then a whale spumes, raising great waves;
Thunder sounds, and causes a purifying whirlwind.
When the whirlwind occurs, how many people in heaven
and on earth know about it?

This case comes from a question that Sansheng, a disciple of Linji, asked Master Xuefeng.

"What shall the golden carp that has passed through the net feed on?"
Xuefeng said, "When you have gotten out of the net, I will tell you."

No matter how often people might say that they have cast off body and mind and become "emptiness" or "nothingness," they have experienced something that is essentially unnecessary. This is what we call "the sickness of enlightenment." It means to fixate on enlightenment. There are none who are deluded, and so there must be no enlightenment. If you say you have attained enlightenment by means of practice, then your delusion has only become the delusion of enlightenment.

Some people come and say, "I feel unsettled by the steady stream of delusive thoughts as they arise in me, so I am doing breathing zazen." Either they have been taught that this sort of zazen is correct and necessary in order to practice, or they have come to think this on their own. We are not usually aware of our breath. Being purposefully aware of the breath means to intentionally put delusive thinking to work. If I say, "It is all right to do breathing zazen when you sit," the students quickly think that following and counting the breath are methods for doing zazen. They think that they must get rid of all of the other thoughts they have had until then. But following and counting the breath and all the other thoughts that they have had until then are the same thing. Whether imagination or rational thought, counting and following the breath, or kōan practice—these are all thoughts that you have produced with your own consciousness. In this way they are the same.

It is also said:

> Sit and look at the true nature of reality. All faults and bad
> deeds will vanish like frost and dew. All darkness will disap-
> pear in the light of wisdom.[72]

"Sit and look at the true nature of reality" means that we are inclined to believe we are doing the most correct thing if we practice a Zen method. In this way, our egoistic thought ends up producing a great illusion. If you become even a little bit settled when you practice following or counting the breath and come to understand this, then you will certainly be able to practice entrusting yourself to your delusive thoughts and feelings, just as they are, without using such props for support. Consequently, if you know this clearly and discern it in practice, then there is no problem at all in using methods such as following or counting the breath or working with a kōan from time to time. However, if you practice without understanding this principle, you will not understand that the correct method of practice is to be completely one with your delusive thoughts and feelings.

Sansheng then said, "Although you are the renowned teacher of fifteen hundred monks, you don't even recognize what I am talking about." At that time there were fifteen hundred monks training at Mt. Xuefeng. Sansheng was saying that although Xuefeng was guiding this great number of monks, he was unable to respond to Sansheng's question. In other words, "You don't understand anything." Xuefeng responds to this charge by saying, "I am the chief abbot and have much to attend to." The chief abbot has many duties to perform. He must read sutras, perform funerals, and attend to matters concerning the lay parishioners. Along with speaking to various people and keeping the monastery clean, these are all duties of a chief priest.

Isn't it a wonderful thing if someone says, "I'm busy now. I don't have time to quietly sit zazen"? If you practice zazen in order to really forget yourself and just become your work itself, then it will be correct from beginning to end. However, those who practice in order to completely eliminate their afflictions so that they can live their everyday life peacefully should remember Xuefeng's response. You should also remember the story about Takamori Saigō who practiced Zen under a master named Musan. One day, Saigō went to see Master Musan and waited half a day. Still Musan did not appear. Saigō became very angry and when he was about to resort to violence, the master finally appeared and used the same line that Master Xuefeng had used: "The chief priest is busy and has much to attend to."

You may have pressing business to attend to and yet perhaps you take time off from work to participate in a sesshin. When you do, do. When you sit zazen, be zazen. How can you be zazen? By forgetting sitting.

But the stone horse still on the way leaves its sand cage suddenly.

"On the way" means on the path. Things on the path are still unclear or unresolved. They are all still in progress, still on the way. In Zen, we also refer to the path as the state of "distinguishing." The ultimate, in contrast, is "sameness." However, we must be able to attain true freedom on the path *within* distinction. Being "on the way" is already everything. So if there are any people here who think, "It's all on the way until there is a conclusion or settlement," they should consider that half believing and half doubting, or when everything is not yet clear, is also already the Dharma.

Beings transmigrate throughout the six realms of delusion: heaven, the human realm, the realm of fighting devils, the animal realm, the hungry ghost realm, and hell. Yet, if we can simply be true beings of these six realms, then there is no need to escape from any of them or to travel to the Buddhist realms of enlightenment. When we are still in doubt and say to ourselves, "Surely, it's like that, but...," then we are totally consumed by this thought. When we can truly believe that "there is no Buddhadharma outside the mind," then we will not seek it elsewhere. It is necessary to freely become a being of hell when we are in hell, or an animal if we are in the realm of animals. We can call this a samādhi of really moving around freely.

The "stone horse" represents the condition of being without a self. The "sand cage" is a flimsy horse shed. The stone horse comes flying out of this small, fragile shed. We cannot usually think or conceive of this. This metaphor applies to our own condition. Even though we seem to be unsettled or in a state of confusion, the morning passes by and during the afternoon we suddenly understand something well because we have learned various things. At such times we don't perceive ourselves in the least. And yet, should we start to sit, the self issues forth from nowhere and we enter a cage we have built called *shikan* or "just," or a cage called "the breath," and we inevitably feel restricted inside it. The meaning of this line is to say, "Is it really acceptable to sit in this cage all day long?"

Why have the meaning of Bodhidharma coming from the West explained in every detail?

To explain something in every detail means that if the explanation is too thorough, then it risks being too complicated to understand. As it is said, "Too much talking damages the wise man's virtue." While Bodhidharma was sitting quietly facing a wall, he would begin to speak only when a person who was prepared to sacrifice even his own arm came to visit him. "Coming from the West" refers to the Way of Buddha, to zazen.

Then, how should the Dharma be explained? A famous expression offers up the image of "bare pillars and lanterns." In the Dharma Hall, there are many such lanterns and pillars. Put ears on the pillars and eyes on the lanterns and just listen. The Dharma can be explained in this way.

At the time of Śākyamuni Buddha, there was a layman named Vimalakīrti who had a celebrated dialogue with the Bodhisattva Mañjuśrī about the Dharma gate of nonduality. Mañjuśrī, who is said to be the ancestor of the Seven buddhas, eloquently stated his views with regard to the Dharma gate of nonduality. Then he asked Vimala to give his views. Vimala, however, remained silent. Later, people said that Vimala's silence was like thunder. This is also a way of expounding the Dharma.

Don't ask about the coming from the West, nor about the East.

The monk Xuansha Shibei had set out on a pilgrimage but along the way attained great enlightenment. He then returned to the temple of Master Xuefeng and said, "Bodhidharma didn't come to China and the Second Ancestor Huike didn't go to India." Master Xuefeng then certified Xuansha's Dharma transmission with the words, "What is gained through external circumstances will never be lost."

Today, just like long ago, people are more interested in filling their stomachs than in listening to the Dharma. They seek a life that will give them a moderate degree of satisfaction. Believing that people wouldn't listen to the Dharma if they were hungry, monks dedicated themselves to social projects. Consequently, the Dharma became second or third in importance. Thus venerable Prajñātārā dispatched his disciple Bodhidharma on a journey to teach the Dharma in China because he sensed that the Dharma was waning in India. But the right conditions did not arise for many years. Only when Bodhidharma obtained the second ancestor, Huike, as his disciple did Zen begin to flourish in China. This is the meaning of the reference to East and West in this line.

However, this line does not mean something comes to the East that was formerly in the West. It expresses, rather, the same idea found in Master Dōgen's statement, "This Dharma is amply endowed in each person, but without practice it doesn't manifest itself, and without verification, it is of no use."[73] Each person is amply endowed with the Mind of the Enlightened Ones. The Mind of the Enlightened Ones is completely full and brimming everywhere at all times. If you have made it your own, you can then be satisfied in any place at any time. Therefore, "Mind of the Enlightened Ones" conveys that there is nothing but the thing itself. "Don't ask about the coming from the West, nor about the East!" The Mind of the Enlightened Ones is completely present everywhere regardless of whether it is east, west, north, or south.

Master Changcha has explained in almost too much detail that there is only one thing to do—namely, to be single-minded and to forget the self everywhere at all times. This second verse says, then, with great solicitude that we must not look outside ourselves but instead be settled in each moment—right now, now, and now again—by looking carefully at where we are standing.

3: The Unfathomable Function

As we consider the *Ten Verses of Unfathomable Depth*, it is not necessary to begin with the first verse and continue on, in a strict order, to the tenth. If you hope to understand the work in its entirety, you need only to attend closely to one of the verses. This fact rings true even beyond the *Ten Verses of Unfathomable Depth*. Inherent in each Buddhist teaching is the ability to encompass the wisdom of all others. Whether one encounters the 84,000 Dharma teachings of Śākyamuni Buddha, or the teachings of Master Dōgen, or kōan collections such as the *Mumonkan*, the *Blue Cliff Record*, or the *Record of Equanimity*—whether you take up a hundred kōans or a thousand—if you truly understand just one kōan, you will understand them all.

The founders of the various Zen sects—Rinzai, Ōbaku, Sōtō, Igyō, and Unmon—were themselves able to cut off at the root the innermost delusions of people with a single word or a phrase. For example, when asked what the essence of Buddhadharma was, Juzhi held up one finger. He went on to answer all questions in this way. Whenever asked why Bodhidharma came from the West, the Imperial Zen Master Daitō always replied "Barrier!" And Master Zhaozhou, recalling his response when asked if a dog has buddha nature, resolved all questions with "Mu!" or "Naught!"

There are many examples of deluded people who have awakened. The monk Xiangyan awoke from a life of ignorance when he heard a rock strike a piece of bamboo. Lingyun cast off body and mind when he smelled the fragrance of a flower. Or there is the story of the master hunter named Shigong Huicang. He was asked by Zen Master Mazu how many deer he could kill with a single arrow.

"No matter how great a hunter," Huicang said, "it is only possible to kill one deer with one arrow."

"What?! And you call yourself a master hunter?!" Mazu replied, "I can kill a whole herd of deer with one arrow."

On hearing this Huicang was suddenly enlightened.

Here was a person who had no prior contact with Zen or with Buddhism or the records of the old masters. Just as in the saying "A hunter chasing a deer doesn't see the mountains," Huicang was singularly focused, continuously and single-mindedly pushing his way toward the goal, without worrying about how high the mountains are or how low the valleys may be. So sudden awakening could occur, without our having been aware of awakening or the possibility of achieving it, upon hearing a statement like "I can kill a whole herd of deer with one arrow."

It is possible to bring to a conclusion the whole text of the *Ten Verses of Unfathomable Depth* by hearing only this one verse, "The Unfathomable Function." I would like you to be mindful of this. Consider the kōan "All dharmas return to one thing."[74] "All dharmas" refers to all things that exist in the universe, both with form and without form. So if all dharmas return to one thing, to one place, then where does the one thing return to? It is important to realize that it is possible for people who have been, until now, completely confused and perplexed to be immediately liberated from suffering and confusion upon hearing such expressions. This is the nature of the Dharma. If you cannot really understand this point, then your zazen will amount to nothing more than "learning meditation."[75]

"Learning meditation" involves imagining that the result or goal is located somewhere far off in the distance. Believing that they must proceed gradually toward the goal, people practice zazen with the thought, "While walking along, each step is the result." The opposite of "learning meditation" is "being beyond learning," which is this moment now. On this point, recall the opening words of the *Song of Realization*:

> Don't you see the person who has abandoned all learning and doing? He neither tries to get rid of delusion nor seeks the Truth.

One must abandon all learning when practicing Zen. Our practice must be such that each breath is everything; there must be liberation in the inhalation of just one breath. Yet this is not something easily noticed. And because it often remains unnoticed, inevitably we seek something "special." As a result our practice amounts to nothing but "learning meditation"—the kind of meditation practice wherein we reach for a faraway goal and acquire various expressions used in Zen and begin to think that playing with and making use of these words means that we have deepened our understanding of Zen.

To avoid this problem, we must be aware that the state of all things existing in this world, in their very condition of differentiation, is referred to as "the differentiation of all dharmas." This state of differentiation itself is the Dharma. The first person to realize that this state of differentiation, including even himself, was the Dharma was Śākyamuni Buddha. There is nothing that is not the Dharma, including oneself. It is impossible to create a separation between oneself and the Dharma. Even when we think of the Dharma as something apart from ourselves, saying "This is the Dharma and this is not," the Dharma is nevertheless seamless. We are practicing the Dharma while in the midst of the Dharma. No matter how fearful or confused or anxious we might be, there exists the Dharma of fear, of confusion, of anxiety, of mental afflictions. If you realize this, then delusion is enlightenment, confusion is realization, and anxiety is peace of mind. This is to say that it is absolutely impossible for something extraneous to the Dharma to enter into our consciousness.

When we hear Buddhist teachings, without being aware of it, we completely lose the ability to distinguish between the Dharma and our self, which we have labeled "a person." If you read or hear something like what I have just said and then think, "This is the Dharma, this is the Dharma," then you are no longer able to distinguish between the Dharma and the self. As a result, you end up making the terrible mistake we call the "naturalist heresy." You begin to play around with expressions like "Everything is good the way it is," or "Nothing to realize, nothing to attain." The authors of the records of the ancestors, like Master Yuanwu Keqin, who commented on the *Blue Cliff Record*, or Master Wumen Huikai, who wrote the *Gateless Barrier*, were only able to leave their writings behind for future generations as a result of constant and unyielding practice. These days, expressions like "making a great effort" or "wholehearted devotion" are nearly dead. The people who wrote down these records did so as a result of really grinding their bodies into powder as they exerted themselves to the utmost. Only as a result of that effort were they able to write that the self and the Dharma are one.

This point can also be made with reference to expressions used in the Sōtō sect, such as "practice and realization are not two"[76] and "subtle practice within original enlightenment." If you have not done any real practice, but are only sitting, and only by virtue of that you say things like "The Dharma and self are one" or "subtle practice within enlightenment," then your self and the Dharma are not really one. It doesn't matter how well you say you have understood, or how enlightened you think you are. All your understanding and enlightenment still occurs on top of a perception of self. In true practice there is no place to plop down and make yourself comfortable.

In Buddhism, we use the words "cause," "condition," and "effect" to explain that there is nothing. Even if there is a cause, there is no result. What does this mean? It means that the present result, as it is, becomes a future cause. When you are sitting, if it so happens that you still feel there is something ambiguous or vague, then that immediately becomes a cause. If you do not change that result, then the ambiguity you feel now will remain thirty minutes from now. This is to say that if you do practice in such a way that you do not change this condition, then it will continue just as it is for an hour, a year, ten years, or even twenty. If you do not understand this well and you continue to sit while holding on to the thought, "Sooner or later, it will come to something if I keep this up," then, without being aware of it, your practice will amount to little more than "learning meditation."

Even if you really practice single-mindedly, sitting through the night without sleeping and so on, there is the danger that you will end up settling into an easy-going way of things where "practice is something that continues until death." You will create this limit called "death," even though people do not die. Practice is definitely not something that continues until death. Birth and death of the self happens moment to moment.

Each evening of the sesshin, the monastery's disciplinarian encourages us with this chant:

Respectfully I appeal to you:
Birth and death are a grave matter,
Everything is impermanent and passes swiftly.
May each of you awaken![77]

We must always keep in mind that present results will certainly be future causes. We must recognize that we are never in the same condition. Our condition is always new. At any given time, a prior condition continues and something new is awaiting. When the future Master Nanyue Huairang paid a visit to the sixth ancestor, Dajian Huineng, Huineng asked, "What thing has thus come?"

This is not something that happened hundreds or thousands of years ago. You must understand that Master Huineng is addressing each of us right now. "I am sitting." "I am burning furiously now in the flames of ignorance." "I am washing my face." "I am eating." These are all things that have thus come. Yet if we are suddenly asked, "What thing has thus come?" we quickly see the "thing" as "me." When someone asks "What thing?" you see what is called a human being because of not being able to let go of the habit of understanding the question as referring to "me." But there is, essentially, nothing and so it is not possible to acknowledge things. Consider the expression:

If this does not exist, that does not exist.
It is because this exists that the other exists.[78]

If there really is no "this," no "me," "I," "myself," and so forth, there is also nothing else. This point, captured in the question "What thing has thus come?" is at the root of today's verse, "The Unfathomable Function."

Nanyue Huairang earnestly grappled with Master Huineng's question for eight years. He really went through great hardship. The result was that he received certified transmission from the sixth ancestor when he expressed his understanding by saying, "If you use even one word of explanation, it will fail to hit the mark." This is called "the Mind Seal." It is to say that he had become a genuine person of the Way. Yet, in a manner of speaking, even that is still a point on the way. What, then, is not a point on the way? What is the final goal? You, yourself, right now. Regardless of whether you are in an unresolved condition or in the midst of ignorance, without fail you are already the "Mind Seal" as you are right now. The place reached through the practice of zazen is your condition right now. This is what is called "the Way of Buddha." Inevitably, though, when you hear of the Way of Buddha, the perception arises that the Way or the Dharma exists somewhere outside of you. This is what is called delusion.

In actual fact, there is no delusion anywhere. Kanzan Egen, the founder of Myōshinji, one of the main Rinzai monasteries in Japan, left us the words:

> All sentient beings are essentially in a state of perfect and complete buddhahood. How, then, have they become deluded?[79]

These words direct our attention to how much we are always looking to something outside ourselves. It is imperative for all of us to closely look at where we now stand—to really check to see whether or not we are practicing "learning meditation" after all. All of the 84,000 Dharma teachings, as well as the words of the ancestors, are fingers pointing at the moon. If we do not act in accord with them, it will not be possible to see the moon. However, when you have seen the moon, then they are no longer necessary, and this is to have returned to your original, essential Self. My hope is that you will keep firmly in mind that the place you reach through practice must be recognized to be you yourself right now.

You cannot rely on looking far ahead to the end of the universe.

"Looking far ahead" is like looking far into the distance with your hand held up to shade your eyes. Time is the same whether it is the distant past or the present. It is eternal. This line refers to a world beyond time, to the infinite. This is what is referred to as "the Unfathomable Function." The deepest source has not moved in the least from the long ago depths of time until now. This thing that does not move is the great function or activity. You must understand that even the slightest movement of this function is nothing but the entrance of the notion of self, the interference or interposition of the "person." If you do not grasp this, mistakes will occur.

The Unfathomable Function is such an immense thing that it cannot be contained. This means that there is no place where it can be settled by statements such as "I've finished it" or "I've seen my true nature" or "I've become enlightened." Consequently, in Zen we say that "there is only one person throughout heaven and earth" in this huge world. The expression "I alone am venerable throughout heaven and earth" also fits completely into the theme of the Unfathomable Function. We can understand this by looking at the human body. The eyes, ears, nose, tongue, body, and mind all function distinctly from one another. We tend to think of sense as one thing being divided, but in fact each of the senses has its own complete function, and this is not in any way the result of human intervention. The human body truly is a splendid microcosm of the universe. If we were to chop ourselves up into small pieces, there would be nothing left of us. Smaller things are made one in the largest thing. There is nothing more intimate than "One."

I am speaking here about different aspects of the Unfathomable Function. My words on the subject may be changing, but the upshot is that they are essentially all one thing. If we make light of this, then we destroy the true meaning of transmission from master to disciple. Nowadays transmission and practice in the Sōtō sect have deteriorated to the point that they no longer have any connection, because it is possible to receive transmission without practicing. A person can enter a temple if he has received transmission. It is then possible for someone who has nothing other than this formalized transmission to enter a temple and give the precepts. This is the worst possible situation. This is the meaning of the first line of this verse.

And why would you tie yourself down to tainted worldliness?

The word "tainted" refers to seeing one thing as two things. As I regularly say, good and bad are not within things. Higher and lower, absolute and relative, do not exist separate from ourselves. Rather, all such things arise based on the notion of "I," the viewpoint from which things are seen as other than us. And so our true mind is clouded. A common expression advises practitioners not to obscure cause and effect. Essentially, there really is nothing that can be obscured, but because we always see things dualistically, we are not aware that we ourselves are creating a dual view. We mistakenly think that the dualistic characteristics are part of the other thing. Such dualistic views are all obstructions or impediments.

There is only one thing, so there is nothing that can be done. That is why in the Sōtō sect we say, "Leave it as it is. If you interfere with it, the confusion will only increase." It is important to know that things are already one even while they are divided. It is not a matter of them becoming one at some point in the future. If you sit thinking that you will become one at some later time, you are merely "learning meditation."

We must change the way we deal with both favorable and unfavorable. Whether we feel satisfied, or we feel dissatisfied, we create comparisons and generate opinions like, "Loss is bad, profit is good," or, "I'll be happy when things are going well, but I'll be miserable when they aren't." In this way, we ourselves bring about our own happiness and suffering. However, the Unfathomable Function is essentially something into which opinions of the ego fundamentally cannot enter, even in the slightest. Since we see things that are essentially one as divided, we create attachments. The expression "Why would you tie yourself down?" captures the absurdity of this situation. It really is not possible to tie ourselves down, yet that is the situation we are in.

"The true nature of things is formless."[80] While things do exist, in actual fact they do not, as such. For all of us bound by the habit of thinking it is impossible to conceive of things as not existing. This is why people become interested in Zen. They think it teaches about this mystery. Their interest deepens even more when they hear about Mu. Many who hear the teachings become interested in actually practicing Zen, and in that way they begin moving away from their former religion toward Zen. They apparently sense that there is a world in which the ego cannot intervene. This is called "the Unfathomable Function."

Essentially, the miraculous body is not bound anywhere.

There are many different names for "the miraculous body." One is "the great mystery," because the miraculous body is a condition that lacks any discernible substance and we cannot acknowledge the existence of anything related to it. When we speak of the miraculous body in terms of "the Unfathomable Function," the whole thing is "the Unfathomable Function." This is true from the standpoint of the Dharma. But from the standpoint of the self it simply is not possible to believe that things do not exist. This is why we say that there are three essential keys to the practice of Zen: great faith, great doubt, and great determination.

With respect to great faith, consider Kanzan Kokushi's kōan:

> All sentient beings are essentially in a state of perfect and complete buddhahood. How, then, have they become deluded?

Essentially we are buddhas, so how, then, are we deluded? We get caught in the language of the kōan. The word "how" makes us feel as if there is some reason or cause behind our delusion, and because we feel this way, we begin to seek again. But before considering reasons or causes, we might wonder what the delusion of sentient beings is and what are they deluded about? Seeing things and hearing things and feeling things—all of these processes take place perfectly without delusion, and we have no trouble understanding that fact. We can even understand that we are deluded, but there is still no resolution of our delusion. Despite the fact that we understand, there is nothing we can do about it. This is truly mysterious.

When we really come to understand, however, we see that this very delusion itself or this very ambiguity itself is "the miraculous body." It is a fact. And yet, what else is it that we want to know? We already know everything, don't we? Someone once said that "reality is the proof of truth." Although we have our facts, and we have our own reality, we just cannot agree to them. We cannot really accept them. We also clearly *know* that we cannot accept or affirm them. So the question is, "What else is it that we want to know?"

When we come to understand, we see that within delusion, within ambiguity, within lack of transparency, everything is already settled.

From the standpoint of the precepts this is called *prātimokṣa*, liberation within each thing. Everything is cast off the way it is. It is not possible, for example, for the eyes to be liberated but not the ears. It is also strange to say, "I've passed Mu, but not the Sound of One Hand Clapping." However, there are some people who do not find anything strange about this and continue to practice in this way until they die. Such people should listen to the words of "The Unfathomable Function" and really apply themselves to a kōan in such a way that they completely become one with it. Otherwise, they will not really be practicing the Buddha Way.

There are many forms of practice that may look like Zen practice, but the practice of the Way of Buddha is nothing other than knowing that, essentially, we are not deluded. If you want to get rid of delusion, or think that your present condition is not so good, and therefore want to transform yourself into someone you can be more content with by practicing Zen, you will only be "learning meditation." Take a good look at yourself. Among the six functioning senses where could there be any place that is not content? Nothing is lacking. Everything is already settled. Among the six senses—seeing, hearing, smelling, tasting, touching, and thinking—nothing is lacking and nothing is superfluous. What, then, cannot be completely satisfied? I would like you to carefully examine this. And if some sense of dissatisfaction still remains, one can only refer to the "miraculous body."

All human problems, as well as the problems of the universe, come from ways of thinking based on the assumption of the existence of a person or a self. Not understanding something, as well as wondering what will happen in the future, are also ways of thinking predicated upon the existence of a person or the positing of a self. There is no way that these ways of thinking can lead to a solution. Essentially, no self exists, and to think that it does is a mistake. Every thought that takes its stand atop a mistake is defective. Understand clearly the principle involved here, and then any sort of practice is fine, whether it be shikantaza or kōan practice.

> It is already throughout the whole body, so what other traces could there be?

"Throughout the whole body" means to become the Unfathomable Function itself with one's entire body, from the top of your head to the tips of your toenails. As you have no doubt noticed by now, we often use the expression "become one" in Zen. Know that becoming one, or becoming "the thing itself," leaves behind no traces of its own process. The result is, as Master Keizan Jōkin, founder of Sōjiji, said, "a black ball rolling around in pitch-black darkness." This is an expression of having become the thing itself, of having merged into it. Yet his statement indicates that he was still only at having become one.

> Keizan's master said, "You are still not finished. You must do more."
>
> Keizan replied, "But I'm doing it single-mindedly. Isn't that all there is?"
>
> His master said, "No, that's not enough."
>
> Master Keizan Zenji said, "When tea is served, drink tea. When rice is served, eat rice."

If you do not leave the realm of having become one and return to the world of differentiation, then "becoming one" ends up being only a matter of "just" or "as-it-is." The problem is what we do after that.

We also use the expression "throughout body and mind."[81] Truly, the Unfathomable Function is this way. But this alone is not enough. Perhaps you are familiar with the expression "the entire body is hands and eyes." This expression conjures the image of Kannon with a thousand arms and a thousand eyes. This is what we call the *dharmakāya* or the Dharma body. Because this body is essentially the "Dharma body," it is possible to explain the Dharma by extending only one of your fingers. It is possible to cast off body and mind by smelling the fragrance of a flower, for the fragrance is also the Dharma itself. If the viewpoint of the ego-self does not intervene, Dharma and Dharma will merge with one another. When there are no seams, everything is the Dharma. It is not possible to become one with things or to realize enlightenment within a body that is perceived to be "me." Yet, since the Dharma body is essentially formless, it is possible for this to merge with it when we come in contact with some condition or other.

It is a funny thing, but when someone farts in a Zen temple, it is not uncommon for the monks to say, "Someone has lit some incense." If it smells a lot, they will even say, "Wow! That is really good incense." In the same way, we can say that the words of Master Dōgen, or even of some other person, resemble incense. This merging with the Dharma body happens to such an extent that all things are the Dharma. We are all already one. So to realize enlightenment through some condition is actually to be hindered or held back. Nevertheless, as long as we do not become one, we remain unsettled.

Inevitably, when we have understood something or have reached a conclusion, something yet remains. This can happen to anyone, but it is especially the case when monks are told to hold on to great doubt, wherein practice and realization are clearly divided. I have heard that when someone's understanding is verified in such cases, the person may even jump around with joy as if mad, and that special rice is served in celebration. This is something that we must all be careful of.

Consider the kōan about the cow passing through a window. Imagine you are a cow in a small cowshed. You manage to move your body, head, and legs out of the shed, but no matter what you try, you cannot get your tail out. There is nothing more contradictory than this! But you have to be able to get your tail out. Enlightenment means to get everything, including your tail, completely out.

But if you do manage to get your tail out, where will it go? From one place to the next. When you exit the shed entirely, you find yourself in another cowshed. You get out of one and go right into the next one. Once you get into the next shed, you won't find a way out of it for the rest of your life. However, you must get out of the kōan. So it's necessary to resort to all sorts of methods in order to completely clean away the sickness of "having understood." This only stands to reason. When you realize it for yourself, you'll understand that this sickness was unnecessary.

A single efficacious word transcends the multitudes.

This refers to the transcendence of previous spiritual boundaries. The word translated here as "efficacious" also means "spiritual." The same term appears in the line from the *Cantongqi* that says:

The spiritual source shines clearly; branching streams flow in the darkness.

We must understand "the spiritual source" to be without limits. The spirit can change into anything since it is unlimited. If we misunderstand the spiritual source to be something like an "eternal soul," that would be questionable. Since this spirit is unlimited, every single act of every single person who has realized the Unfathomable Function down through the ages appears in it in all clarity. Rinzai sect temples traditionally hang a sign that reads: "There is a true man who transcends all distinctions. He constantly goes in and out through your sense functions."[82] Freely going in and out through the sense functions is the activity of a person of the "Unfathomable Function."

It is far beyond the Three Vehicles and does not require cultivation.

Here, "far beyond" means that the Unfathomable Function is not proven or verified by means of practice, nor is it a matter of "becoming one" from now on. It is a problem that precedes practice and verification. It is what is referred to in Zen as "before the birth of your mother and father"—that is, something that precedes everything else.

"Vehicles" refers to conveyances we either ride on or are given a ride on. It is acceptable to think that we are riding to our final destination on either the "Vehicle of the Listeners" (śrāvaka-yāna), the "Vehicle of the Solitary Enlightened Ones" (pratyeka-buddha-yāna), or the "Vehicle of the Bodhisattvas" (bodhisattva-yāna). The "Vehicle of the Listeners" is also referred to as the "Small Vehicle" (hīnayāna). This is a form of practice in which a person merely listens to all sorts of teachings, and because of that, the teachings never really become his or her own. Since listeners are only looking at the finger pointing at the moon, we must ask ourselves how long will it take before they will be able to see the moon? As a result, it takes quite a long time to arrive at enlightenment practicing with this vehicle. Master Dōgen attacked this sort of practice fiercely, saying that practice should not be like that. As for the Vehicle of the Solitary Enlightened Ones, those who practice with this vehicle do not teach others that it is necessary to come to enlightenment.

They are only concerned with their own satisfaction. The Vehicle of the Bodhisattvas is the one that emphasizes practice for the benefit of others. This vehicle is also called the "Great Vehicle" or Mahāyāna. Such distinctions are primarily the concern of the academic world, but we must know this much at least to understand "It is far beyond the Three Vehicles."

We human beings have long thought about how to transform our feelings of dissatisfaction into feelings of satisfaction, and in the process we have tested many methods for achieving that transformation. Now we have arrived at the Way of Buddha. The phrase "does not require cultivation" in this line means that the Way of Buddha itself, even though it is referred to as the "Supreme Vehicle," is unnecessary. We may even go so far as to say "it is far beyond being the Three Vehicles, and not contingent on practice." Until we truly realize that we were already always all right just as we were, we will try the Vehicle of the Listeners or the Vehicle of the Solitary Enlightened Ones or the Vehicle of the Bodhisattvas. In the end, though, we must realize that everything was already all right just as it was.

When he traveled to China Master Dōgen entered the monastery of Master Tiantong Rujing, where for three years he did not lie down to rest. He was so single-minded in his sitting that he didn't even know the faces of the monks who were sitting next to him in the meditation hall. What did he say when he returned to Japan from China?

I have realized that the eyes are horizontal and the nose is vertical. I will not be fooled by others.[83]

And:

Be one with the community in activity and in stillness . . . there is no benefit in standing out.[84]

"Be one with the community in activity and in stillness" means that when the monks go to bed at night, we should also go to bed. Nowhere does Master Dōgen say that we must sit up late at night or sit without sleeping. When the last bell is rung, we should sleep with the others.

When the work drum is struck, we should go out to work. When the bell for zazen is struck, we should go to the meditation hall and sit. It is also said:

> When the drum is struck for meals, go to the dining room.
> When the bell for ceremonies is struck, go to the Dharma hall.

In other words, there is nothing to be gained by doing something special.

There appears to be a contradiction between the way that Master Dōgen himself behaved and the way that he instructs us to behave. We know that Master Dōgen did not lie down to rest for three years, yet he tells us not to stand out or go to extremes. How can he say this? He can say this because he made the great effort of not lying down to sleep. Because of his own great effort he was able to instruct us, to tell us, "You needn't experience the same hardships that I have. I've realized that it's all about now. So the most important thing is to realize that everything is already the way it should be. It isn't good to look for something special."

But we should be careful. Just because Master Dōgen said this doesn't mean that we needn't do *anything*. A delicious piece of cake will not simply fall into our lap by just thinking about it. Cake is not going to fall out of the sky, no matter how long we wait for it to. We won't fill our stomachs that way. Only after having made great effort is someone able to say, "The practice of the Three Vehicles is totally unnecessary." If you cannot understand my previous statements that Dharma and self are similar but not the same, you won't really be able to grasp this.

Shake off your hands and get away from the sages of all ages.

This line describes someone who seeks nothing from the Buddha, the Dharma, or the Sangha. It refers to one who doesn't ask for help from anyone, one who has shaken off everything and is thus truly alone throughout heaven and earth. It was precisely with the hope that we could accept this condition that our forbearers wrote various records. The following dialogue between Master Nanquan Puyuan and the future Master Zhaozhou captures this point well:

Zhaozhou asked Nanquan, "What is the Way?"
"Everyday mind is the Way," replied Nanquan.
Zhaozhou asked, "What is everyday mind?"
"It is your condition right now," replied Nanquan.
Zhaozhou asked, "How can I strive after everyday mind?"
"If you strive after it, you will go in the opposite direction,"
    replied Nanquan.

When we talk about "everyday mind" it seems to suggest that there is no need for practice, doesn't it? Wondering at this, Zhaozhou asked how, then, should we understand everyday mind? Everyday mind is our condition right now. If we strive after it, we will think that we are headed east but will actually be headed west. It we strive after anything, we will end up working directly against our goal. This is the point that Master Nanquan and Master Zhaozhou's dialogue illustrates.

In the Rinzai sect, such dialogues serve as kōans, like Zhaozhou's "Mu":

A monk asked Zhaozhou, "Does a dog have buddha nature?"
Zhaozhou answered, "Mu!" (No!)

By saying this, he meant, "Sit with this as a great doubt!" Here at Hosshinji, I have never said to people who practice with a kōan, "Kōans are no good. You should practice shikantaza." Instead, I let each person practice the type of zazen that is suitable to them. The important thing is that the opinions of the ego-self do not intervene in your zazen. Any method is all right so long as you forget the self. The important point of practice is not in choosing the type of zazen but in forgetting the self. Those who practice with a kōan are just fine.

If you choose to look at a kōan, however, one is enough. Just examine it thoroughly. Knowledge and analytical thinking will inevitably intervene. If you choose to practice with Mu, you must ask yourself where the unresolved problem, the thing that you cannot really accept, lies? There is nothing within Mu that you don't understand or that gives you a sense of dissatisfaction. It is simply Mu and that is all. It's neither delusion nor enlightenment. The "No!" of Mu is not nonexistence, as in existing and not existing. If the perspective of the self does not intervene, it is not a question of understanding or not understanding. Nor is it a matter of being satisfied or unsatisfied. So just try to let go of everything. If you do, then what do you say is your Mu? What is the mind of faith? It is something that you can do nothing about, that you cannot manipulate. Isn't it?

Hakuin, who would later become a Rinzai master, failed in this regard when his master, Dōkyō Etan, asked, "How do you look at Zhaozhou's Mu?" When Hakuin replied, "It is impossible to put your hands on it," Master Etan suddenly reached out and grabbed Hakuin's nose, twisting it. "See how I can put my hands on it. Why do you say that it cannot be handled?" Hakuin, for the first time, realized that he had been only "learning meditation," that he and the kōan were still separate. From then on, he was able to begin his own practice.

Daitō Kokushi, founder of Daitokuji Monastery in Kyoto, as a precaution to Zen practice said, "Relentlessly and thoroughly investigate that which is beyond understanding."[85] In other words, practice zazen with your goal firmly settled where reason cannot enter. You must be thorough and complete in your practice. Those who have really reached the final point speak not even a single extra word. If you can practice persistently, firmly focusing on that place wherein reason cannot enter, you will understand that essentially there is no distinction between zazen-within-stillness and zazen-within-activity. You will also be able to understand that everything is one. In short, you will understand that the Dharma body is indeed formless.

We hear terms like "unborn" and "unperishing" in places like the Heart Sutra, but we must be careful with regard to such words. "Unborn, unperishing" does not refer to that which we perceive to exist, including ourselves. Rather, these words indicate that essentially nothing is born, and therefore nothing can perish. With regard to ourselves, we say that "this thing" is living, and so we also say that "this thing" perishes when it ceases to function. But "this thing" does not know whether it is alive or dead. It has no idea that it is talking or seeing or thinking, or that because this body exists, those functions are attached to it. Since it does not know that it is living, it cannot know when it is dead. And yet it is easy to mistakenly understand impermanence to mean that things exist and that things change, undergoing repeated cycles of life and death. But this isn't how it is. From the very beginning there is nothing that could be an unchanging center, so change itself is called impermanence. It is easy to misunderstand this. We must really understand and accept the principle of this or else we will be led astray.

So with regard to the Mu kōan, there is nothing about it that you must understand, nor anything that it is all right not to know about it. Nor is there anything in it that we could just say is "Mu." This is why Master Zhaozhou answered "Mu!" On other occasions, he answered "U!" (Yes!) It may seem that this leaves some ambiguity between having or not having existence or being or not being existent. But Master Zhaozhou's answers come from a place where there is nothing. So whether we say "U!" or "Mu!" what is left when we uncouple all words from what exists in this world? All of these problems become, by themselves, wonderful kōans.

A kōan is something that cannot be touched or interfered with. So in Zen we say that we understand when we realize that we really can't understand what we can't understand. This is what it means when we say there is no other way of escaping something than to attend only to the thing itself.

Then your path of return will resemble an ox in the midst of fire.

The "path of return" refers to what happens when we have gone around and around, tried out various things, and then returned. "Fire" is that which burns up everything, so that nothing remains. It is an expression of extreme purity. "An ox" represents the condition of complete liberation, where all offensive smells such as the "self" or "Buddha" have dissipated. Master Guishan Lingyou once said, "When I die and am reborn, I will become a farmer's cow outside the temple gate."[86] Here, Master Guishan Lingyou uses the image of a cow instead of an ox to express the condition where all foul smells of "self," the "Dharma," or "Buddha" have disappeared. We can understand this as a metaphor for liberation or enlightenment.

We are always in the midst of fire. The various mental afflictions, the state of "I really don't understand," and so on—these are all fire. It is a mysterious thing to be inside of fire. If the Dharma body is fire, then whatever suffers from "I really don't understand" is the Dharma body, too. Even though all sorts of delusions exist, we are absolutely not harmed in any way. There is nothing more mysterious than this.

Even though it may seem that we are repeating the same things over and over as we practice, they are by no means the same. Each day a new self continuously goes through cycles of birth and death. Everything is impermanent. So even if we have been deluded up until now, it is certainly possible to be free of delusion. The same condition never persists. The only problem is that we do not flow along with this continual change.

The only thing we really need is diligence. Don't look for anything and don't throw anything away. It is enough just to endeavor. When you grow weary and get sick of this simple activity, all sorts of things will happen. Viewpoints of the self will arise. "I must do something," you'll think. Then if still nothing happens, fatigue will set in and various thoughts appear. When these thoughts appear, you'll start saying to yourself, "I shouldn't be thinking this." It's easy to become more and more covered with dirt in this way. So please be very careful of this and just continue your efforts. Even if you're looking for something in particular, it's not as if it will come flying in from the outside. And even if you think of getting rid of something, of throwing something out, you must still ask yourself, "Where will I throw it, anyway?"

The point is to make effort without wasting your time and energy. This is "the Unfathomable Function." As long as you don't understand this, it will only be "the function of dust and dirt." So it is important to keep in mind that, ultimately, both understanding and not understanding come from the same source.

4: The Transcendent within Dust and Dirt

It is really quite difficult to be completely focused. Looking back, I remember that I clearly understood what my teachers were saying, and it was my intention to practice zazen just as they had instructed me, but when it came down to it, things were not going the way I was told they would. Even though I was practicing just as I had been told without entertaining any doubts about it, I was still not getting anywhere. For my part, I neither completely accepted nor assented. There was either something extra or something lacking in my practice. So I became desperate, and I practiced frantically without caring how my efforts appeared to others.

During Rōhatsu *sesshin*,[87] I often tell people, "Regardless of whether you practice shikantaza or with a kōan, or whether you follow the breath or count the breath, you have to forget yourself." When you are told to forget the self, you must do it. This was my objective as well: to forget the self. Nevertheless, even though I practiced single-mindedly just as I was told, no matter how much I exerted myself I was still fixed on the idea that I hadn't accomplished this forgetting yet. I realized, then, that somewhere I was adding my own force or energy. I had to let go of myself, so to speak, and yet somewhere in zazen I was using myself. I became more and more earnest in the knowledge that I had to be totally focused, but no matter what I did, the self did not disappear. Whether during zazen or in the midst of practicing other methods, I gradually came to understand that consciousness of my self was somewhere involved.

"What should I do?" I asked myself. I knew, however, that the only thing I could do was be one with zazen—to be one with the method. So that is how I sat. Still, even though I tried to sit this way, it didn't work out easily. Again and again I had to start from the beginning. While repeating this over and over, I gradually no longer thought in terms of correct or incorrect, right or wrong. When I did so I entered the samadhi of method. Of course, I wasn't conscious of my condition of samadhi. Being in accord with this condition, I became it. As soon as this happened, I was then aware that it had certainly happened. I immediately used my vantage point of having realized something to reflect on what had become of the doubts I had felt before. Right away, the self reappeared.

Forgetting what I had realized, I then made one more effort. This process of forgetting, and forgetting again, and beginning again, was crucial. Even though I knew the expression "Taking one step off a hundred-foot pole," I couldn't really do it. Inevitably, I got stuck in what I had realized. And so, over and over, I began again. Acknowledging the good condition that I had achieved, I started to sit with this good condition as my objective.

Of course, there is no such thing as a good condition anywhere, so this was a mistake. When you decide that a certain condition is good, then that condition becomes the objective, and so you sit repeating the same thing over and over with your misguided objective in mind. Still, you shouldn't stop here, for it is only by pressing on that you gradually come to notice your mistake. This is the only way that I myself managed to be able to proceed, and also to quietly reflect on where I was. As I did this, I became aware that I was adding my own force or energy, which I hadn't noticed before.

In the process of repeating this practice over and over, I forgot the method of zazen as well as zazen itself. The condition of forgetting the self is expressed as "being one." Just as we are not always consciously aware that we are breathing, when we "become one," our awareness of zazen disappears. We don't even notice that it has disappeared. Then when we come into contact with some condition, suddenly everything disappears, including the condition with which we have come into contact.

At this point, we might think, "Is this it?" I knew the words "to dance about with joy," but I didn't feel that way. So I wondered, "Is this really it? Or have I still not forgotten myself?" When I thought that, I thought what I ought not to have thought of and then was unable to let the thought go. Gradually this state gave way and it was possible to maintain a condition entirely beyond delusion and enlightenment, just as enlightened people have taught since time immemorial. It was a condition in which I did not reflect on my condition at the moment, in which there was not even any "thing" like "just this thing, just this thing." I came to understand the condition of "only that"—no matter what I was doing, or when, or where I was doing it. It was no longer necessary to look back. I was able to assent to this condition completely. This will inevitably happen if you persist with the right practice.

This is the true practice of consciousness: truly being one, being one, being one, and forgetting that you are one. Focused and sustained effort is necessary. It cannot be achieved by doing nothing. As I have been saying, Zen teachings—the teachings of suchness—come from those who have actually attained it. Master Dōgen was so devoted to his practice that he practiced without even lying down, and he couldn't even recognize the faces of the monks who sat next to him in the meditation hall. This ethos is expressed in the word shikantaza, "just sitting," which implies that it is enough to "just" sit.

It is easy, however, to overlook the fact that the expression was uttered by someone who had forgotten precisely this "just." So we misinterpret the expression to mean, "It's fine to just sit without thinking anything, without looking for anything, and without giving anything up." By interpreting shikantaza in this way we create a limit called "just" and then sit within this self-created limit. In that case, we really do gain and lose nothing. This is why I say that a clearer distinction must be made between the "self" and the "Dharma." Otherwise it is easy to make mistakes.

If we sit with this "thing" that understands as the basis of our practice, then we lay a foundation. We set up an awareness of having understood something, then we watch our zazen and constantly judge it. This habit is an obstacle. So I would like you to sit in a strong and steadfast way, no matter what happens, so that you won't be swayed by external circumstances.

It is said, "Those who are true to the Buddhadharma are also true to the way of the world." This means that those who are really able to devote themselves entirely to their Zen practice are also able to devote themselves entirely to worldly affairs, such as work and family life, which are subject to dualistic thinking. If you are in business, just do business. If you are wholeheartedly devoted to your work and do it without thinking of zazen or religion or profit or loss, you will also be able to just sit, without seeking results and without thinking of the past, just being one when you come to the temple. The Buddhadharma and the way of the world are not separate. As it is said, "The true nature of things is without form. The Dharma body is formless."

When you don't understand, it's okay not to understand and to completely become one with not understanding. There is nothing wrong with not understanding. The fact of not understanding is simply beyond good or bad. The idea that not understanding is bad and understanding is good is based on thoughts that arise from the self. In Zen we practice such that we transcend the thought of the self. Please accept not understanding in this way.

We often hear news about countries at war. Each country says that it is in the right and that its fight is just. But how can the right and just fight with others who are right and just? It is a contradiction. In reality, everyone who fights believes that they are right. Such fighting occurs because of the intervention of the ego-self. Good and bad, right and wrong—these terms are created with the thought of the ego. This is also true with zazen. Everyone has his or her own view of zazen, so nobody thinks that they are mistaken about it.

If we translate the title of the fourth verse literally, it would say "Dust and Dirt and That Which Is Different." "Dust and dirt" refer to those things that obstruct practice. "That which is different" is a phrase that we must understand to mean "that which transcends one thing." In our current condition, delusion, discrimination, self-consciousness, and the ego all belong to the category of "dust and dirt." But this verse tells us that "dust and dirt" are the same as "transcendence."

> That which is impure is impure by itself; that which is pure is pure by itself.

This line explains that "dust and dirt" and "enlightenment" are indeed one thing.

We usually talk about things in terms of whether they are pure or not, but they really aren't like that. When a thing is impure, it belongs to the realm of impurity, and when a thing is pure, it belongs to the realm of purity. These two realms cannot be compared.

Clean sheets get dirty, we wash them, and they become clean. Later they become dirty again, and we wash them again. We wash something that is dirty and it becomes clean; we wash something that is dirty and it becomes clean. If that's how it is, we begin to wonder what all the washing is for. When something is clean there is nothing about it that is dirty. There is nothing within it that can be compared to its cleanness. On the other hand, when something is dirty there is nothing in the least that is clean about it. The objective of washing something is not to make it clean, it is just to wash it. This alone is sufficient to the task. This washing on its own is a realm completely beyond dualistic thoughts that compare the cleanness of things.

This observation also applies to our lives. Seeing, hearing, smelling, tasting, touching, and thinking are the functions of the six senses. The mind is a tool that discerns things, unlike the eyes, the ears, the nose, or the skin, which only perceive things. Still, the mind only discerns things. It does not judge whether things are good or bad. Likewise, the six senses only perceive things. So our bodies are able to take everything in just as it is. This is called the Dharma body. Since everything is the Dharma body, it is possible to notice that we are one with things by coming in contact with some condition.

The ego—something that we have unconsciously come to think of as existent—stands in the way of this process. The function of the ego is to perceive existence in something that does not exist and to become attached to thinking of it in that way. The ego refers not only to human beings but to all things that exist in the world, both with form and formless. This is even so when it comes to our practice.

> When the fifth ancestor, Daman Hongren, was about to choose his successor, all the monks thought that the head monk, Datong Shenxiu, would surely become the sixth ancestor. Master Hongren challenged those who would be his successor to write a pure verse of Zen on the temple wall to express their understanding.
>
> In response to Master Hongren's challenge, Shenxiu wrote:

"Always make an effort to keep the mirror clean."

The other monks found this persuasive, saying, "Yes, if we don't continually keep cleaning, things will become dirty." In contrast to Shenxiu, Master Dajian Huineng wrote: "Essentially, there is not one thing. How, then, can dust collect?"[88]

Dajian Huineng was chosen as the sixth patriarch.

Things today are just as they were long ago. Shenxiu's verse expresses that "zazen," "the method," or "practice" are like cleaning implements that we must use to keep ourselves from becoming dirty. This is why he failed to be chosen as Master Hongren's successor. It is not possible for dust or dirt to collect on something that does not exist. Dust and dirt are beyond comparison, and so neither dust nor dirt truly exist. Since there is nothing pure in the world of dust—nothing that can be compared to it—dust vanishes on its own. Ours is truly a world where there is nothing.

We call this understanding the "great round mirror wisdom" or "perfect wisdom." This is why, when there is delusive thinking, we totally become delusive thinking. The Dharma of delusion, the Dharma of confusion, the Dharma of discrimination—that is all there is. So when discriminative mind arises, make the effort to be discrimination as-it-is without thinking, "I shouldn't be thinking this." If you become the thing itself, then you will disappear. This applies equally to sickness and death and all other things. It is necessary to be one with each thing.

Beings who are still at the rank of bodhisattva, such as Bodhisattva Avalokiteśvara or Bodhisattva Kṣitigarbha, have yet to become buddhas. Thus, they still have no way of knowing what enlightenment or highest wisdom is. Because they do not know it, even the bodhisattvas call it delusion! As long as we are not yet buddhas, we call enlightenment delusion. When we understand this, the very same delusion will become enlightenment. Remember, whether we talk about enlightenment or delusion, these things have no substance, so they cannot be compared.

This is the meaning of the terms "pure" and "impure" in this line of the verse. Because we compare things, pure and impure appear. Even to simply acknowledge things as existing is to turn away from the Dharma.

If the thought of "just" or "suchness" arises even a little, then this is already to go against the Dharma. As soon as we think "I'm just hearing" or "I'm just seeing," we add something on to our awareness. Now you see how very difficult it is to really be one, be one, be one. To even speak of "just hearing," "just seeing," or of "becoming one" means that the intention to do so is there. Even the thought that you "must become one" is in opposition to the Dharma. This is what is meant by "That which is impure is impure by itself. That which is pure is pure by itself." Even to acknowledge the existence of "pure" or "impure" goes against the Dharma.

Highest wisdom and delusion are likewise empty and even.

This line seeks to impress upon us, as the first line did, that although things have different names, they are essentially one. We hear about "emptiness" or "the absolute," and tend to think that this is the essence or end point of Buddhism. But even to think about Buddhadharma is to get caught up in names, and this act is already a source of delusion, isn't it? It is truly difficult to deal with words. Nevertheless, we have no choice but to use them.

I often mention the saying that "Buddhadharma is this very moment now." We find in this line, as is the case in many such sayings, the word "now." Yet there is no substance to it. But we have no other choice but to use the word "now," to make this word without substance our own. You see, we must travel to the end by acting in accordance with the "Way of Buddha." It is a great contradiction for us to be seeking the Way while in the midst of the Way, but this is what we must do. We must make the Buddha Way that lacks any substance our own. To do so is, in reality, extraneous, unnecessary. But if we don't do it, then we can't truly be who we are right now.

The solution, however, is not to think, "Oh well, I guess this is all there is in the end. It doesn't really matter what happens." Those who complacently think like this don't notice that they are actually stuck. They will never realize that their whole body contains the entire universe. You must be careful about thinking in this way, because you will make yourself small with your own thoughts. This second line is intended to show us just how much words are sources of delusion. Since this point is easy to misunderstand, Master Changcha explained it further in the next line.

Who could say that nobody can appreciate Bianhe's jade?

To understand this line, we must know the ancient Chinese story of Bianhe:

> Long ago in the Kingdom of Chu, there lived a farmer named Bianhe. One day while tilling his vegetable field, he came across a large rock. Upon looking at it closely, he saw that it was actually a large piece of jade. So sure was Bianhe that the stone was jade, he decided to give it as a gift to the king, Ling.
>
> On receiving the gift, the king asked an expert to give his opinion on whether or not the rock was genuine jade. When the expert told the king that it was just an ordinary rock, the king had one of Bianhe's legs cut off as a punishment.
>
> Later, Wu became the king and once again Bianhe offered the stone to the king, saying, "This is a splendid jewel." But King Wu said, "This man is trying to trick me," and had the farmer's other leg cut off. Bianhe was overwhelmed with sadness. Clutching the stone in his hands, he sobbed and sobbed until his tears ran out and drops of blood replaced them.
>
> The next king, King Wen, found Bianhe in this state and asked his retainer, "Why does that farmer cry so?" The retainer told him Bianhe's story, and King Wen again summoned an expert to appraise the stone. This time the expert confirmed that the stone was indeed a wonderful jewel. Facing Bianhe, the king asked, "Why do you cry so?"
>
> Bianhe replied, "I don't cry because my legs have been cut off, but because prior kings could not recognize that this stone was in fact real jade. I cried out of exasperation at this situation."
>
> Thus, it was that, during the reign of King Wen, Bianhe's

stone was first proven to actually be jade. Later, King Zhao, ruler of the Kingdom of Qin, attempted to acquire the jade in exchange for fifteen castles. Thus the jade came to be known as the "Many Castles Jade."

Bianhe's story shows us that it is hard to be totally confident about the truth of something. However, without such confidence we won't really be able to believe that we will certainly reach the final point as we do Zen practice. We have already made our departure, but what is our destination? It is ourselves right now. There is no other point of arrival than these various thoughts we are having, feelings of confusion, and so on, right now. Who decides that being confused isn't good? When we are confused or feeling completely lost, that's all there is. When we think, it's just thinking. That's all. There can be no other place of arrival.

Śākyamuni Buddha verified that mental afflictions are themselves enlightenment. He ascertained this for himself. And yet, why is it that we cannot accept ourselves as we are? Why did Śākyamuni Buddha say that this condition we occupy—of being lost and confused—is enlightenment? This isn't the Buddha's problem. It's something we must be able to resolve for ourselves. Recall the words of Kanzan Kokushi, founder of Myōshinji:

> All sentient beings are essentially in a state of perfect and complete buddhahood. How, then, have they become deluded?

Yet, even if we notice that enlightenment is all about our condition just as it is, we are still unable to unwaveringly continue the true practice. As Dōgen says, "This Dharma is amply endowed in each person, but without practice it doesn't manifest itself, and without verification, it is of no use." His statement applies to everyone. Everything is certainly just as it is, but this fact will not manifest itself without practice. If we properly practice and follow the way of the ancient ones, it will surely manifest itself. We must practice or it will never happen. Simply saying "Everything is all right just as it is" is only to have made up your own mind that everything is all right. This type of surrender will not result in the real thing.

Master Changcha likens our situation to Bianhe's jade. Each of us possesses a precious jade. Śākyamuni Buddha and all enlightened ones have verified that everything is the Dharma body, that essentially all sentient beings are buddhas. We have all heard this, and we have all resolved to practice the Way of Zen. Some of us have even been ordained as monks. Therefore, our destination is fixed. That we are still in our current condition means that we have not reached our destination yet. This is because the scenery along the way seems so pleasing. We think *It will eventually happen, it will eventually happen*. But this isn't enough. If we do not persevere in walking this path, we will not reach our destination.

I say that the jewel of the black dragon shines everywhere.

"The jewel of the black dragon" is a priceless jewel. Here it is used metaphorically to indicate an attempt to gain great profit through dangerous risk. And yet, from the perspective of the Dharma, dust and dirt are priceless jewels as well. Therefore, "There is a bright ball of jade wherever you go." This priceless jewel shines everywhere. Nothing is concealed.

However, just like the rich man's prodigal son in the Lotus Sutra, we don't recognize ourselves to be born to wealth. Instead, we seek wealth elsewhere. The various and sundry conditions appear due to various and sundry causes. The prodigal son in the Lotus Sutra ended up in his condition of not recognizing the wealth to which he was born due to the conjunction of certain causes. Regardless of whether we meet with success or failure, from the perspective that "all dharmas firmly take their place,"[89] both success and failure are the jewel of the black dragon. So you must not say, "A person like me can't do it," or "I'm such a worthless person." Nor should you look anywhere else to find the value you are seeking.

Dwell firmly in each thing, at each place. Whatever you see, whatever you deal with, you must notice that it is the jewel of the black dragon, through and through. Thus it is said that the jewel of the black dragon and a thing covered with dust and dirt are exactly the same. In other words, the dreams we see in sleep and the dreams we see in our waking lives are exactly the same.

Thus far I have provided several examples that indicate that things have no substance. Indeed, there exists no substance at all within things. Not a single one of us was aware when we were born. And then, without being aware of it at all, because we were given names, we who once knew nothing began to assume that this thing was us—that we ourselves exist. After that, this thing that did not know itself began to see and hear things; it began to understand and to not understand; it sometimes felt sad and lonely. Many different things happened. However, the true Self has absolutely no knowledge of any of this. The self that bears the name that was given to us is only a symbol of ourselves. Delusion appears because this symbolic self always creates conflict with the true Self.

> Only when the myriad dharmas disappear does the whole thing appear.

"Myriad dharmas" refers to everything you see with the eyes, hear with the ears, taste with the tongue, smell with the nose, feel with the body, and think with the mind. The word we translate here as "disappear" literally means "to come apart at the seams," like a piece of clothing being torn into its parts. The disappearance of myriad dharmas refers to discrimination of the differences between them and their being broken apart into their parts, and their parts being ground into dust. Nowadays, the word *discrimination* has a bad connotation, but discrimination *against* certain things or other people is not the sense meant here. Difference simply exists, so it is not possible to say that differences are truly good or bad, or to make comparisons. What this means is that in the face of the utter distinction of each of the myriad dharmas, all thoughts and illusions come apart and disappear. In other words, since we find no source or origin for these myriad dharmas, whatever remains of them disappears. This line—"Only when the myriad dharmas disappear does the whole thing appear"—expresses the condition wherein things are crushed up just as they are.

What, then, is it that appears? It is the jewel of the black dragon, the priceless jewel of unborn wealth, appearing even in the midst of dust and dirt. "The whole thing" refers to this splendid jewel. As things gradually disappear, they are each already completely the jewel of the black dragon. When a thing comes apart, it finally disappears. Yet practice is not a matter of the self gradually disappearing such that, in the end, nothing remains. Even though we say "gradually," our destination is in fact already wholly us, the final point is always here. It is not something that lies ahead in the future.

The Three Vehicles split up and assumed only provisional names.

"The Three Vehicles" are, again, the same vehicles introduced in the previous verse: the Vehicle of the Listeners, the Vehicle of the Solitary Enlightened Ones, and the Vehicle of the Bodhisattvas. In terms of these three, we see that there are various means and methods of coming apart and gradually disappearing. Some people cut off ignorance by taking the Vehicle of the Listeners, some by taking the Vehicle of the Solitary Enlightened Ones, and others by taking the Vehicle of the Bodhisattvas. Each vehicle cuts off ignorance by means of its own practices. However, although we set up different names for the different branches of Buddhism, when we reflect on them, we see that they are in reality all one thing. That one thing is zazen, sitting.

Consider the kōan:

All things return to one thing. To where does the one thing return?

This kōan refers to the fact that there are many different ways to practice but they are ultimately all about becoming one. In Japan, for example, there exist various Buddhist sects, such as Tendai, Shingon, Nichiren, and so on. Each sect has its own practices, such as chanting a certain phrase or title of a sutra, and so on. Nevertheless, Śākyamuni Buddha ultimately taught only one thing—namely, to forget the self. Do not be confused by names. Instead, take the saying "Grass, tree, and earth are all realized buddhas"[90] and make it your own.

Consider also the following poem:

> If even the grass and the trees are said to be buddha,
> How reassuring for a being that has a mind.[91]

Who wrote this? It is said that a cow wrote it with her saliva. Śākyamuni Buddha said, "Mountains, rivers, grass, and trees are all realized buddhas." And yet, why is it that we human beings, with minds confused about this, look elsewhere? It is because when we notice that we are deluded, we then have the delusion that there is enlightenment. It isn't the case that anxiety transforms into peace of mind. Rather, anxiety becomes delusion so long as we do not understand it. However, once we understand anxiety, we see that anxiety, just as it is, is already enlightenment.

Truly outstanding people have determination that knows no bounds.

Without extraordinary aspiration, without the aspiration to do something by any means possible, it will be difficult to reach our goal. In any case, we must notice for ourselves that our own Dharma has always been here. As I often say, anyone should be able to do this. Feeling perplexed is not a problem. If the energy and determination to achieve your goal increase, then it is only natural that the depth of your perplexity also increases. This is why I say, *Just do it.*

Do not try to go where the buddhas have already gone.

This means that we must not blindly follow others. Only we can do it. Master Changcha urges us to be independent, to walk alone and be that one person throughout heaven and earth. In the Sutra of the Three Thousand Names of the Buddhas of the Three Ages, we find the Buddha of Great Courage and Ferocious Effort. You, just as you are right now, are the Buddha of Great Courage and Ferocious Effort. Consider the expression:

A person of great courage can realize buddhahood in an instant. For a lazy person it takes three eternities to reach *nirvana*.[92]

We think of a *tathāgata* as someone who is totally remote from ourselves, but it isn't so. The state of a tathāgata is a state that anyone can achieve. *Tathāgata* literally means "one who has thus come." Isn't this the same as "What thing has thus come?" Anytime, anywhere, it is always, "What thing has thus come? What is it that is thus?"

From long ago, it has been said:

Far more virtuous than making an offering to millions of buddhas is it to make an offering to one person of the Way with a liberated mind.

However, the first verse of the *Ten Verses of Unfathomable Depth* tells us that "A free and empty mind is still separated from it by a great barrier." So separation still remains even with a free and empty mind. This is because our real objective is always our condition right now. Up to the fourth verse, Master Changcha has been explaining the same thing from various angles so that we can, in one way or another, arrive at our own condition right now.

But we must ask ourselves why we endure so much hardship in this place that is closest to us—a place without space, separation, or time. Our hardships are such that Master Changcha must even go so far as to say that "A free and empty mind is still separated from the Mind Seal by a great barrier." Why can't we assent to that place still, even though we know that it must be just this? We hear what we must do and we try it, but we do not succeed. We try again, but still, we can't assent to it. Listen, then practice; listen, then practice. While doing so, you must have confidence that there will certainly come a time when you will be able to "just do it." Put life into your sitting from this moment on.

5: THE BUDDHIST TEACHING

> A monk asked Master Zhaozhou, "What happens when there is even the slightest difference?" Zhaozhou replied, "Heaven and earth are far apart."
>
> The monk then asked, "What about when there is no distinction at all?"
>
> Zhaozhou again replied, "Heaven and earth are far apart."

WHAT HAPPENS IF there is the slightest distinction, the slightest distance, the slightest separation in time between self and other? The slightest separation between self and other is as great as the distance between heaven and earth. And what if there is not the slightest distinction, the slightest distance, the slightest separation in time between self and other? It is also a distance as great as that between heaven and earth. Everything, all the various contents of your thought, is the activity of mind. This activity of mind itself says neither "existing" nor "not existing." To perceive things as existent is to turn away from the Dharma. To turn away from the Dharma means to become separate from it.

Dahui Zonggao, a disciple of Master Yuanwu Keqin, said about the *kyōsaku*, the warning stick, "If you call this a kyōsaku, you go against it." But what if we don't call it a kyōsaku? The same logic applies: we also turn away from it. If we acknowledge the existence of something, even in the slightest, we create a separation between it and the Dharma, and the truth disappears. It will no longer be the fact itself anymore. This is what we can take away from these words.

Likewise, if we say, "Now, I am sitting zazen," we create distance. But what if we said, "I'm not sitting"? We would also separate ourselves from it in the same way. Why is it like this? The monk Changsha Jingcen explained this matter in the following verse:

> Those studying the Way do not realize the Truth,
> because they acknowledge a center of consciousness.
> This is the seed of birth and death through endless time,
> but the fool calls it the original self.[93]

The phrase "center of consciousness" refers to our tendency to think that there is a control tower inside of us that is at the center of the six sense functions. When we think something, we inevitably imagine that there is a space within the body where the activity of thought takes place. It is difficult to accept that we think with the whole body, such that the whole body is the thought.

Similarly, when we see something, we see it not only with our eyes, and when we speak, we speak not only with our mouths. We speak, see, and hear with our whole bodies. When we think, speak, taste, smell, feel, or hear, whether we know it or not, an ego-self is nowhere involved. Regardless of whether we commit good or bad deeds, no harm can be done to the Dharma body. We must understand clearly that this is a firmly established principle of the Dharma.

The title of this, the fourth verse, is "The Buddhist Teaching." It has always been said that the sutras—that is, the forty-nine years worth of Śākyamuni Buddha's teaching or the "84,000 Dharma Gates"—are all finger-like explanations that point to the moon of the original Dharma body. The original Dharma body is us. Although the sutras are like fingers that point at the moon, enabling us to see it, it is not possible for us to see the moon by looking only at the fingers. We must see the Dharma body in accordance with the sutras, but we shouldn't feel as though we have seen it when, in fact, all we have done is study the sutras.

Seeing the moon, becoming the moon—this is Zen. Without a finger pointing at the moon, it wouldn't be possible to see it. Once you have actually seen the moon, the finger is no longer necessary and the moon itself will also disappear. You must admit this much. The moon disappears upon being seen because the source of all things—be it the moon or be it the sutras—is one with them. Sutra titles may differ, but they are all one in the end. By means of the Buddha's teachings, we come to know the Buddhadharma. By means of zazen—the practice of buddhas—we learn that we ourselves are buddhas. Once we know this, we can truly use this Dharma body freely.

There are some priests who say, "Scholars know a lot about the sutras, but they don't know much about reality." But many scholars do have a deep understanding of the principles of the teaching. In order to be able to speak with people who know such things, we must also understand for ourselves what scholars know. So it is important to read books. Of course, it is also important to sit. It is necessary to combine both elements in our practice. I regularly emphasize this.

Many monks begin their careers studying Buddhism and make great efforts in doing so. Deshan Xuanjian, known in his time as the king of the Diamond Sutra, was one such monk. He began as a scholar but later gave that up and sought refuge in Zen.

> Once Deshan was approached by the proprietor of a teashop. The man said, "The Diamond Sutra says that it is impossible to grasp the mind of the three worlds."[94] He then quoted the passage from the Diamond Sutra that says, "Because the past mind cannot be gotten hold of, the future mind cannot be gotten hold of, and the present mind cannot be gotten hold of..." and asked Deshan, "With which mind will you eat this meal?"
>
> Deshan found himself unable to answer. He therefore went to see Longtan, a Zen priest. Deshan stayed speaking with Longtan until late into the night. When he was ready to take his leave, Deshan noticed that it was dark outside and asked Longtan for a light.
>
> Longtan lit a candle for Deshan, but when Deshan reached to take the candle, Longtan blew it out and Deshan was suddenly enlightened.

Deshan's story is quite well known. In this way, many enter the Way through the gate of doctrine. But when they find that study alone does not liberate, they seek refuge in Zen. As Master Dōgen said:

> You delude yourself with the sutras. The sutras don't delude you. If you think you have to throw away the sutras, won't you then also have to throw away the Buddha mind and the Buddha body? And if you throw away the mind and body

of Buddha, won't you then have to throw away the disciples of Buddha? And if you throw away the disciples of Buddha, won't you then have to throw away the Way of the Buddha? And if you throw away the Way of the Buddha, won't you also have to throw away the Way of the Ancestors?[95]

What Master Dōgen is teaching us is that saying that one doesn't need the teachings of the Buddha is tantamount to throwing away the Buddha mind.

The Three Vehicles spoke golden words one after another.

The first teaching that Śākyamuni Buddha expounded, the Avatamsaka or "Flower Garland" Sutra, is very difficult. When he taught it no one could understand it, because Buddha delivered it from the vantage point of his own high level of realization. Noticing how incomprehensible the sutra seemed to his disciples, Buddha consulted the Bodhisattva Mañjushrī, who is commonly said to be the teacher of the Seven buddhas.

"No one seems to understand at all what I'm saying," Buddha said, "what should I do?"

Mañjushrī advised him saying, "What I say is not solely advice for you, World-Honored One: I have advised all of the past buddhas in the same way. Why not make it easier for others to understand by expounding your teaching two or three levels lower?"

From then on, Buddha taught his doctrine according to the Three Vehicles: the Vehicle of the Listeners, the Vehicle of the Solitary Enlightened Ones, and the Vehicle of the Bodhisattvas.

But the buddhas of the past, present, and future only declared the same thing.

Here Master Changcha is saying that as we study Buddhism, we must gradually come to understand the Three Vehicles as being ultimately one. How do we do this? In Zen we use the expression "enter samadhi through listening, thinking, and practicing."[96] The "Listeners" in the Vehicle of Listeners are those who only listen. They understand that practice is a good thing and that it is something that they must do, but it never comes to anything because they end up only listening to the teaching for ten, twenty, or thirty years.

Rather than simply be satisfied with listening to the teaching, we must listen, think through carefully what we have heard, make up our minds that we really agree with it, wish to put it into practice, and then, finally, actually put it into practice. This is what it means to "enter samadhi through listening, thinking, and practicing." In the end, we ourselves must practice and feel satisfied with it.

> In the beginning, when they expounded the reality of skandhas
> and then complete emptiness, everyone grew attached to it.

"Reality" here refers to difference or discrimination, and "emptiness" refers to equality or sameness. In dualistic thought, difference and sameness are always in opposition and so they cannot be in harmony, and because they cannot be in harmony, they cannot merge. I notice that people often end up emphasizing either difference or sameness. This is precisely what it means "to be attached to the Dharma."

In order to become freed from this attachment and to be truly at ease, we must first throw away this body we call our "self." As we gradually continue with our practice, we must come to realize that "understanding," "not understanding," "ambiguity remains," "something yet remains that must drop away," and so on, are all distinctions that we ourselves have created. These distinctions, as such, are empty. There is nothing except everything just being there as it is, for itself.

We are empty, and so each thing ends with each thing. Think of something you have seen. Does it remain in the eye? Does something you have heard remain in the ear? Likewise, nothing remains in the mind. Even if you have lived for decades, the ears are completely clean, the eyes are completely clean, and the mind is completely clean. Nothing from the past is piled up. This is so because all of these sense functions are empty.

During the Nirvana Day ceremony, we read the Sutra of the Last Teaching, where the following passage appears:

> Respectfully and carefully observe the precepts leading to
>   liberation in each activity,
> like finding a light in the darkness, or a poor man finding a
>   treasure.

What this means is that difference itself is empty. But if we think to ourselves, "Oh, now I see: the teaching of Buddhism is emptiness," and grow attached to this idea, everything we have learned up to that point will only be useful to ourselves alone. If we are attached to the self, we will only have the knowledge that we are attached to. If we let go of that, our knowledge becomes something much, much larger, such that it can then benefit others and the world. But we will not be able to do such great work for others unless we totally throw the self away. This notion not only applies to Buddhism. Since everything we have learned up until now is attached to us, it only has a small effect. If we let go of the self, it is possible for each of us, with our own dispositions and abilities, to be of service to all sentient beings.

In fact, if we let go of attachment, even that which is mistaken can be of use to others. "Heresy" may be an ugly word, but there were all sorts of heretical teachings during the time of Śākyamuni Buddha. Yet once those who held different views took refuge in Śākyamuni Buddha, their supposedly heretical teachings all became part of Buddhism.

Later, when they negated both reality and emptiness, everyone discarded it again.

The Diamond Sutra expounds many sorts of emptiness. While this is true of Buddhist sutras in general, the Diamond Sutra, in particular, explains emptiness in especially great detail. We find in its pages the phrase:

> The world is not in fact the world. That is why it is called
> the world.[97]

We might paraphrase this as "The world that we usually refer to as the world is not in fact the world. This world that is not in fact the world is the world." This is a complicated way of stating things. But if we replace the word "world" with synonyms for the self, such as "I" and "me," we will more easily understand it. "The 'I' that I usually refer to as my self is not in fact me. This 'I' that is not in fact me is my self."

The Diamond Sutra also says:

> The true nature of things is without form. The Dharma body
> is formless.

These types of teachings on emptiness are read by all types of Japanese Buddhists. In the Zen sect, we read this sort of thing in the Diamond Sutra. In the Nichiren sect, they read this sort of thing in the Lotus Sutra. In the Tendai sect, too, they read about emptiness in a variety of sutras. But reading these teachings, alone, is like browsing a menu at a restaurant. When we go to a restaurant, we look at the menu. But we won't enjoy a good meal simply by reading the menu. We must actually put food into our mouths. The practice of Zen is to taste the teachings for ourselves.

The teachings are also like a prescription for medicine. Simply reading a prescription will not cure a headache, nor soothe a stomachache. Yet we need to know what medicine we must take to cure our illness. On the other hand, we have no need of medicine when we are not sick. The situation alluded to in this line of today's verse is something like this. Since we are essentially not deluded, the medicine of Dharma isn't really necessary. Yet practice begins when, thinking we are deluded, we read the prescriptions laid out in the sutras and realize that we must actually take the medicine.

This line of the verse uses the word "discard" to convey that after reality and emptiness are first compared, we must subsequently throw them away. In other words, after we realize that we are essentially not sick, we must quit taking the medicine.

**The complete treasury of sutras in the Dragon Palace is meant
to be prescriptions.**

The Dragon's Palace is said to be an ideal place for a human being to live. According to another interpretation, however, it is the place where the Dragon clan lived, and where many of the Perfection of Wisdom sutras were stored following the Buddha's entry into nirvana. The words "complete treasury of sutras" conjure the image of a treasury filled to the brim with books. This image symbolizes that words lack something, that they are unable to express their subject exhaustively. Words like "the Middle Way," "the true nature of things," and "perfect—lacking nothing" are all unable to fully express their subjects. We might feel that such phrases aren't lacking at all, but precisely by saying them we prove that something is lacking.

That the treasury of sutras is meant to be prescriptions indicates that the sutras show us what to put into practice, but once we have applied their teachings, we need not cling to them. Master Yunmen's "Medicine and sickness cure each other," Case 87 of the *Blue Cliff Record*, will help us to understand that this line is indeed the heart of all Buddhist teaching. The case and its attendant verse read as follows:

Case 87
Yunmen said to his disciples: "Medicine and sickness cure each other. The whole universe is medicine. What, then, is the Self?"

Xuedou's Verse
All the earth is medicine—how mistaken people of all times
     have been!
They close the gate and build no cart, though the Way is wide
     open.
What a mistake! What a mistake! Even if your nose is up high
     as the sky, you'll still be taken in tow.

The kōan asks, "If all the universe is medicine, what is the Self?" When there is sickness, it is possible to cure it using medicine. But if we continue to take the medicine after the sickness has been cured, the effects of the medicine actually become harmful, and the harm caused by it may even be more severe than the sickness. If you are deluded, you should take the appropriate medicine, namely zazen. When you take the medicine, it works, and delusion disappears. This is called enlightenment.

So those who think to themselves *I'm still not enlightened* are yet at the stage of practicing before enlightenment. But when they become enlightened, both delusion and enlightenment must disappear. Otherwise, we cannot say that it is true enlightenment. If enlightenment does not disappear, it becomes a delusion called "enlightenment." Enlightenment itself can therefore become an obstacle.

When viewed from this perspective, we can see that while medicine is clearly medicine, sickness is in fact medicine as well. In reality, our sickness is extremely powerful medicine. In the end, although Yunmen's "Medicine and Sickness" encourages us to ask where sickness really is, where delusion really is, we are also encouraged to ask where enlightenment really is. We speak of the "self" or "the view of ego-self," but what are they and where are they after all?

> Even the Buddha's last teaching does not reach the
>   unfathomable.

The Nirvana Sutra is said to be the last sermon that the Buddha gave on the day and night before he died. This final Dharma teaching is also referred to as "Upholding the Precepts and Expounding the Infinity of Buddha nature."[98] In short, this sutra is both a teaching on the precepts and also a clear expression of buddha nature. That is to say that therein, the precepts are used as a means to clearly explain buddha nature. However, even this last sermon "does not reach the unfathomable."

> If even one deluded thought arises in the world of true purity,
> This already means spending eight thousand years in the world
>   of human beings.

In Zen, the idea that everything is completely pure and free of delusion is expressed in the phrase "the world of true purity." We also say "essentially, there is not one thing." The negation in this expression articulates the condition of transcending existing and not existing. As Master Huineng said, "How, then, can dust settle?"

But simply by saying "everything is completely pure and free of delusion," "the world of true purity," or "essentially, there is not one thing," something already flows out. If we acknowledge the existence of something for even an instant—for the duration of one thought—by uttering "the world of true purity," we imply that it actually exists. But this phrase does not indicate any positively existent thing at all. Because something spills out in a single moment of thought, there is instantly a separation between it and the truth as large as that between heaven and earth.

Because it is said that Zen is "without thought and the drawing of distinctions," people tend to think that there must be no thought or drawing of distinctions during zazen. But if we were to say, "There must be no thought during zazen," there already is a thought. It is similarly said, "When in samadhi, you are unaware of it." That is, if you know you are in samadhi, you are unaware that your knowing it moves you outside of samadhi. Once you are parted from samadhi, you end up watching it.

I regularly ask students not to judge their zazen. If you always watch your zazen while sitting—judging it to be good or bad, thinking that you are sitting well or not sitting well—then you are not really practicing zazen. The objective of zazen is to forget the self, and yet you are clearly watching it. If you find yourself thinking, "This isn't good. I've got do x, y, or z instead," then you are not practicing zazen. You must not speculate about the condition of your zazen. If even a single thought briefly appears, it becomes delusion and true wisdom is lost. In this regard, "8,000 years" is a way of describing the great distance or gap that could be opened up on account of a single thought.

Recall the case of Bodhidharma, who truly endured what was difficult to endure, practiced what was difficult to practice, and risked his life as he crossed over from India to China. He did this single-mindedly only for the sake of the Dharma. Luckily "five petals appeared from one flower." We must impress this deeply on our minds. We are at a critical moment, where the question has become whether we ourselves will continue to pass Zen on to future generations or whether it will disappear.

6: THE SONG OF RETURNING HOME

Master Dōgen, founder of the Sōtō sect in Japan, said:

> It isn't that we do zazen; zazen lets us do zazen.

I also say this to you now, whether you are new to Zen or an old practitioner. I regularly emphasize that there can be no gap in our practice of zazen for "me" to enter. We must really be zazen itself. Consequently, if we have the idea that we should put some force or strength into the lower belly or concentrate on something, then precisely this force or effort will somewhere defile your zazen. Even the thought *I've got to make an effort* is excessive, from the standpoint of purity. Our condition right now, at this very moment, is truly transparent, clean, and clear. Dirt cannot adhere to it. It cannot be tarnished.

Remember that when head monk Shenxiu said, "Always make the effort to keep the mirror clean. Never let dust or dirt collect," Master Huineng responded with, "Essentially, there is not one thing. Where, then, can dust collect?" Shenxiu's thought is that if we persistently clean the mirror of our minds, dust and dirt will not collect, and sometime in the future we will realize buddhahood. But "sometime in the future" could mean tomorrow, the day after tomorrow, or it may mean that we never actually meet the true Dharma. Our human lives are uncertain—they could even end tomorrow. As we say, "Birth and death are the great matter. Time passes swiftly." So it isn't good to bank on "sometime in the future."

This was already clear when Shenxiu was passed over as successor to the fifth ancestor, long ago in China, before Zen had even branched into the separate Sōtō and Rinzai sects. Yet even among the successive generations of ancestors, there were few who had a great aspiration to attain enlightenment, who did zazen all night without sleeping, or who from the beginning sat in zazen without lying down. These days as well, many practice zazen, even though they have no true aspiration to practice it. They simply try it out when someone says, "Zazen is a good thing to do. Won't you sit with us?" People who practice like this waver, wondering all the while if someone who has attained enlightenment, like the masters of old, actually exists. Many end up practicing zazen half believing and half doubting.

Not everyone is like this, though. There are also quite a few who are earnest right from the beginning. In any case, if you persist, without neglecting the practice, then zazen will teach you zazen. I often say this. Zazen itself is the teacher of zazen, not a person. Zazen will teach you about zazen and therefore it is necessary to continue persistently and without negligence. Zazen is not a matter of understanding the nature of delusion. If zazen itself does not end up becoming delusion, how will it be possible to ascertain the nature of delusion? This applies not only to delusion but to anxiety, fear, and other mental afflictions, or to conflict between self and other. If the ego-self does not intervene, then it is certainly possible for affliction to become delusion—to become greed, anger, and ignorance. Then we will be able to understand the nature of the thing itself. The strength to push on to this understanding is called the "Way-seeking mind."

In order to construct a fine building, we must lay a strong foundation. Likewise, we may sit in zazen correctly, as it was transmitted by the buddhas and ancestors, but if our practice amounts to little more than counting periods of sitting or trying to sit for as long as possible, it will be of little use. This type of practice is an indication that our foundation is weak. If we lack a strong personal aspiration to practice zazen, then our zazen will be limited to the times when we sit.

True zazen pervades all activities in which we engage throughout the day. When this becomes apparent, we come to firmly and stably practice zazen-within-stillness. All of our work throughout the day—whether using our heads to think or using our bodies to move—will also become zazen. At all times and during all activities "zazen will be zazen." In short, everything we do will become zazen.

We mustn't let the self and the Dharma grow apart with thoughts like, "I am working," or "I am sitting in zazen." We must practice zazen with our whole bodies, we must do our work with our whole body. We must become one with our work to the extent that there is no gap for "me" to enter. This has nothing to do with the length of our periods of practice.

So as soon as you have availed yourself of the great opportunity to participate in sesshin, I urge you not to waste it. You must sit without raising "me" in the slightest. We say in Zen:

> Whether speaking or silent, whether moving or still, the Self is calm and at peace.[99]

Regardless of whether we speak or are silent, are still or move about, there is a Self that is truly settled, a Self that is neither completely moving nor completely still.

Bodhidharma sat for nine years facing the wall, waiting for someone to come who was really seeking the Way. Huike, who would become the second ancestor, appeared and asked, "Would you please tell me about the Dharma Seal of all the buddhas?" Bodhidharma, realizing that Huike wanted to hear about the Dharma directly transmitted from Śākyamuni Buddha, replied, "You cannot get the Dharma Seal of the buddhas from someone else. It can only come from yourself." Zazen is something that only you can do. In the same way that only you can breathe through your nose, only you can really seek the Way. What is the Way? The Way is you yourself. You are the Dharma body, and the Dharma body is something without limit. It is infinite; it is boundless. That is your nature. But because we perceive the existence of a "self" or a "me," we do not notice that we are this boundless thing.

What is commonly known as kenshō (enlightenment) is not simply a matter of knowing the true nature of something in a single leap. Rather, it is necessary to know the principles of the Dharma. In order to know the nature of something, we must follow the sequence of "listening, thinking, and practicing." We must understand that it is absolutely necessary to first listen to the teachings, think them through well, and then to put them into practice. Even with questions like, "Why must I look at one kōan after another, rather than look at just a single kōan?" there are many aspects that we must intently think through.

> Don't be distracted by the King of Emptiness when you are still
> on the Way.

This line conveys just how difficult it is to persist with the practice of zazen. Suppose a traveler on the road says, "I must get to Tokyo, but the scenery along the way is so beautiful! I'm going to take a break to enjoy it." If this happens frequently along the way, it will make it quite difficult for the traveler to reach his or her destination. Now suppose someone who is in the midst of sitting says, "Seeing this profound view, I feel as if I've achieved the objective of my sitting. So what need is there to continue on toward the goal?" As you progress in sitting in zazen, you may find yourself growing quite content, achieving a certain peace of mind that invites you to settle down. It isn't good to get stuck in such a place. This line warns us against practicing like a person who, while still on the way, settles down to enjoy the scenery.

Usually we only feel like persisting with what is good, with what is satisfying and brings contentment. But both good and bad are medicine for our zazen. Since both good things and bad things lack substance, we can gather both and convert them into energy for our zazen.

The Lotus Sutra demonstrates this point with the parable of the Phantom Castle, wherein a traveler along the five hundred mile road to his hometown encounters a series of enchanting, phantom castles along the way. With each castle encountered, the traveler is long delayed, wondering at the beauty and majesty of the castle, and in this way is prevented from reaching his home. We should understand this parable to mean that we must not stop our practice when we feel that we have gone far enough. If we think about it, we depart from a place that does not essentially exist. We must then realize, too, that whatever we acquire, throw away, or grasp along the way, is likewise not real.

> You must drive your staff forward, moving on until you reach
> home.

Driving forward our staff, we return home to our true Self. Our true Self is empty, formless, like a vibration that we hear in the distance or a shadow that we see on the ground. We say, "The mind realizes itself on its own accord."[100] However, when you think you have realized or awakened to something, you must quickly cast that notion aside. It is imperative not to approve of yourself, but to always tell yourself that it is not yet enough.

Dahui Zonggao, a disciple of Yuanwu Keqin, the Zen master who compiled the *Blue Cliff Record*, said that he had experienced "eighteen great enlightenments and countless smaller ones."[101] He said that he had all of these enlightenments, but that none of them were the real thing. They were all "serving the King of Emptiness"—they were mistaken. Later he burned his master's book. Hakuin Zenji said the same thing about his enlightenment experiences.

When I recall my own practice, I see a similar pattern. I, too, sat single-mindedly. Occasionally, I would find myself in a very unusual state and I would think, "Oh! This must be what it's like when the self has disappeared!" But because I knew I was seeing something, it was not the real thing. My ego-self was simply coming to the fore and seeing this state, wondering if this might be enlightenment or liberation.

Since that state was so different from anything I had experienced before, I went to my master and asked, "Is this it?"

"Throw it away," he said.

But it was really difficult for me to throw it away. I got into the habit of seeking out that condition again. *If I sit like that*, I thought, *then I can forget my self.* So I sat trying to experience that unusual condition again. This was the most dangerous thing I could have done. Immediately, everything became very difficult. When desiring to inhabit a certain state, you think that you have found "it," you will only get as far as that state, and your zazen then becomes bound by that limitation. At that time I suffered unbearable mental anguish. Even if I were struck over and over again or verbally abused, I clung to that state. If I were told, "Let it go! Let it go!" it became even more difficult for me to let go. I couldn't really become empty or return to the source. I endured great hardship in this way. So it is really important to sit, dwelling in emptiness.

If you travel for a long time like clouds and water, don't get attached to it.

"Clouds and water" refers to clouds that float freely through the sky and water that flows freely to the sea. Although in Japanese culture monks are sometimes referred to euphemistically as "clouds and water," in this case the phrase is not used to refer to monks. Clouds come and go with a free and empty mind and water likewise flows freely without a care. Since neither of them ever remain fixed in one place, their condition seems wonderful.

Consider the kōan:

> When wind blows the willow catkins, the wooly seeds sail
> away;
> When rain strikes the pear blossoms, butterflies take flight.[102]

When a gust of wind blows, the fluffy seeds of the willow catkins are carried away. When rain suddenly falls, the butterflies that had landed on pear blossoms quickly fly away. These words describe the state of being unattached to anything.

Yet while the state of clouds and water appears to be one of nonattachment, they are still only partly resolved. If we wander as mendicant monks for a long time, we come to dislike remaining in one place. We come to feel somehow restricted by having a roof over our heads. This is a bad habit, and something we must be careful about. It isn't necessarily the case that living freely like a floating cloud or flowing water is the best way to live. If it were, then we would grow unable to enter the three worlds so as to guide sentient beings. So we should be careful not to narrowly define a Zen monk as someone who is unattached to anything and always independent and carefree. In the end, this state as well is no more than another unresolved condition.

The great Rinzai master Daitō Kokushi once said, "Relentlessly and thoroughly investigate that which is beyond understanding." That which is "unthinkably beyond understanding" is the place where ego-thought cannot enter. We ought to enter that place and practice there with Mu or counting the breath. In the Sōtō sect, we say, "Sit in a dignified way, without dealing with or being disturbed by anything." This also refers to the unthinkable. On the other hand, it's no good to sit quietly forever in an enclosure called "just." Only those who have really reached that particular place can use this "just." It is unacceptable for someone who hasn't reached it to enter a box labeled "just," and to sit there quietly thinking that this is all there is to it.

Master Zhaozhou, who answered "Mu!" (No!) when asked if a dog has buddha nature, also said:

> If you see a place where there is a Buddha, quickly pass
> through it.
> As for places without Buddha, you mustn't dwell there
> either.[103]

A "buddha" is something beautiful, something wonderful. Even if we become a buddha—a being undisturbed by anything and filled with deep compassion—we must not stay there. We must quickly pass through that state. We also mustn't stop at a place where there is no buddha. In the end, we must get away from emptiness or nothingness, or buddha, or hell. If we don't get away from everything, then we'll not return to the source. This is what "travel for a long time like clouds and water" means. We must let go of everything as we travel, without getting attached to traveling itself.

Even in the deep recesses of snowy mountains, don't forget your mission.

Here Tong'an Changcha reminisces about the past. Formerly he was a guest of the Buddha, but he now feels pity for such guests. Master Changcha is saying here, "I practiced single-mindedly as a guest at a certain monastery, but now I've become my true Self. I feel compassion for those people who are guests in the same way I used to be." This line suggests that Master Changcha caught a glimpse of enlightenment, or something like it, yet he was still limited by enlightenment. He only caught a glimpse of a place that was neither boundless nor limited, here expressed as "snow." Early on, he stepped into mountains where there was deep snow. He didn't know then that the hometown to which he hoped to return still lay far off "in the deep recesses of snowy mountains." So here he reminisces about a time when he got lost and wandered deep into snowy mountains.

We see many people in Zen who end up getting lost in zazen and the method. The better a condition is, or seems to be, the greater the risk that we will become lost in it. This is why we must make an effort to move on beyond that state. However, it can be very difficult to keep going. We may find ourselves thinking, "I've done this much zazen but I still can't accomplish it. Many people practice zazen, why is it that no one is able to accomplish it?" Thinking in this way, we grow concerned with the practice of others. Then we might think, "Well, if they can't do it, then neither can I." Misleading ourselves in this way, we end up sanctioning our own inability to accomplish anything. This is not how it should be.

Master Yangshan Huiji, one of the founders of the Guiyang sect of Zen, distinguished between the "rank of absolute faith" and the "rank of saving people."[104] He based his distinction on how much a person was able to believe. We can believe that there certainly is such a thing as enlightenment, and that we can accomplish it if we practice in a certain way, but our belief would still be dualistic. Śākyamuni Buddha, Bodhidharma, and Master Dōgen definitely attained enlightenment, and we can believe that they did. The real question is whether or not we will actually be able to accomplish it.

Master Huiji would say, "You have a very firm resolution, and I have no doubt that you are really one with your faith, but you are still far removed from the rank of saving people." He would not acknowledge the enlightenment of such a person. All beings truly do have buddha nature. But it is not enough simply to believe that because Śākyamuni Buddha or Dōgen said it. We must know that for ourselves if we hope to achieve the "rank of saving others."

When people are told, "First, you must believe," many stop at the "rank of belief." What Master Huiji is saying here is that if we fail to reach the "rank of saving people," we will not return to the source. Consider the expression "Proceed one step from a one-hundred-foot pole and your whole body appears all over the universe." That is how I would like you to do it. It is said that at the rank of belief we can enter the Buddha's world, but we can't enter the devil's world. In other words, we will be in the company of buddhas, but we become one who cannot enter into the three worst realms of delusion—namely those of hell beings, hungry ghosts, and animals. People may say of us that we are like Buddha, but it will be very difficult for us to free beings in the lowest realms.

Since we are all endowed with buddha nature it is possible that we can become bodhisattvas or buddhas. It is also possible for us to descend into one of the three lowest realms. Master Dōgen said that zazen is the practice of killing buddhas. Here "killing" means "becoming one with things." Many of us may be practicing zazen in order to become buddhas, but Dōgen said that zazen involves killing buddhas. This is exactly how it is. We must die completely on our sitting cushion.

Ah! I regretted that in past days my face was like jade.

Again, Master Changcha reflects on the progress of his practice, confessing that he has his regrets, too. Long ago, prior to writing the Ten Verses, he traveled from place to place for practice. Sometimes, when he would meet with conditions that made it seem as if he had forgotten the self, he would wonder if this wasn't enlightenment. When we encounter something we have never encountered before, it can certainly be difficult to let go of it and toss it aside. This is doubly so if we have not met a master who tells us, "A self yet remains who has had this experience." Or we may remember experiences we have had in the past, even before we started practicing Zen, wherein we felt as though we may have forgotten ourselves. We may then want to experience that state again. If we get stuck on such experiences and make revisiting them our objective, that will always be the limit of our practice.

But, again, the thing we must be most careful of is the concept of "just." We human beings fundamentally do not like limits, but for some reason or other, "just" seems like the real thing. We cannot grasp that it is still incomplete. We create the illusion that "just," "now," or "the present moment" is separate from impermanence, thinking that it exists apart from what is constantly changing. But "just" is not the end point. It is a condition that is still unresolved.

> And I lamented that at the time of my return my hair had
> turned white.

Recall the expression, "Time flies like an arrow. It waits for no one." Years pass by before we know it, and even though we want to persevere, it becomes difficult for us to stick with our practice. "Years ago," we say, "I used to cut down all the miscellaneous delusive thoughts with the Dharma sword of Mu and had the courage to strive for enlightenment, but now that has disappeared."

Lamenting that at the time of return his hair had turned white has two meanings. One is that time flies. Our hair becomes grey without our noticing it. Our legs and back grow weaker. As we grow older we may no longer have the courage or vigor to strive for enlightenment, and we might completely forget about the practice we have done until now. The other meaning has to do with our ability to really practice well after we have lost our vigor. With these words, Master Changcha is saying, "Now you are finally able to enter the circle of Zen people, people of the Way."

Do you understand? You may say that you have grown old and become so lazy that you cannot do anything, that it is no longer possible for you to strive for enlightenment or to practice zazen. You may say that you once had the desire to understand the Mu kōan by any means possible, but you now admit that you have forgotten it. And yet, only now that it has finally come to this can you enter into the circle of people of the Way, people of Zen. The "stink" of enlightenment, or practice, or zazen has been removed.

> Returning to my old home with dangling arms, there was no
> one who recognized me.

This line describes the perspective of someone who has completely thrown away everything that he or she has acquired through practice and now lays claim to nothing. Having thrown away what they have acquired, everything has now truly disappeared. They no longer resemble the person who at the beginning was so full of vigor and perseverance. That is why no one in their hometown recognizes them. They have totally changed. The Dharma, the self, and everything outside of the self have disappeared.

Yet, although it may seem like the ego has been removed so that only the Dharma remains, it is not possible. Nevertheless, they think that through practice they have disappeared, while the Dharma remains. This is the "stage of faith," and it is a difficult point. If the ego-self disappears, then both ego-self and the Dharma must disappear. Yet at this stage something glittering, something splendid, something buddha-like or bodhisattva-like remains. This is what it is like when the self has disappeared, but the Dharma remains. It is not possible in this condition to enter the circle of Zen people. We must completely let go of both "self" and "Dharma" in order to finally be called a Zen person or a person of the Way. But if we look very closely, the self remains. If we do not know how to put out the fire, all the methods and means will only be those of a person for whom the Dharma still remains.

Also, I had nothing to offer my parents.

Here is finally described the condition in which everything has been thrown away, including wisdom, methods, and means. In other words, there is no Buddha, no Way, no Zen, and no Dharma, now that we have returned to our original self, the self that once didn't know anything. The ancient story of the Chinese master Guling Shenzan is illustrative of this:

> Master Guling Shenzan returned to his home temple after years of practice. When he returned, his master said, "I have had no word from you for a long time. What have you been doing out there all this time?"
>
> "I haven't been practicing at all," Master Guling replied, "I've only been walking here and there."
>
> Thinking Master Guling a not particularly good monk, the master put him in charge of the temple bath. One day, while Guling was washing his master's back in the bath, he murmured, "You really have a great temple, but I think the buddha inside has been neglected."

"It may seem neglected," the master said, "but if it is washed it will become clean."

Then the two began to speak of the Dharma in earnest. After they spoke for some time, the master realized that the person he was now speaking to was not the disciple he had known before.

"Where have you been and what have you been doing?" the master asked.

Master Guling Shenzan answered, "Actually, I have been practicing with a certain master. I was at last able to throw everything away. I wanted to return here to repay my debt of gratitude to you for ordaining me as a monk, so as not to be forgetful of it. Please forgive me for what I said when I was washing your back."

"No, no," the master said to his disciple, "Don't worry about it. From now on I plan to practice myself."

The old monk set out to practice and it is said that he became a fine Zen priest.

It is unusual to hear of a master treating his disciple as a teacher in this way, but this kind of odd behavior happened in an exceptional situation, unique only to these particular people. Master Guling's statement that he hadn't been practicing at all, but only wandering around, has the same meaning as, "Returning to my old home with dangling arms, there was no one who recognized me." When he spoke those words in reply to his master's question, they had great significance, but his master did not understand it.

Lines seven and eight of this verse have mostly the same meaning. However, the phrase "there was no one who recognized me" has particular significance. What it means is that our practice is not something we do in order to get something. Practice is done in order to throw things away. Otherwise zazen will simply be a means to become learned, and it will only end with the accumulation of stories about Zen and the Dharma. I would like you to continue endeavoring at sesshin so that you do not become such a person.

7: The Song of Not Returning Home

THE SEVENTH VERSE of *Ten Verses of Unfathomable Depth* is a particularly challenging verse. Before I delve into it, I would first like to make some comments about how to properly practice with kōans.

There are many people who indiscriminately look at kōans. Some think that Zen involves investigating and then passing through kōans, but this is a very shallow view. "Zen is the center of the Buddha-dharma,"[105] as Master Dōgen said. This means that Zen is really the essence of Buddhism. Having said that, however, we must not think that it is the only teaching of Buddhism. If we do not see Zen from the broader vantage point of Buddhism at large, we will lose sight of the whole of Buddhist teaching. So I would like you to study Zen with a flexible mind, without developing a fixed or rigid conceptual viewpoint with regard to it. If we are told to look at a kōan without really understanding why, and we think that practicing with a kōan like Mu, for example, is the only way to practice zazen or Zen, we risk being mistaken in our thinking. Thus, in order to practice correctly, you must think for yourself. You must ask your master, "Why must I look at Mu?" Otherwise your delusion might increase as a result of your Zen practice.

A kōan is something that is extremely useful when it comes to devoting yourself to practice of the Way. Kōans also serve as tools to see whether or not a person has reached the final point. It used to be that there were no kōans. But people's perseverance gradually began to ebb because they could no longer endure sitting quietly. It became unavoidable that students had to be given questions with which to grapple. This had already happened in China, even before Zen came to Japan.

Kōans are neither good nor bad in and of themselves. Their quality depends, rather, on the person working with them. It is, therefore, quite possible that someone who has been practicing wholeheartedly may become worse off by being given a kōan. This is why it is necessary to work completely with a single kōan.

Kōan practice is not a matter of coming to understand the kōan by various means of practice. Instead, it is to totally become the kōan with one's whole body, from the top of the head to the tips of the toes. Resolution of the kōan means to so thoroughly become the kōan that there is nothing left but the kōan. Then, when the kōan disappears, you will also disappear. When one side of a dualistic viewpoint disappears, it is not possible for the other to remain. When the kōan and the self disappear simultaneously, we call this "body and mind cast off—cast off body and mind."[106]

Zhaozhou's Mu kōan is one that is relatively easy to become one with, and that is why new practitioners are often given this kōan first. They are told, "Just be the kōan. Be one with it." And yet, it is still difficult to really penetrate it since many random and idle thoughts arise. Ultimately, though, both shikantaza and kōan practice are employed in an effort to forget the ego-self, by whatever means possible. So it is fine to sometimes practice with a kōan, and fine at other times to practice with shikantaza. There is no need to be partial to one or the other, and we should not argue about which is better or worse.

Simply put, it is important to be clear that the objective of sitting in zazen is to forget the self, not to study kōans. As Master Dōgen said:

> To forget the self is to be enlightened by myriad things. To be enlightened by myriad things is to cast off the body and mind of oneself, as well as that of all things.[107]

It might be useful here to consider a story from China. This story is about Master Zhaozhou and the woman who owned a teashop on the road to Mt. Wutai.

> At a certain time every year, many people make a pilgrimage to sacred Mt. Wutai. Along the road leading to the mountain there was a teashop at which many travelers would stop to ask for directions to the mountain. The owner of the shop

only ever answered such questions with "Just go straight." No matter who asked her, all she would say was, "Just go straight and you will get to Mt. Wutai."

It happened that a monk who was training under Master Zhaozhou made a pilgrimage to Mt. Wutai during a break between practice periods. He also asked the shop owner, "How can I get to Mt. Wutai?"

"Just go straight and you will get there," she answered.

"Is that so," he said, and continued walking.

Watching him leave, the shop owner said, "Ah! He is also a good monk. He is going straight just as I told him, without going down any side roads."

Since the shop owner always said the same thing, it eventually became a topic of conversation among monks who made the pilgrimage. "The shop owner doesn't seem like an ordinary person. She must have practiced quite a bit of Zen," they would say. Eventually, the monks told Master Zhaozhou the story and asked, "Won't you go there and check on her for us?"

Thus, one day, Zhaozhou took to the road with a crowd of other pilgrims to visit Mt. Wutai. The owner of the teashop was there, just as the monks had said she would be. Zhaozhou said to her, "I'd like to ask you the way to Mt. Wutai."

As always, the shop owner replied, "Just go straight. If you take any side roads, you will not get to Mt. Wutai."

When Zhaozhou returned to the monastery, he reported to the monks, "Since you asked me, I went to investigate whether the shop owner was genuine or not. It was just as you had told me. When I asked the way to Mt. Wutai, she said, 'Just go straight.'"

All of the monks listened intently, waiting to hear what more Master Zhaozhou would say. But rather than saying "She's an imposter" or "She's genuine," he said only, "I've seen through her."

Zhaozhou did not say that the teashop owner was mistaken, nor did he say that her understanding was still shallow, nor did he comment upon whether or not she was enlightened. Of course, the monks were surprised. They all wanted Master Zhaozhou to speak to the teashop owner's credibility, but all he said was, "I've seen through her." Well, this became a problem. In a word, it became a kōan. The monks felt utterly helpless because Zhaozhou said so little. They would have understood him if he had spoken in terms of good and bad, but because he only answered them with the enigmatic "I've seen through her," they didn't know what to make of it.

How should we look at Zhaozhou's statement? We can say that this kōan is similar to Zhaozhou's Mu, in that it is a relatively easy kōan to practice with. Whatever the case may be, a kōan is devised in such a way that it activates our consciousness. In fact, these stories are chosen precisely for this reason. The essential characteristic of a kōan is that it continually activates our thought processes and then snatches away thought until consciousness no longer arises. This is why his very simple and clear answer—"I've have seen through her"—appears. When difficult thoughts and feelings appear while sitting, and you think, "This isn't really zazen," there is nothing wrong with trying to practice with Zhaozhou's "I've seen through her" or "Mu." But you shouldn't approach such things with the intent of understanding them. The kōan only truly comes to life when the whole body ends up becoming the kōan.

Having the intention of going to the source, of returning to the origin, is already a mistake.

You may wonder where the "source" or the "origin" to which one hopes to return actually is. I always say that there is neither a beginning nor an end to things. All things, including human beings, have no beginning, no end. Everything arises from causes and conditions. Things continually come together and then separate, come together and then separate. Things stick together for only a fleeting moment before they again part ways. Given that this is the case, how can we even begin to know where, exactly, the source is?

Yet, although we do not understand what "returning to the source" means, we still say that everything we experience and observe is the ego. But no matter where we look for it, we can find no ego. We speak of the true Self, but we don't know which self is the true Self. We listen to the various things that Zen masters and the ancestors have said—and they all do speak of the ego or of the true Self—but what is the ego, really, after all? What is the true Self? This is something we must investigate closely.

As long as we say, "I don't know," or "I don't understand," we still have seeking mind. But how do we know if this seeking mind is the voice of the ego or the voice of the true Self? The question remains. So having the intention of going to the source, of returning to the origin, is already a mistake. In the last lines of the preceding verse, Master Changcha spoke about his own practice, but in this verse, he speaks to us about the mistake of intending to return to the source. The title of this verse is "The Song of Not Returning Home," and the main idea that Master Changcha addresses here is not getting stuck on the idea of returning to the origin.

The well-known Buddhist layman Su Tongpo touches upon this same topic in a poem:

Mt. Lu famous for its mist
Zhejiang Bay for its tides.
If I hadn't gone there, I would have regretted it forever.
When I actually went and returned
There was nothing special
The mist of Mt. Lu,
The tides of Zhejiang Bay.

The fame of Mt. Lu and of Zhejiang Bay is a way of describing how we long for the experience of awakening to our true Self. Mt. Lu is a place of exceptional beauty and represents the desire to return to see the place of the true Self. It symbolizes what nirvana, or enlightenment, or forgetting the self means for us. The smoke-like mists of Mt. Lu are a seasonal phenomenon that occur when seawater in the district of Zhejiang flows back upstream. We can think of this splendidly beautiful scenery as nirvana, our final destination, or the Buddhadharma. "If I hadn't gone there" expresses the deep desire to go to the place oneself, to see that beautiful place with these very eyes, while living in this body—by any means possible. Saying that one would have regretted it forever is to say that one's desire to get to Mt. Lu and Zhejiang Bay one way or another never disappears. Even though we may have seen or heard of other beautiful places, only Mt. Lu and Zhejiang Bay remain always on your mind. We would certainly regret not going there, and so we think that we absolutely must see it at least once. I would like you to recognize and accept that this poem represents our condition right now.

But in the end, Su Tongpo writes, "When I actually went and returned, there was nothing special." This means that finally, when our wish to see the scenic beauty of Mt. Lu and Zhejiang Bay with our own eyes finally comes true, we find that there was nothing special about them. "What? Mt. Lu and Zhejiang Bay?" we say, "I can see that kind of scenery anywhere." In Zen, we call this "everyday mind." Although we intently sought enlightenment, and felt that we absolutely had to reach it, in the end we find that it is not at all different from our daily lives, the lives we live each day. Despite our deep and long-held yearning to reach it, it turns out to be nothing special, nothing out of the ordinary.

On the other hand, if we were to ask whether everyday mind is the final point of the Way of Buddha or the essence of the Buddhadharma, the answer is that it is not. Everyday mind certainly is the destination of Zen and of Buddhism, but it is a mistake to simply recognize the existence of something like everyday mind and think, "Oh, now I see. That's what it's all about." "Everyday mind is the Way" is certainly the ultimate principle of the Buddhadharma, but looking at it from the perspective of Buddhism as a whole, the point is that "the true nature of things is formless." There must be no Way, no Dharma, and no Buddha. The home to which we must return is a place where there is nothing. This is what this particularly challenging verse called "The Song of Not Returning Home" expresses: we mustn't get stuck in the idea of returning home.

Essentially, there is nowhere to settle down, no place to call one's home.

Every person is registered somewhere. In the national registry there is a record of each person's date of birth and legal residence. However— and this is just a metaphor—a person who has studied Zen and reached the final point must not be registered. This is to say that the place where you are registered is not your real home. You should be well aware of this as you pursue Zen. So even if you do come to know that "Everyday mind is the Way," you must realize for yourself that this is still something along the way. It is not the final point. Otherwise, it will be easy to fall into distorted ways of thinking, in which you think that Zen is just "all about the now," and that's all there is to it.

The condition in which things have really disappeared is the original condition. So if we understand something, the thing to do is to throw it away. If we understand or do not understand, we do so with the same exact awareness. It isn't that it's good to understand and bad to not understand: both must be discarded. This is what Master Zhaozhou meant by "I've seen through her." He didn't say that the shop owner was good or bad or mistaken. In truth, it can't be said.

So, whether we are working with "I've seen through her" or "Everyday mind is the Way," it is a mistake to say, "Everyday, ordinary mind is the Way. There is no Way other than what you are seeing and hearing and feeling right now. That is the Way of Buddha." Instead, we must practice from that perspective so as to let go of the Way, too. It is difficult to get that far, but first we must understand that "Everyday mind is the Way" is not the final point of the Buddhadharma. We must continue with shikantaza or kōan practice. Otherwise, we'll stop before coming to the end.

The ancient path through the pines is covered with deep snow.

No matter how hard you look for the essential self or the essential thing, you cannot find it. The entanglements and conflicts in your mind are like being in snow so deep that you cannot step into it. It is a place where nobody has yet gone. Various thoughts and delusions are likened to a snow-covered landscape that you cannot escape once you enter it.

The long range of mountain peaks is furthermore blocked by clouds.

Master Changcha continues building a scene in which not only has the snow piled up but it is not possible to see anything beyond the snow. These lines depict the scene very beautifully. No matter how much we walk around in such a setting hoping to see something, we won't be able to. The more we want to see something, the less able we are to see it. Near and far are matters of our perception. Within things themselves there is neither near nor far. These words express the state of having transcended space and time as separation disappears. The meaning of this fourth line is, in short, that we should think deeply and be clear about the fact that we must not exert ourselves in vain to understand something.

> When host and guest are tranquil and serene, everything is incongruous.

The pair "host and guest" carries its usual meaning. But these words also indicate a differential relationship, not unlike the word pairs "senior and junior," "teacher and student," and so forth. These days, when we speak about sameness and difference, we think about difference as something negative, as related to "discrimination." However, we run into problems with difference and distinction if we don't clearly distinguish host and guest. It is said that the wisdom of sameness is relatively easy to understand, but that the wisdom of difference is very difficult to see. But in fact, since all things are just one thing divided, we won't really understand sameness if we don't clearly understand the wisdom of difference.

In Zen, we say, "Wherever we are throughout our lives is sufficient in itself."[108]

"Wherever we are" means wherever we live and wherever we go. The place where each of us lives and our position in life are sufficient. However, since most of us cannot be truly satisfied in our hearts, it often happens that we distort the relationship between "host and guest," or if we don't distort it, we at least make everything incongruous. No matter how intimate our mutual relationship may be, if we decide that I am the host and you are the guest, our relation becomes formal or distant. You'll chafe, asking, "Why do you have to be so formal, so stiff?"

So it is strange, given sameness, to establish mutual vows or the notion of trusting one another. That would be something extra. Everything is essentially one, so it is a mistake to think that we must believe in each other or make vows. When a relationship is truly intimate, there is no need to say, "Why do you have to be so formal, so stiff?" When things become indistinguishable, they are one. So it is mistaken and delusional to expressly establish "host" in opposition to "guest." These are just names.

When we were born, we knew no names. But because we have attached names to things, conflict arises. If we were to remove all the names in our life—guest, host, teacher, student, zazen, delusion, discrimination— what would remain? "Host and guest" is just another way of expressing difference and sameness, sameness and difference. The problem of difference also arises on the way to reaching the final point. There are quite a few in the world of Zen who think that they have reached the end point, but by making distinctions such as "I understand, but you still don't understand," they create conflict.

> When lord and vassal are united, there is wrong in the midst
>   of right.

Here, "right" and "in the midst of" stand for sameness. We no longer use archaic words like "lord and vassal," but they simply stand for mutual relationship. Even from our own point of view, nowadays relationships between father and mother, brother and sister, seniors and juniors have become disordered. We emphasize sameness, but it is a "bad sameness," where there is neither equality nor distinction. The world has become a place in which people insist on always getting their own way. We read in the newspapers that in some schools there is no longer any distance between those who teach and those who are taught. It is precisely this kind of thing that encapsulates "wrong in the midst of right." When there is neither sameness nor difference, everything is thrown into disarray. We shouldn't call this "unity" or "equality."

Good things don't pass for good things. We call this the sahā world,[109] but if we can't enter the six realms—birth in heaven, among human beings, fighting devils, animals, hungry ghosts, or in hell—then how could we possibly free sentient beings? So while it is necessary to enter the mountains and foster "one or a half disciple," we must also simultaneously teach the Dharma to many people by secretly going to town. It is important to do both, but if we end up going too far or too frequently into the world, we run the risk of losing the source itself.

We must be aware that the Dharma is something that can disappear. The Way is something that exists everywhere, and not only here in Japan. The Way exists everywhere, but its mere existence is of little use. That alone does not help us. We might even say that it would be better if it just didn't exist in such cases. Each thing is certainly endowed with its own dharma, with its own "duty." Laypeople must be of service to as many people as possible. Ordained people must be able to guide people to faith. In order to lead people to faith, you must first become ordained. In order to become such a person, it is necessary to do zazen, to forget the self, and to be willing to enter into any of the realms of suffering, and to then be of sufficient help to the beings that inhabit each world. This is the duty of someone who is ordained. When it comes to things other than inspiring faith, anyone can do them.

> When Master Linji Yixuan was about to die, he asked his disciple, Sansheng, "Is everything all right?"
> Sansheng said, "Don't worry. You can die in peace."
> Linji then replied, "Who would have thought that my true Dharma eye would be destroyed by this blind ass?!"

It was thus that Master Linji verified his disciple Sansheng Huiran, the "blind ass," by essentially saying, "You have destroyed the Rinzai sect, and that's why I can die in peace." This is quite different from situations we hear about these days. Linji was not saying, "I found a good disciple who will pass on my Dharma, so now I feel at peace." Rather, he was able to die with peace of mind because the Dharma had been crushed. It is no wonder, then, that the Rinzai sect has continued on until the present day in this manner. We must practice with the aim of inheriting the Dharma in the same way that Sansheng did. If we do not, we cannot really "return home and sit peacefully." This is something that ordained people in particular must be well aware of.

How will you sing the song of returning home?
In bright moonlight, the dead tree is blooming in front of
the hall.

Master Linji really returned home when he said, "Who would have thought that my true Dharma eye would be destroyed by this blind ass?!" This is what is meant by "the dead tree is blooming"—to put an end to it, to completely shatter it so there is nothing left. Only then is the Dharma truly transmitted from master to disciple for the first time. The master's Dharma is transmitted without one drop being lost. This is what is meant by "destroying" or "extinguishing" the Dharma. It isn't just that something has been passed on through a connection. You must impress this deeply on your mind. Otherwise, you won't be able to think of flowers blooming on a dead tree.

Up until now, we may have been sitting with our own ideas about zazen. However, to put it in rather extreme terms, we practice zazen in order to forget zazen. From now on, endeavor with the strong determination to realize this goal.

8: The Revolving Function

VERSE EIGHT is about sameness and difference or discrimination and equality, and you'll note that the wording of the verse is a bit complicated. In some editions, this verse has been titled "Change in Rank" instead of "The Revolving Function." The difference is one of before and after, like the front foot and back foot that continually change places when walking. In the same way, sameness and difference are but a single thing. I think that this is something we can understand by reading this verse.

In the Sōtō Zen sect we frequently use the word shikantaza, which means "to sit single-mindedly." We use methods such as shikantaza or kōan practice to make it easier to concentrate. Speaking in terms of practice, the syllable *shi*, "one" or "only," signifies difference. At the same time, it verifies "as-it-is." The function of verification is sameness, as in the Sōtō sect teaching that states, "Practice and realization are not two."

The function of "practice" is difference and the function of "verification" is sameness, so there is no leaning to one side or the other. We inevitably have preconceptions, so we may lean toward a one-sided sameness, expressed by words such as "just" or "as-it-is" or "the way things are." This is why it has been long said that the wisdom of sameness is relatively easy to clarify and understand. But it is also said that the wisdom of difference is quite difficult to clarify and understand. I would like you to be well aware when you study this verse that while "just," "only," and "as-it-is" are sometimes used as ways and means, they are also at the same time the ultimate. They possess both of these aspects.

It is still dangerous even inside the castle of nirvana.

Nirvana is a state of neither arising nor ceasing. This refers not only to the birth and death of human beings but to all things with form that are right in front of us—things we can see, as well as the movements of the mind. All such things neither arise nor cease. Having neither arisen nor ceased is the ultimate condition of things. We ourselves, just as we are right now, are the ultimate. Deluded, anxious, afraid—we are the ultimate even with these things. That is all there is. Otherwise there is nothing. This is called "the highest rank of sameness," the ultimate endpoint.

Because there is nothing in this state, there is everything. Whatever happens to come into it is all there is. Moreover, since this state is all there is, there is nothing it can be compared with. This is the result or effect of the Way. In Buddhism, we speak of causes, conditions, and effects, but since an effect immediately becomes a cause that gives rise to the next result, we shouldn't get stuck solely on the result. This applies to reality as well. We cannot stop or hold on to any of it, because it is always unfolding within change.

People who practice zazen tend to be particularly inflexible or unadaptable. This is because they are always trying to be in a quiet state of "emptiness," where nothing arises. But, as this line says, this is "still dangerous," because something yet remains. There must be nothing that remains in the state of being neither arisen nor ceased. Whether we call it emptiness, difference, or sameness, this beautiful condition exists within human consciousness and is dangerous because "emptiness" or "just" or "Dharma" remain.

In Zen we often say that the self and Dharma are separate. Yet within the aspect of difference, the self must be the self and Dharma must be Dharma. This is clear. However, there must be neither the self nor Dharma, as far as things are concerned. Both the self and Dharma must really disappear. I have already said that it is a mistake to think that we are already in the state where everyday mind is the Way. "Everyday mind is the way" is the ultimate we arrive at as a result of Buddhist practice. It is a major problem to fall into thinking that "Everyday mind is the Way" means our own present condition. I would like you to see things from the standpoint that all things essentially neither arise nor cease, and to be very careful of the trap of thinking that "just be" or "things are just as they should be" reflect the ultimate teaching of Śākyamuni Buddha and the ancestors. Rather, it is a matter of "neither arising nor ceasing."

There is a well known story about the sixth ancestor, Dajian Huineng, who went to study at the monastery of the Daman Hongren, the fifth ancestor, after having only heard a single line from the Diamond Sutra— "Let your mind function without dwelling on anything."[110] There is no place from where the mind appears and there is no source to which it returns or into which it disappears. If there is neither a place from where the mind arises nor a place into which it ceases, then it must only be a matter of suddenly appearing due to the coalescing of conditions. Many think that mind and body are separate, but when a thought arises, there is only that thought. It isn't the case that the body or mind think; there is only the thought.

However, when the self intervenes, thought does not remain just thought. Awareness of good or bad, like or dislike adheres to it. So when you sit in zazen, don't build up castle walls around yourself by falling into thinking, "I must be empty, I must be quiet." These thoughts become the "castle of Nirvana," or castles of "neither arising nor ceasing," "emptiness," or "nothingness." These sorts of conditions are comfortable, crisp, and clean and they are surely quiet, too, but in the end they are only what you have created for yourself.

The source isn't like this. If we knew nothing about Zen or the Dharma you wouldn't think of it as being like this. We should only single-mindedly do our practice without knowing about these things. Otherwise we get caught up in ideas about emptiness or nothingness. This is what "it is still dangerous" means: that something yet remains. No matter how clean we may have become, there is something "clean" that remains.

Even if we say, "I'm no longer hung up on anything," we need to notice whether or not we are now hung up on not being hung up.

Even if you really aren't stuck, such a latent condition could continue for two, three, five, or even ten years, and then many years later, you may indeed become unexpectedly hung up on something and lose everything you had achieved up to that point. All your effort might still end in vain. So you must understand this line to mean "really do it until nothing remains."

In Japan, we usually use a washcloth in the bath. After using it, we wring this wet cloth again and again until all the water has been wrung out. It seems that we have gotten all the water out, but if we wait for a while and wring it again, more drops of water will appear. Ultimately, it isn't easy to wring out all of the water. This is what "it is still dangerous" means.

Strangers come across each other without appointment.

This line refers to the various paths that we take in our lives, whether they are in towns or in the countryside, or in the north, south, east, or west. "Without appointment" means that nothing is certain along these paths. We don't know what we will encounter. There isn't one thing we can say is fixed or decided. This is also to say, again, that sameness and difference are not separate; within sameness there is always difference and within difference there must be sameness.

In a company, for example, there are CEOs and employees, the workers and the management. It is not possible for an organization to consist solely of management or solely of workers. So no matter how equal the world may be, it is not possible to say that equality and discrimination, management and workers, teachers and students, parents and children are the same. It is not possible for things to consist of solely one side.

A person who understands well the principles of things gets along well with others, but he neither panders nor forms factions. Such a person firmly lives his life determined by his own way of thinking. If he didn't, his life would become an "evil sameness." We must be harmonious with others, but not identical. The way of the world is such that things are not fixed or settled, and if we try to make them into one thing, dangers arise.

People call someone who provisionally puts on a dirty robe
    "a buddha."

The Buddha's teachings are said to be divisible into true teachings and provisional teachings. Provisional teachings refer to teachings wherein means and methods contradict principles. In the Sōtō sect, for example, one teaching says that there is nothing to realize and nothing to attain. It is certainly this way, but we only come to understand what to take up and what to give up when we attain the result of practice. From the standpoint that there is "nothing to realize, nothing to attain," we needn't do shikantaza or kōan practice or count the breath or follow the breath. But we must skillfully use these things in order to affirm for ourselves the fact that they are unnecessary. They are unnecessary, but their results are in accord with the Way. This is why we say that true understanding is when we make our not understanding what we do not understand completely our own. To think of using this or that method to understand what we don't understand is a mistake. True understanding is said to be understanding that what we don't understand is what we don't understand.

We can understand the meaning of "putting on a dirty robe" by looking at the example of the bodhisattva Avalokiteśvara, who frees sentient beings by changing into thirty-three different forms. Likewise, Śākyamuni Buddha would adopt a teaching style suited to the classes of people he was teaching, using various context-specific methods for each audience. Śākyamuni Buddha's "entry into nirvana" was also an expedient means of teaching. From the standpoint of "neither arising nor ceasing," how could it be? Yet without his entering nirvana, people would not have followed him, nor would they have been able to believe in him. Even our lives as monks and nuns may function as provisional means of teaching. At funerals, for example, we have a good opportunity to teach people about Buddhism. We always place the words "newly returned to the source" above the precept name of the deceased. To which source do they return? Is there such a thing as a source? Everyone wants to know such things. In order to lead people to faith, we must chew up and digest these provisional means. By understanding the ultimate and incorporating it in his teachings, the Buddha made it useful. But merely saying "neither arising nor ceasing" or "nothing to realize, nothing to attain" without really knowing the final point will come to nothing. If someone who understands the final point teaches "neither arising nor ceasing," "nothing to realize, nothing to attain," and explains that others are provisional teachings, there will be a clear course or order to their teaching. However, if someone who doesn't know the destination teaches only the methods, they will not be able to lead people to the true destination. This is a big mistake, as expressed in the saying, "If there is a hairbreadth's deviation, it is like the gap between heaven and earth."[111]

Certain teachers who use the terms "provisionally" or "expedient" are able to use them to point to the truth. If the one who teaches others does not really understand these concepts, then even the methods as such will be mistaken, and students will be guided in a false direction. Even if you say, "I'm only using these methods temporarily," it is a serious error to use methods without really understanding them to be only methods, only means.

> But if someone wears precious clothes, what should you call
> him?

Once, long ago, Śākyamuni Buddha happened upon a hunter who had netted and was just about to shoot a pregnant deer. The Buddha transfigured himself into a golden-hued deer. When he had explained the laws of karma and rebirth to the hunter, he pitied the deer and released it. Thereupon, the king at the time reportedly said, "I am a deer with the head of a human being. You are a human being with the head of a deer." Do you understand? The king had the head of a human, but the body of an animal. Śākyamuni Buddha was just the opposite. His head was that of a deer, but his body was that of a human being. Ever since then, it was prohibited to hunt deer in that kingdom. This is to say that with regard to sameness and difference or discrimination and equality, it is necessary to reach a level where you can use things freely.

There is a saying "Zen when not doing zazen." If the condition of your everyday zazen is not really your own, then all of the merit that you have accumulated over a long time can suddenly vanish upon coming in contact with specific conditions. Buddhism abounds with stories of people losing long-term friendships or the trust of others because of sudden fits of anger. There is nothing more frightening than anger. Anger can turn everything to ashes; it can destroy everything. That is why it is often said that the most difficult precept to observe is the precept "Do not get angry." It is important in daily life to forget anger by not perceiving "the other"—that is, by not creating distance between oneself and others.

This applies to good things as well as bad things. We call this "endurance for the sake of the Dharma." If people say that they get angry for the sake of the Dharma, this is an indication of how difficult it is to forget both self and the Dharma. At the same time, this shows that we cannot be negligent in our everyday practice. During sesshin, we can sit comparatively peacefully and quietly, but everything disappears when sesshin is over. This also affirms the great difficulty of reaching the ultimate point.

> In the middle of the night, the wooden man puts on shoes and leaves.

These allegories are also another way of saying that sameness and difference, discrimination and equality, are always one thing. "The wooden man" describes a condition where there is not even the slightest particle of self. This also applies to the "stone woman" that appears in the next line. "The middle of the night" is pitch-black, so it is not possible to see things clearly. This is sameness or equality. "The middle of the night" is sameness. "Puts on his shoes and leaves" means that even in the pitch-black of night, we don't mistake our own shoes and those of others. If the shoes are taken off in the appropriate place, then we can quickly put them on again. In this way, "the wooden man" is the function of a person who is truly without self and in any situation clearly recognizes his own things as opposed to what belongs to others. This verse expresses difference and sameness in harmony.

> At dawn, the stone woman puts on a hat and goes home.

The *Song of the Jewel Mirror Samadhi* contains the image of the stone woman as well. One of its lines says, "The wooden man starts to sing, the stone woman gets up to dance."[112] Just as with the wooden man above, the stone woman has no self and so is unhindered. She represents being totally free.

"At dawn" is the opposite of "in the middle of the night" and is, therefore, a reference to difference or discrimination. The two lines "in the middle of the night" and "at dawn" are parallel in reference to equality and discrimination. "Puts on her hat and goes home" refers to sameness—that there is sameness within difference. In the *Song of the Jewel Mirror Samadhi*, this is expressed in the line that says, "Hiding your practice, functioning secretly, like a fool, like an idiot—to continue just in this way is called the host within the host."[113]

The wooden man and *the stone woman, in the middle of the night* and *at dawn, puts on his shoes* and *puts on her hat*: each of these refers to something very difficult to carry out, namely the quiet continuation of the right practice of zazen when not doing zazen. We don't continue because someone forces us to. Rather, we are single-mindedly diligent as we pursue our method of practice. This sounds easy but is in fact quite difficult. It is tempting to fall into thinking that "Everyday mind is the Way and so whatever I do is zazen." Those who dislike doing zazen say, "If everything is zazen anyway, why should we do it?"

But this is a mistake. If whatever we do is zazen, then zazen is also a part of whatever we do. Whatever we are doing—sitting, lying down, walking, talking, and so forth—it must all be a continuation of mindful practice. It is truly difficult to do, but this is the type of effort we must make. Sameness and difference are indeed very difficult to practice, but it would also be wrong to try to always be consciously aware of them, such that we end up thinking, "Now I must practice sameness," or "Now I must practice difference." We must be able to practice them naturally.

An ancient emerald pool, the moon in the empty sky.

The word "ancient" frequently appears in Zen sayings. "Ancient" in this case does not mean "old" or "in old times" but refers to something eternal, something that does not change. The moon shining in the water is a common allegory. Which is reflecting which? Is the water reflecting the moon, or is the moon reflecting the water? This also applies to a shape and its shadow. One thing is divided but while divided is still one thing. For the water, the reflected moon is also the water. For the moon, the water is also the moon. It is something that never changes. This is why we can say it's "ancient."

Because you cannot really know the thing itself as the thing itself, you cannot really believe that it's just that and nothing else. This is why trouble arises in the world. But in fact trouble isn't difficult, it's only a matter of accepting things as they are.

When we don't understand, we simply don't understand. But we have been taught to think that there must be nothing that we don't understand, so we make every effort to understand. To truly understand, however, is to really know for ourselves that not understanding is not understanding. Until we understand in this way, our understanding will always change. We will end up understanding, then not understanding, then understanding, then not understanding, and so on. To abide by a way of understanding that does not change, you must understand that not understanding is not understanding.

The delusion of doubt appears because we think that various words conceal various things. This is why it is never possible to be free of doubt. We must become "a wooden man" and "a stone woman." That is why we practice zazen.

When we use the words "good" or "bad," we tend to think that there actually is something "good" or something "bad." But there is no difference with regard to things themselves. We use words to discriminate, but within things themselves, there is neither good nor bad, like nor dislike, beautiful nor ugly. These judgments are only within our minds. Things themselves do not change.

> Screening and filtering over and over to catch the moon, for the first time you will really know.

"Screening and filtering" refers to a process, like the one used in paper making, wherein a medium is filtered again and again in order to remove impurities. It isn't okay to feel satisfied, thinking that we have reached your goal, when we have merely glimpsed it. We must completely and continually, "over and over," throw away whatever we have attained. This is the meaning of "screening and filtering." The same sentiment is expressed in the Zen saying "You must even throw away that which is not there."

The *Ten Verses of Unfathomable Depth* present ten profundities that are expressed in different ways, but they are all about the same origin or source. In the end, the *Ten Verses of Unfathomable Depth* lead to the same ultimate—the infinite. If the origin does not disappear as well, then we will be caught in words. The *Ten Verses of Unfathomable Depth* are ten modes of expression that bring both the origin and the unfathomable depths to an end. This is why Master Tong'an Changcha left these verses to us. This point is exemplified in the story of Master Guishan Lingyou and his disciple, Xiangyan.

Xiangyan was very earnest in his study of Zen and frequently came to Master Lingyou for *dokusan*. But the master never approved of him. He would say neither that Xiangyan was still on the Way nor that he had reached the final point but would only repeat the admonition, "Throw away that which is not there." In this way he made Xiangyan persist in his practice for twenty years.

One day Master Lingyou said to Xiangyan, "Say one word from that place where you have completely eliminated everything you have learned or understood, from before your mother and father were born."

Xiangyan, although he had practiced diligently using various methods with unflinching courage up to that point, was unable to reply. Seeing that he was unable to become enlightened, he vowed, "If I cannot be enlightened in this life, I will never give up in all future lives to come."

He then asked to take his leave from the monastery and went to the home of the late Zen master Nanyang Huizhong, where he tended the master's grave while continuing his practice alone with untiring zeal.

One day, while Xiangyan was sweeping the grounds, a small stone that had been caught in the tip of the broom flew up and hit a piece of bamboo, making a sound.

Suddenly Xiangyan thought, "Oh! Is this the ultimate point of the Buddhadharma that Master Lingyou speaks about?"

He analyzed himself in various ways. The more he thought that it might be this or it might be that, the more his theories and words were exhausted. He found himself in a predicament from which he could find no way out. He ended up in a state from which he could neither proceed nor withdraw. He had driven himself that far into a corner.

Upon hearing the sound of a stone striking a piece of bamboo, he forgot everything he had learned.

When Xiangyan returned to Master Lingyou, the master approved of him.

In Zen, Master Lingyou's refusal to approve of Xiangyan for twenty years is called the greatest kindness. The fact that Master Lingyou did not easily approve of his disciple is a sign of his great compassion. The problem that the master posed to Xiangyan uses the words "mother and father," which we automatically associate with parents. But in this case the phrase "before your mother and father were born" refers to the essence of Buddhadharma. The master was asking his disciple to express the essence of Buddhadharma in words.

In Xiangyan's case, it took twenty years of repeatedly using his "filtering screen" to purify himself. He had resolutely put everything he was taught into practice for twenty years, without giving up at all, until he was finally able to attain his master's approval. People rarely practice in this way these days—to practice after giving up all practice. When he finally received his master's approval, Xiangyan said to Lingyou, "I don't value your Way, but I'm very grateful that you didn't give me your seal of approval for twenty years."

When Xiangyan began to teach his own disciples, he posed the following problem:

Imagine a situation where you hang by your clenched teeth from a branch of a tall tree into which you have climbed. Neither your hands nor feet have any support. Then, from below, someone says, "Hey! Say one word of Buddhadharma." If you cannot answer, you have no value as a monk. But if you do answer, you must open your mouth and fall straight down from the tree and die. What do you do?

When we hear "a tall tree," we are apt to immediately think of ourselves in a tall tree with trunk and branches. But here, "a tall tree" is not something separate from us. I would like you to reflect on this: think about what it means to cling to a branch with your teeth, risking death should you open your mouth to speak one word. Xiangyan made his disciples practice with this harrowing problem, and using it, forced them to generate aspiration. It is a good problem. Perhaps he adopted this means because he himself could not respond when he had been asked to say a word from before his parents were born. Use problems like this, think of these kōans as your own, and then really persevere in your efforts.

9: CHANGING RANKS

THE NINTH VERSE, titled "Changing Ranks," deals primarily with the problem of how easy it is to fall into a one-sided sameness or equality. We can understand "sameness" in this context as referring to the realm of *satori*, emptiness, or nothingness.

One of the teachings passed down in the Sōtō Zen tradition is that of the five ranks.[114] The "five ranks" referred to are the relative within the absolute, the absolute within the relative, coming from within the absolute, arrival at mutual integration, and unity attained. It is possible to cure all manner of illness with these ranks. The rank referred to in "changing ranks" is the "rank of truth," sometimes called the "front" of things, which the Heart Sutra and others refer to as "the realm of emptiness." It is said that the true nature of things is formless in the realm of emptiness and that the things we now see are phantoms without substance. The point of this verse is to change such ranks.

When we say "the whole world is a dream," we mean that the dreams we see in our sleep and the dream that is the whole world are of the same nature. Both types of dream lack substance. This is the true form of things. Everything is constantly changing, so there is no way to lay hold of them. This is what it means to not have any substance. This is sameness or the absolute—equality. The relative, on the other hand, is the realm of difference. Although things do not have any substance, we see all sorts of things right now in front of us—there may be a window, a desk, this book, and so on. We call all of this variety that we see and experience "the world of form." Form is difference.

The Heart Sutra contains the famous lines: "Form is emptiness. Emptiness is form." This is a way of referring to things as both absolute and relative at the same time. What it means is that it isn't really possible to lean toward one or the other extreme. Certainly, there are the realms of emptiness and of form, but there is no substance within either. The sutra of The Merging Difference and Sameness, and others, refer to this as "interacting" or "blending." They say that this world is not comprised of just one thing, but rather that all things are mutually interdependent and support each other. In other words, everything is mutually interdependent.

Many who practice zazen for a long time understand this principle well and are thus able to freely use concepts like "the realm of emptiness," "the realm of form," "mutual interdependence," "absolute and relative," and "interacting." Keizan Jōkin, founder of Sōjiji, when asked by his master about his practice, said, "A black ball rolls around in pitch-black darkness." When his master resonded, "That isn't enough," speaking from the aspect of difference or the relative, Keizan said, "When tea is served, drink tea. When rice is served, eat rice." Thereupon Keizan was given his certificate of Dharma transmission.

"When rice is served, eat rice" means that we eat when meals are served. Certainly, it is this way: what is hot is hot, what is cold is cold. Truly, there is nothing else. At this point, however, we come to an impasse at "this is all there is." We let our understanding end at "There are no things," regardless of the fact that the Dharma is boundless and without limit. Since we think of the fact of nothingness as a fact, and therefore acknowledge it as existent, we easily fall into the trap of "nothingness." If we don't overcome this trap of nothingness, then things that do exist will not truly disappear for you. The danger is that we will end up understanding "When rice is served, eat rice. When tea is served, drink tea," and simply stop at thinking, "Yes, that's the way it is." The result is that we won't really live up to this and will inevitably get stuck at this point.

I would like you to be aware that since concepts like "everything just as it is right now," "everyday mind is the Way," "Dharma," or "Zen" are quite easy to understand, we are apt to fall into a one-sided sameness and stop there. It's easy to fall into thinking "I do zazen. I practice my method. Isn't this condition now all there is?" We call this "the wisdom of sameness" or "the rank of the absolute." We must go one step beyond this rank to a world of boundless flexibility. There are many different ways of meeting and dealing with people, and this is why we must change ranks. It would be strange to say that there is a world separate from the absolute, but we must practice in such a way that we become separate from the world of the absolute.

Growing hair and horns, you enter town,

"Growing hair and horns" means that we must, to put it simply, become a cow—that is, we must have a realization that goes beyond discrimination. As for "town," when we say with regard to monastic life that today we are allowed to enter town, it means that we are allowed to go shopping for half the day because it is a rest day. The rest day indicates sameness, and going into town indicates difference. So to go into town, we must become a cow, or some other animal, which represents a state that transcends discriminative consciousness. Furthermore, this line implies that if you do not also transcend the condition of the cow, you will not truly be able to go into town and buy things freely.

Daitō Kokushi, one of the ancestors, lived for twenty years in Kyoto as a mendicant monk. This whole period was "growing hair and horns." It is said that he endeavored at this also because his master had told him that it was necessary to do so if he really wanted to enter the aspect of the relative. This, in short, is "changing ranks."

This also applies to life in the monastery. A senior monk will tell a junior monk, "I've been here for many years and you just arrived here yesterday, so it's only natural that you have to do such and such. It's only natural that you should show reservation with regard to this or that." In this way, the older person emphasizes only the aspect of difference. This is also true of society as a whole. It seems that the emphasis is inevitably put on vertical relations in life. The point is that if we continue to dwell on these ranks forever, we must be careful. If we forget senior and junior ranks, it becomes possible to do anything. This is the practice we must do. This is the point of "Changing Ranks." We must practice in such a way that we become a person who can, by changing ranks, become anything.

A long time ago, there was a Japanese monk named Shunchō. He purposely stole something so he would be put in prison. Once he was in prison, he began to teach the other prisoners using the Lotus Sutra.

We may wonder whether or not he was going too far, but his actions also constitute "changing ranks."

To say that "everything has to be within zazen" means that ideally all of your life should take place within zazen, not that you should try to somehow integrate zazen into your life. This is what "Growing hair and horns, you enter town" means. It's easy to talk about "growing hair and horns," but it is actually difficult to do.

As you come in the front entrance of Hosshinji, the following inscription can be seen on the right: "One grain of donated rice has the weight of Mt. Sumeru. If a person doesn't realize the Way, he will end up becoming an animal." Master Dōgen used very strong words in connection to this point, even going so far as to say, "A person who does nothing and only eats what is given to him is merely a shit-making machine." He also used the phrase "a stinking leather bag" to severely rebuke those who live by accepting the donations of others without practicing.

Resembling a blue lotus flower blooming in the midst of fire.

A blue lotus flower, called *utpala* in Sanskrit, is a kind of mythical water lily said to bloom only once every 3,000 years. The blue lotus flower not only blooms just once every 3,000 years, but it also does so in the midst of fire, which burns up all things. Here "all things" refers to delusions, enlightenment, sameness, difference, and so on, which are burned up until nothing remains. I would like you to understand this state as being most pure.

The flower is us—we ourselves are in the midst of fire. We are, each of us, an exceedingly rare flower that blooms only once every 3,000 years in utmost purity. This means that those people who seek zazen, or the Way, or the Dharma are truly few, and since you are among those few, your state of mind is like this rare utpala flower.

The buddhas and ancestors are those who have awakened to the Dharma by means of Dharma. They have awakened to zazen by means of zazen. However, as I mentioned earlier, if one's zazen only ends at awakening, then one gets stuck at that rank of awakening. So in letting go of that rank the Way is attained. When the Way is attained, having attained the Way disappears. Why? Because in the midst of the fire that burns everything, "having attained the Way" is completely burned up. So the meaning of these two first lines is that it is really very difficult to do away with the total "nothing" that you have attained.

Understand that the image of falling into the realms of lower sentient beings, such as cows, horses, dogs, or cats, means "transcending all things." It has nothing to do with becoming such things, but rather with transcending them. We must go one step beyond what we have understood. This applies also to what we have attained, as well as to what we have not. What you think you have understood and what you do not understand are completely the same.

At this point, I often say, "It is fine simply to warm your sitting cushion," or "You must concentrate on one thing," or "It is not good to do something practice-like," or "Leave your thinking unto itself," or "Just sit as you are; there is no need for a method, no need to come to see me in dokusan." I say these things because I would like you to transcend them. It is not as if you should simply do these things as you have been told. Rather, I would like you to sit in such a way that you transcend even these things. Then you can come to dokusan. We also mustn't be stuck between understanding and not understanding forever. That happens when we cannot transcend and get hung up on something because of it.

Letting oneself be reduced to an animal can also be understood to mean "to take by surprise in a way that cannot be fathomed by human thought." This means that collecting alms just because monks from long ago collected alms is not everything. You have to transcend both what you understand and what you do not understand, and beyond that even transcend what you have transcended. This is all "changing ranks."

Long ago during the time of the Buddha, before we had developed the ability to construct bridges, rafts were used to cross large bodies of water. Buddha used the imagery of leaving the raft behind when one had reached the other shore to illustrate leaving behind the method. It is exactly the same with zazen. A time certainly comes when zazen is no longer necessary. No longer necessary means that whatever we do is zazen, whatever we do is Dharma, whatever we do is right in the middle of the Way. It is incorrect to say that practice continues until death, given that there is no death. All things have neither beginning nor end. And so it goes for practice. Thoroughly mastering the Way is the same as saying that it never ends. All traces must disappear or it is not truly mastered.

It is truly difficult to forget everything completely and then go on to forget even what you have forgotten. It isn't a matter of practice after enlightenment or practice before enlightenment. Essentially, practice is unnecessary. It is a mistake, to begin with, to think that delusion exists, and so to bring delusions we mistakenly believe to exist to an end is to make a twofold mistake. If you don't notice this, you won't see the mistake. It's only natural, then, that when you haven't attained enlightenment you won't be able to make it your own.

Joy is the most difficult thing from which to detach. When practicing, we often experience joy because of what is happening to us. But if there is joy, then there is also sadness and regret and all sorts of emotions. It is important not to stagnate on account of emotions. If we stagnate at any point, it becomes transmigration through the six realms, and we become separate from transmigration. But if we can become transmigration itself, then we can become people who can use transmigration. It's possible to attain this great freedom.

Master Zhaozhou once said, "In the past, I was used by time, but from the moment I forgot the self, I was able to use time."[115] I am speaking of a condition in which we have become "empty," which is to say our condition now. Whatever thoughts arise, whatever the condition of our zazen, this applies to each of us. It is all the moment "now." We are in a world where there is nothing, but we lean in one direction or another. Right now, we are dwelling in a certain rank. The point is that we need to assent to this rank and not seek elsewhere.

In the Sōtō sect, we emphasize that practice and realization are not separate. Practice itself is the manifestation of realization. This is "purity," and we call this intrinsically, totally quiet and pure thing the "now." But this has led to a misinterpretation of the concept of "sitting single-mindedly," and shikantaza has come to be understood primarily as a certain sitting posture about which many people say, "This alone is sufficient. There must be nothing to attain, nothing to realize." The result is that a certain consciousness accompanies the idea of sitting single-mindedly, and we think, "It's enough to just do our shikantaza and just sit." It is true that it is enough to just sit, but these words only make sense in the case of someone who has seen the result. Shikantaza is enough, but what happens is that for us "just" remains and we come to an impasse. We say, "Just, just, just," and that is where it ends. This is neither the Buddhist teaching of "emptiness" nor of "nothingness." We are simply playing with "just" to help ourselves abide always in a clean and beautiful place.

Consider the expression "It is easy to become a buddha, but difficult to become a devil." Indeed, many Zen priests are not able to enter the realms of heaven, human beings, fighting devils, animals, hungry ghosts, and hell. They instead call out from a high place, "Come up to me here, come up to me here!" This is called "the illness of purity" or "falling into one-sided sameness of emptiness and enlightenment." This type of illness is the most difficult one to cure.

People are taught things like, "To sit zazen in a clean and beautiful place is to be the purest buddha," or "If you sit for a little bit, you are a buddha for a little bit." In this way, people inevitably become attached to sitting and think there is nothing to attain and nothing to throw away. You must notice that it is a great mistake simply to make do with "everything is all right as-it-is." Otherwise, there is the danger that you will really just sit there, and that is all it will come to. If you are not sufficiently careful of this point, you'll only endeavor in vain.

On the other hand, sometimes teachers put various delicious looking things on the table such as, "If you do zazen, it will become like this; you will experience this kind of condition." In this way, zazen ends up becoming a kind of pleasure, wherein we seek for enlightenment or nirvana. It's easy to fall into this type of illness, so while "growing hair and horns" we must receive instruction on how to become free of such a condition. There are various Zen illnesses, but you must be especially careful of this "illness of purity."

In the old days, people would plow the fields with their cows and horses and manually plant grains of rice, one by one. We must work single-mindedly in this manner and endeavor like a wooden man or a stone woman. The Japanese word for "work" can be etymologized to mean "making the land comfortable." The point is to work in order to exhaust bodhi-mind. There is no other work than working for others. Buddhist priests in particular have a job that no one else can do, namely to guide others to faith. So instead of expending your energy doing all sorts of other things, I ask you to just be diligent in leading others to faith.

The following words confirm Dharma transmission (*inka shōmei*):

> A cow goes into the mountains and has enough water to
>   drink and grass to eat.
> The cow leaves the mountains, touching the East, touching
>   the West.

In short, this is to "grow hair and horns" and go into the city. Furthermore, this also relates to the phrase "a blue lotus flower blooms in the midst of fire." Please become a cow, become a horse, and sit quietly, steadily in zazen.

Some people say, "It's frightening to think of getting rid of the self," but this is only because we hold on to the self and imagine what it would be like if it disappeared. It's the same with death. This body will die completely, and when it does so, there is no reason to expect that you will know that you are dead. Still, there are some people who say, "I'm afraid of death," or "Death makes me anxious," but this is a mistake. Death is not only the "death of a person." We are being born and dying over and over again right now. We are always repeating birth and death, and because of this repetition, we must not make the mistake of thinking conceptually that "death" refers only to the time when a person's functions stop and the body becomes cold.

In any case, to be able to practice like an animal is to reach the culmination of practice. You must be reduced to such a condition and then transcend having been brought down to that level. This is the problem posed in "Changing Ranks."

All afflictions become like rain and dew in the vast sea.

This line says that if we transcend all things and in the process become a blue lotus flower blooming in the midst of fire, we obliterate or grind up all delusions by means of the 84,000 Dharma gates. In other words, the 84,000 teachings that Śākyamuni Buddha expounded during his life can be said to be 84,000 delusions. "All afflictions become like rain and dew in the vast sea" means that all delusions flow away with the rain and the dew. This is a condition of total transcendence, such that transcending is complete.

All ignorance becomes like clouds and thunder on a mountain.

Ignorance is expressed in Buddhism as "lack of light," as when there is total darkness. Since it is dark, it is not possible to see clearly or to understand. And so this becomes delusion. Among delusions, ignorance is what we could call a prior or innate delusion. We can call it "beginningless," something that accompanies us even before we are in our mother's womb. This ignorance follows us around, and it is something that we enter the world with from the moment we leave the womb. To break down this inborn delusion, it is necessary to practice wholeheartedly, even at the risk of your life.

You completely blow out the furnace below the cauldron of hell,

"The furnace" refers to the fires of hell. All bad karma is created by the delusion of ignorance, and this is why we suffer the karmic fires of hell. But conversely, this means that if there is no self it is possible to blow out this conflagration with a single breath.

Once, a certain criminal fell into hell and the devils threw him into a cauldron of boiling water. A blue lotus flower immediately bloomed and a cool breeze blew in. The devils quickly gathered together and asked Yama, the ruler of hell, "What happened?!"

Lord Yama investigated the life of this person and found that while he was alive a single character from a sutra called Dhāraṇī of the Great Protectress Queen of Mantras (Mahāpratisarā-Dhāraṇī) had fallen down on him. As a result he was spared being thrown into the boiling cauldrons of hell.

Japanese priests often use this story as material for sermons. The point of the story is that familiarity with even a single line of a sutra or from one of the ancestors' records will suffice to save us. Even if we fall into the realms of hell, of hungry ghosts, or of animals, recalling even a single line of Buddha's teaching may prove to be the condition thanks to which we are suddenly saved. The image of completely blowing out the furnace below the cauldron of hell emphasizes the importance of such a condition.

> Long ago, during the Buddha's lifetime, a certain woman played with the outer robe of a monk. As a result of that condition, she fell into hell. However, the condition that caused her to fall into hell finally became, after many rebirths, the very condition whereby she became a nun called Utpalavarnā and attained enlightenment.

Since it was the same condition, this story conveys how it is necessary to endeavor to meet "buddha-conditions."

Even if you write the single word "wisdom" from the Heart Sutra on a scrap of paper, that is enough. It is written in the Dhāranī of the Great Protectress Queen of Mantras that it is possible to be liberated in this way. The power of one person can reach a great number of sentient beings.

Smashing to pieces a forest of swords and a mountain of daggers[116] with a single shout

This line refers to the hell in which beings must walk barefoot on a forest of swords and a mountain of daggers, as an expression of the great difficulty of practice. These words also refer to things like being scolded by your teacher or enduring various sorts of abuse while practicing. In order to wake himself up, the monk Ciming would stick an awl into his thigh whenever he felt sleepy. Another monk was known for sitting with a lump of iron on his head. These are both examples of "walking on a forest of swords." Nevertheless, if your eyes are opened by means of one condition, it will be possible to break up all such things. Those people who do not have this experience will not understand this.

Even golden chains cannot hold you back at the entrance.

Because practitioners in the Sōtō sect only sit quietly, people in the Rinzai sect sometimes call this kind of Zen "barren tree Zen of silent illumination."[117] On the other hand, because Rinzai practitioners follow a practice of looking at one kōan after another in order to arouse aspiration, practitioners in the Sōtō sect sometimes call the practice of the Rinzai sect "the entrance of golden chains." "Dead-tree Zen" is not good, but neither is a Zen wherein no matter how far we go, we are told "more, more," without understanding the final destination. The expression "legs without eyes" refers to this sort of situation. If we were to walk on and on, without the ability to see where we are going, running into this, colliding with that, we will never get where we are going.

These days there are also great numbers of people who sit zazen without a teacher, who nonetheless say that they have experience practicing zazen. I'm not sure where such people have received guidance. It seems that many have read about practices such as following the breath and counting the breath, and then claim that they have actual experience practicing zazen. Groups of two, three, five, or ten people like this sit together. There are neither precepts nor Zen for them. They are simply a group of people coming together, and when they are finished with their activity, they disband and go home. It is only a matter of meeting and then parting. A flock of crows gathers at night, and when it becomes light again the next day, they leave. This is a serious danger.

In the end, the three elements of "asking a master about the Dharma," "the practice of zazen," and "maintaining the precepts" are absolutely necessary. Without these three things you are walking without eyes, and although you will end up walking, you have no idea where you are heading.

Going into the realm of other beings, you transmigrate for
a while.

Some time ago someone came to me and asked, "What is the difference between delusion and enlightenment?" There is the rank of bodhisattva, a rank applied to a person who still has not truly become a buddha. Why doesn't he or she become a buddha? Bodhisattvas, that is, those who always work for other people, acknowledge the existence of others as separate from themselves. So the idea of having to do good by helping others never disappears. On the other hand, a buddha is a person for whom any notion of acting for some purpose—like saving sentient beings—has disappeared. This is called the Dharma. For a person at the rank of bodhisattva, enlightenment is delusion. They are the same thing. But when you practice and become a buddha, delusion, as it is, becomes enlightenment. Enlightenment and delusion are not separate. A great gulf exists between those who see things dualistically and those who do not.

We often hear about the endless cycle of birth and death and transmigration through the six realms, but in Zen each step in the cycle of birth and death is said to be liberation. There is neither good nor bad karma in transmigration itself. There is only that condition being repeated over and over, and so the condition of great liberation is called "the endless cycle of birth and death and transmigration through the six realms." All this again describes what is meant by "entering town."

A certain priest once said, "Greed is a fact, anger is a fact, and ignorance is a fact." In other words, greed, anger, and ignorance, as they are, are already reality. And so it is truly a mistake to think, "I must do this. I must do that." Because by doing so we acknowledge the existence of ourselves and think of improving ourselves by moving in a good direction. But if you ask me, "Does that mean everything is all right as-it-is right now?" saying as much would be to acknowledge the existence of something called "as-it-is right now." In short, we must always look closely at our practice and be careful as we engage in zazen with regard to this point.

"Changing ranks" is a rather difficult topic, but I would like you to understand that you must not stop at your present standpoint. It is necessary for all of you who practice Zen, regardless of whether or not you are monks or nuns, to endeavor at helping others by leading them to faith. We do this by being reduced to an animal and going wherever necessary.

10: Before the Rank of the Absolute

In his *Points to Watch in Studying the Way*, Eihei Dōgen writes:

> Those who practice the Buddha Way must first of all believe
> in the Buddha Way. Those who believe in the Buddha Way
> should believe that they have been within the Way from the
> very beginning, without deviating or wavering, without gain
> or loss, or any mistake. Generating belief like this, clarify
> the Way and practice accordingly. This is the foundation for
> studying the Way.[118]

We must believe that all things—even anxiety, irritation, anger, and
complaining—are already the Way, Zen, and Dharma that the buddhas
and ancestors taught. This practice of first believing and then grinding
up this belief is one that can only be found through the Way of Buddha.
In other religions, it appears that faith is everything. Buddhism teaches
that we first seek the Way in accordance with faith. Then, by grinding
up that faith, the Way, Dharma, enlightenment, and delusion, everything disappears.

In other religions, believers must place their faith in a person—Jesus
Christ, God, or Allah. But nowhere did Buddha command us, "Believe
in me." Rather, he said, "Follow the Dharma and make the Dharma
the standard and the goal." The Dharma is not a person. Śākyamuni
Buddha and the ancestors who followed him have always, and without
exception, been awakened by means of Dharma, rather than a person.

At the moment Śākyamuni Buddha glimpsed the morning star, he
became one with it. When Xiangyan heard the sound of a pebble strike
some bamboo, he awakened. Others have attained enlightenment upon
smelling the fragrance of a peach blossom; some have realized liberation at the moment of entering their bath. Through the Dharma, each

became aware of his or her own Dharma body, the condition in which the self has disappeared. This means that the seam between Dharma body and Dharma body disappeared entirely, and the two Dharma bodies completely merged and harmonized.

Analytically speaking, all matter, including human beings, is composed of the four major elements—earth, water, fire, and air. As *The Merging of Difference and Sameness* says, "Fire heats, wind moves, water wets, earth is solid." The practice of Zen makes us realize that we are already one with all of this. It is not a matter of getting something new through practice. In fact, in Zen the worst sort of illness is that of thinking that we have achieved something or become something different due to practice. On account of thoughts like this, Zen illness or Dharma illness befalls us. As Master Dōgen says, we should only begin our practice when we believe that we have been within the Way from the very beginning, without deviating or wavering, without gain or loss, or any mistake.

Yet because of past customs and habits, we inevitably end up trying to manipulate our present condition based on some learned or instinctive way of thinking. Even those who strive single-mindedly to see ego thought at work try to manipulate themselves with judgments of good or bad. We must completely grind this mistake up by means of sitting. For as long as we indulge this way of judging and manipulating our condition, we will never find real satisfaction in the Buddha Way. Mere belief or faith is not enough. Remind yourself of this, and understand that whatever you feel you may have achieved, it is still not the end point.

Now and then, someone will come to me and ask, "I've been sitting for a long time. Is it wrong to look at a kōan?" We should note that all of the words and teachings of the buddhas and ancestors are kōans. The most essential, the most basic kōan is the teaching that all sentient beings are endowed with buddha nature. All things—including you— are tathāgata, are gone to thusness. This is something that cannot be changed. Everyone has buddha nature. Everything is eternal and does not change.

Śākyamuni Buddha taught that all sentient beings are endowed with buddha nature. Subsequent teachers like Bodhidharma taught "independence from anything written" and "transmission outside the teaching." Still other masters taught things like "Directly point at the mind, see into one's nature, and realize buddhahood."[119] These are all kōans.

When you practice single-mindedly, you may come to feel that sitting, alone, is insufficient. If that is the case, you can pick up one part of Śākyamuni Buddha's teaching or a phrase from one of the ancestors' records. Persisting in your doubt, you think, "What does this really mean after all? What can this be?" You continue to hold on to this inquiring, questioning mind. We should not think that kōan practice is only for the Rinzai sect and not for the Sōtō sect, or that shikantaza is enough for the Sōtō sect.

Buddhist practice begins with repentance and continues with taking refuge in the Three Treasures, namely the Buddha, the Dharma, and the Sangha. From there we take up and observe the Three Pure Precepts and the Ten Major Precepts. It is difficult to put these into practice one by one, so in Zen we sit single-mindedly. This single-minded sitting is itself, in fact, complete repentance, taking refuge in the Three Treasures, and observing the precepts. Since all of the precepts are included in sitting, we can practice the entire path by sitting.

Now, true repentance is said to result in the disappearance of the self. If, however, we confess by means of discriminative thought that "I did this" and "I did that," then the self will still remain. True repentance involves making the self truly empty, such that not even a single drop of the self remains. Since, if we do this, the self disappears, it then becomes possible to be one with all other things. In our world there are no enemies.

Even though we say, "Love your enemy," it is in fact not possible to acknowledge the existence of an "other" to love. From the beginning, we cannot perceive any person whosoever who could be our enemy. This is what we Buddhists call "big love." When we forget the self, we can really understand that the world is one.

Even as we sit wholeheartedly, it is still very difficult to cure the illness of "I exist." This is why we need the teachings of the buddhas and the ancestors. The Buddha Way, zazen, Dharma, and so on, are all medicine. Practice is the medicine that we provisionally use. Know, however, that if we continue to take the medicine when the illness is cured, we will be poisoned by the medicine and end up worse off than when we started. This is the "Zen illness," so difficult to cure. The worst form of this illness comes in the form of sitting before a calligraphy scroll in one's living room, speaking endlessly about Zen, having memorized a great many of the words of the buddhas and ancestors.

When there is delusion, we must cure it with medicine. Counting the breath or following the breath is the medicine called "Buddha's teaching." When we cure it, delusion disappears. The condition in which delusion has disappeared is called enlightenment. We call a cure "complete" when the harm caused by both the medicine and the illness disappears. It would be strange if enlightenment did not disappear along with delusion. Since illness is cured by means of medicine, we should then understand that medicine is in fact the very illness itself. This is why we say that the true nature of things is formless.

In any case, Zen is medicine, but if it lingers when we've already removed the sickness of delusion, then the harmful effects of the medicine will also linger.

> In front of many dead trees and steep boulders, there are many wrong tracks heading off course.

"Dead trees" refers to a condition in which all ornaments and decorations such as Zen, enlightenment, the Way, and the Dharma have completely disappeared. This is what it means to return to the source—to become like a baby that doesn't know anything, not a single thing, about the Dharma, or Zen, or the Way, or religion. Dead trees don't know about dead trees. They don't even know if they understand or if they don't understand. This condition of not knowing anything is called "Before the Rank of the Absolute." The rank of the absolute is sameness, emptiness, nothingness. So "Before the Rank of the Absolute" refers to a state in which we really know nothing about existence or nonexistence, delusion or enlightenment.

But even when we reach this condition, we are still not safe because we still haven't reached the final destination. It is like the following allegory:

A turtle comes up from the sea and lays eggs on a sandy
beach. It skillfully digs a hole and then lays its eggs in it.
It then carefully covers the eggs with sand and returns to
the sea. The turtle's tail, however, unbeknown to the turtle, leaves an imprint in the sand as it returns to the sea.
The turtle thinks that no one will know where it has laid its
eggs. But a person looking for turtle eggs need only trace the
clearly visible imprint that the turtle's tail left in the sand to
find them.

The illness of enlightenment is just like this. Little by little, without
our knowing it, it appears in our lives.

**Those travelers who have reached this place all trip and
stumble.**

Whereas "wrong tracks" in the first line indicate a situation of being
completely mistaken about the direction in which we are heading, as
in when we believe we are headed east but are actually headed west,
"trip and stumble" in this line indicates a situation of suffering the
consequences of being completely mistaken. If we were walking straight
ahead, for example, thinking, "Continuing in this way is totally unmis-
taken," we may be caught utterly unaware by obstacles in the path, such
as a hole or boulder, and thereby injure ourselves. The injury is often
worse when we have little hesitancy with regard to our step or the pace
at which we move.

The problem here is that after we have experienced enlightenment,
something still remains of that experience—something we think of as
"good." Even if we've been able to throw away everything else, something yet remains that we are absolutely unwilling or unable to throw
away. This remainder tends to be something we judge to be good. This
is why we must be especially mindful of the fact that medicine can easily
linger, becoming poison, once the illness is cured.

A crane stands in the snow but does not have the same color.

This line refers to causality. A crane is white and so is snow. They are both white, but because of causes and conditions, one is snow and one is a bird. Since only the color of two completely different things is the same, the issue of sameness and difference is highlighted here. It is certainly impossible that there be only sameness with regard to these two things. Sameness is always accompanied by difference. It is likewise impossible for there to be only difference. Difference is always accompanied by sameness. This is an explanation of the absolute and the relative interacting and transposing.

> The bright moon and the flower of reeds do not really resemble each other.

This line echoes the one above. The flowers of reeds are white and the moon is white. Due to causality, they share the same color. They look the same, but they are not the same. In the Baojing Sanmei, we find the lines, "A heron hidden in the moon. Taken as similar, they are not the same." If we look closely, we can see that they really have a different nature. So even "when mixed together, their places are still known." If we pay attention to things individually, we can see "sameness within difference."

As I have said before, we must transcend what has already been transcended. The need to transcend the transcended is also relevant here. The expression "put a head on top of the one you already have"[120] refers to the fact that although things resemble each other, various forms of phenomena appear because of causality. So these two lines about things appearing the same, but being different, are about phenomena arising through causes and circumstances.

Consider the following song:

> A sweetfish lives in the rapids of a river,
> A bird nests in a tree,
> A human being dwells in the world of kindness and sympathy.[121]

Early summer is the season that we associate with sweetfish, a type of fish that lives in the rapids of small rivers. Birds nest in trees, and people live amid kindness and sympathy. Everything is one. However, because of causality, a fish, a bird, and a human being each live in different places. Essentially, everything is one, but through causes and conditions, things live in different places and take different forms.

Likewise, in a monastery, sitting zazen is the same for everyone, yet there are different roles for different people. Order is maintained by means of affirming each person's respective position or standpoint. When the bell is struck, we go to the Dharma hall. When it is time for a meal, we go to the dining room. When the drum is struck, we go to work. When we look closely, we can see that everyone endeavors single-mindedly in their respective areas. This is causality, or arising through causes and circumstances. Although everything is one, that one thing is divided because of different conditions. Yet while divided, it is still one thing.

> "I'm finished, I'm finished, I'm finished!" When you think so, you cannot really be finished.

"Finished" means to come to an end. When we arrive at our destination, we say we are "finished." It would be foolish to look for water while in the midst of water. Water does not say, "I am water," but we end up being used by the concept of water when we say, "This is water." This line means to say that it is strange to announce that we are finished when we are already in the midst of a condition where everything is already finished from the very start. This is similar to the saying "zazen is zazen."[122] It is strange to announce that you are doing zazen when you are doing zazen. If we truly penetrate "zazen is zazen," we can see that looking at our zazen and saying "I am doing zazen" is to be used by the concept of zazen. Someone who describes their condition with these words is still outside of zazen.

When we are not used by the concept of zazen, then zazen must be moving, standing, sitting, and lying down—that is, every activity in our lives must be zazen. This seems to be a contradiction, but it actually happens that we unknowingly watch the condition of our zazen, and this is something we should be careful about.

> If you say, "This is it! This is the ultimate source!" you also need
> a good shout.

"A good shout" means that someone scolds you loudly and tells you that this is no good.

"The source" is the origin, the very beginning. We often speak of "the essential Self" or "the true Self" or of "returning to the source." But what is the source of the Self? If you think about it, I think you will understand it. We use the expression "before your father and mother were born." Where were we before our parents were born? We Buddhists often use the term "beginningless" as an important kōan in everyday life. Where did we come from? We must thoroughly study this question and seriously contemplate whether or not there really is a source.

From the vantage point of "Before the Rank of the Absolute," wherein there is really nothing, it is easy for "nothing" to remain. Many settle everything for themselves by saying things like, "There is nothing, just nothing," or "Just do it." But then "just" exists. This means that there is still a source left. We must notice this. At this point, the question must be about what we should study, what we should pursue in our practice of Zen. Once we know what we must study, we must grind that knowledge up. If we can truly grind it up, such that not a trace is left, there will nevertheless still be some remaining sediment or powder. We must press on until even that sediment has completely disappeared.

The following is a well-known dialogue between Master Nanyue Huairang and his disciple, Mazu Daoyi:

> One day, Mazu was sitting in zazen when his master Huairang came along and asked him, "What are you doing?"
>
> "I'm doing zazen in order to become a buddha," Mazu replied.
>
> Master Huairang picked up a piece of tile and began to scrape it vigorously with a rock.
>
> Mazu then asked, "What are you doing? What do you hope to do by scraping that piece of tile with a rock?"

"I'm making a mirror," Master Huairang answered.

Mazu asked, "Can you really make a piece of tile into a mirror?"

Master Huairang replied, "Can you really become a buddha by doing zazen?"

Later on Mazu became a great Zen master, but when he heard this he simply could not grasp that delusion, as-it-is, is already the result, or buddhahood. Sometimes the right condition simply doesn't arise. Therefore, we must continue making great effort no matter how far we have come.

> From the bottom of your heart, you play a melody on the harp
> with no strings.

"Playing a harp with no strings" suggests giving voice to that which is inherently silent. The bodhisattva Mañjushrī and the layman Vimala once engaged in a debate over the question of "the Dharma gate of nonduality." At the end of his turn, Mañjushrī said, "That's all I can say. Now, Vimala, please expound your understanding." Then Vimala expounded the Dharma without opening his mouth. He simply remained quiet. Later it was said that Vimala's silence was like a mighty clap of thunder. The "harp with no strings" alludes to this condition in which Vimala's silence resounded like thunder.

> How would it be possible to grasp the moonlight shining in the
> empty sky?

Moonlight is just like the vibration of sound: if a bell is rung, the vibration is certainly there, but there is no substance to it. Existing, but without real substance—this is the condition of all things, including us human beings. It is the same when we say "the universe." Certainly, there is this word "universe." It refers to what is endless, boundless, and without limits. But from the standpoint of Buddhism, this word refers to ourselves. From the standpoint of the self, it is the Buddha;

from the standpoint of Dharma, it is what is boundless and unlimited. We ourselves are the Dharma body that is boundless and unlimited, and we can awaken to this fact and verify it by sitting.

One way or another, sesshin and the practice of zazen aim to clarify this. This Way has barely survived transmission from India to China to Japan, but because it has been passed down to us we are now able to do sesshin. Please be fully aware that we have the responsibility to pass it on to future generations. We must have this aspiration, otherwise the Dharma will disappear. Some say, "I'm not so sure about that. How could the Dharma ever disappear?" But only those who do not know the Dharma say this.

> Once, Master Huangbo said to some monks, "Do you know that there are no Zen masters in China?"
>
> One of the monks asked, "There are many Zen monks. What do you mean when you say there are no Zen masters?"
>
> Master Huangbo replied, "I didn't say that there isn't any Zen, only that there are no masters."

This dialogue appears in the *Blue Cliff Record* and describes the grave situation now prevalent throughout the world. It is truly a curious and strange thing to see so many people recklessly practice shikantaza or employ kōans without any real understanding of Buddhadharma or of Zen.

Practice is medicine. If you use medicine haphazardly, such misuse can truly cause irrevocable harm. Today, enough people already suffer from the harmful effects of taking this medicine, so we must be very careful about this. Only when we are able to remove the delusive attachment to the ego by means of practice will we then be able to use all of the knowledge that we've learned up to that point. This is the *Eye and Treasury of the True Dharma*, the *Shōbōgenzō*. "Shōbōgenzō" is not merely the name of a book written by Master Dōgen. We ourselves are truly the Eye and Treasury of the True Dharma. In the end, I would like you to resolve that you will realize this as soon as possible and continue to endeavor single-mindedly.

Appendices and Tables

十玄談

原田雪溪 普説

Appendix I: Chinese Edition of the *Ten Verses of Unfathomable Depth* (*Shixuantan*)

S: Sibu Song ed.; K: Korean Canon ed.;
D: Dongchansi Song ed.; M: Ming Canon ed.
L: Liandeng Huiyao ed.; T: Modern Taishō Canon (*Daizōkyō*) ed.

THE APPENDIX SHOWS the variants of the text in all major editions of the Ten Verses that we were able to locate and that have been mentioned above. They do not allow many conclusions about the relatedness of the texts. It is only clear that the Ming version is maximally distinct from the Sibu and the Korean version, which is expected, and that the modern Taishō canon version is based on a close relative of the Zongmen Liandeng Huiyao version. Overall it is obvious that from early on editors made their own choices, probably comparing two or more versions of the text. This makes it difficult to distinguish clear lineages among the different versions.

Sekkei Harada did not choose the text alone but collaborated with the Chinese Zen monk Guanjun. Since the version of the text he worked with is carefully edited and does not coincide with any edition known to us (including the Japanese Taishō canon), we believe that he and Guanjun did the same as all the editors of the various Zen records in different canons did before him, namely edit out a new "best" version from extant previous editions.

同安察禅師十玄談并序[L,T]

同安察禅師詩十首十玄談并序[M]

詩八首　同安禅師[S]

詩十首　同安禅師[K,D]

序

叢林所行十玄談皆無序引。思曩游廬阜。得其序於同安影堂。
今▪之。云。夫玄談妙句。迥出三乘。既不混▪。亦非獨立。
當臺應用。如朗月以晶空。轉影泯機。似明珠而隱海。且學徒有等。
妙理無窮。達事者稀。迷源者眾。森羅萬象。物物上明。
或即理事雙祛。名言▪喪。是以殷勤指月。莫錯端倪。不迷透水之鍼。可付開
拳之寶。略序微言。以彰事理。

心印

問君心印作何顏　　　　　　　心印誰[何[L,T]]人敢授傳
歷劫坦然無異色　　　　　　　呼爲心印早虛言
須知體[本[D,M,K,T]]自虛[靈[D,M,K,S]]　　將喻紅爐火[焰[D,M,K,S]]裏蓮
空性
勿[莫[D,M,K,T]]謂無心云[便[D,M]]是道　　無心猶隔一重關

祖意

祖意如空不是空　　　　　　　玄[靈[D,M,L,T];真[K]]機爭墮有無功
三賢尚[固[T]]未明斯旨　　　　　十聖那能達此宗
透網金鱗猶滯水　　　　　　　廻[回[K,M,L,T]]途石馬出沙籠
慇懃爲説西來意　　　　　　　莫問西來及與東

玄機

迢迢空劫勿能收　　　　　　　通身何更有[問[D,K]]蹤由
妙體本來無處所　　　　　　　迥出三乘不假修
靈然一句超群象[眾[L]]　　　　廻[回[L]]程堪作火中牛
撒手那邊千[諸[D,M,S]]聖外
豈爲[與[L]]塵機作繫留

塵異
濁者自濁清者清　　　　　　菩提煩惱等空平
誰言卞璧無人鑒　　　　　　我道驪珠到處晶
萬法泯時全體現　　　　　　三乘分處假[別強(L, T)]安名
丈夫自[皆(S, L, T);字(M)]有衝天志　　莫向如來行處行
[氣(K, D, M, L)]

佛教[演教(T)]　　　　　　　　後非空有眾皆捐[緣(T, M, S)]
三乘次第演金言　　　　　　鶴樹終談理未玄
三世如來亦共宣　　　　　　閻浮早已八千年
初説有空人盡執
龍宮滿藏醫方義
眞淨界中纔一念

還鄉曲[達本(LT)]
勿於中路事空王　　　　　　策杖還[咸(D, K)]須達[歸(D, S)]本鄉
雲水隔時君莫住　　　　　　雪山深處我非忘玉
堪嗟[尋思(S, D, M, T)]去日顏如　　却[嗟(S, D, M, T);]歡[嘆(L)]迴[回(L)]來
[時(L)]鬢似霜
撒手到家人不識　　　　　　更無一物獻尊堂

破還鄉曲[還源(T)]
返本還源事已[立(M), 亦(D, K, S)]差　　本來無住不名家
萬年松径[逕(M, T)]雪深覆　　　一帶峯巒雲更遮
賓主穆[默(D, M, S)]時全[純(S, K, D, M)]是妄　君臣合處[道合(D, M)]正中邪
還鄉曲調如何唱[物(D)]　　　明月堂前枯樹[木(K, S, D, M)]華[花(L)]

迴機[回機(L);轉位歸(D, M, S)]
涅槃城裏尚猶危　　　　　　却裝珍御復名誰
權挂垢衣云是佛　　　　　　石女天明戴帽歸
木人夜半穿靴去　　　　　　再三撈[澇(D, K, S)]漉[摝(M, L)]始應知

萬古碧潭空界月

陌[驀⁽ᴷ⁾]路相逢沒定[了⁽ᴰ·ᴷ·ˢ⁾]期

··

轉位[廻機⁽ᴰ·ᴹ⁾，轉位帰⁽ᴷ⁾]

披毛戴角入廓[塵⁽ᴷ·ᴸ⁾]來　　　　無明山上作雲雷

煩惱海中爲雨露　　　　　　剱[劍⁽ᴷ·ᴰ·ᴹ·ᴸ·ᵀ⁾]樹刀山喝使摧

鑊湯爐炭吹教滅　　　　　　行於異類且輪迴[回⁽ᴸ⁾]

金鎖玄關留不住

優鉢羅華[花⁽ᴰ⁾]火裏開

··

正位前[一色⁽ᴸ·ᵀ⁾；一色過後⁽ᴷ⁾]

枯木巖前差[茇⁽ᴷ⁾]路多　　　　行人到此盡蹉跎

鷺鷥[鵞⁽ᴷ·ᴰ·ᴸ⁾]立雪非同色　　明月蘆華不似他

了了了時無可[所⁽ᴹ⁾]了　　　玄玄玄處亦須呵[訶⁽ᵀ·ᴹ⁾]

慇懃[殷勤⁽ᴷ·ˢ·ᴹ·ᵀ⁾]爲唱玄中曲　空裏蟾光撮得麼

Appendix II: Contemporary Comments on the *Ten Verses of Unfathomable Depth*

AT LEAST TEN commentaries on the Ten Verses are known: four in Chinese, two in Korean, and four in Japanese. As for China, besides the two commentaries translated in full at the end of this part of the appendix, there also exists a commentary from the tenth century, which is no longer extant, and a commentary from the seventeenth century by Weilin Daopei. The two Korean commentaries are one from the fifteenth century by Kim Si-seop and one from the early twentieth century by Han Yong-un (cf. Sim 2009). The four Japanese commentaries were all produced in the Edo-period. Two of these were authored by Shigetsu E'in, one by Senjō Jitsugan, and one by Genrō Ōryū.

Here, however, we are primarily interested in those views that are historically closest to Changcha's own times, as they may also be closest to Changcha's own understanding of the work, and thus provide us the best evidence for accurately interpreting his poems. We use the word "contemporary" in a broad sense, including the period of the Northern Song dynasty. The two commentaries still extant in Chan records of the Song dynasty appear in the *Chrestomathy from the Ancestors' Hall* and in the *Record from the Chan Groves*. We will here translate both in full. The commentary found in the Chrestomathy has special significance, as it is written by Mu'an Shanqing, who claims to be the one who reinstated the preface to the poems.

Aside from the two long commentaries by the Song period scholar-monks Shanqing and Huigong that will be given in the latter half of this appendix, and countless quotations of lines from the Ten Verses in other Chan records, the Ten Verses are also occasionally referred to in dialogues and poems as a text. The following story is found in at least seven Chan records in some variation. The version presented here is from the *Record of Anecdotes from Lake Luo* (1160):

> Master Miyin Anmin of Huacang temple in Jinling first lec-
> tured about the Surangama Sutra at Chengdu. The audience
> was flourishing. At that time Master Yuanwu lived at Zhao-
> jue. Master Anmin and his friend, Duke Sheng, spread the
> doctrine of "transmission outside the teaching."
>
> A monk asked for instruction about the *Ten Verses of
> Unfathomable Depth*. When he asked, "How does the Mind
> Seal look?" Yuanwu said in a sharp voice, "The patterns are
> already manifest!" When Anmin heard this he was suddenly
> struck. He said to himself that he had reached it.

Master Anmin is depicted as already being a Buddhist teacher but not
yet fully accomplished. Anmin gains sudden realization due to Master
Yuanwu's response to his reading of the Ten Verses. His realization,
however, turns out not to be sufficient yet, so he decides to follow
Yuanwu and eventually inherits his dharma.

One noticeable fact about these and other references to the Ten Verses
in Chan records is that they do not appear earlier than the twelfth century. The earliest clearly datable reference is from 1124. This indicates
that in conjunction with the gradual increase of Chan dialogues involving Tong'an Changcha, the reputation of Changcha's poems expanded
gradually through the eleventh century, becoming firmly established
in the twelfth century. This reputation and fame lasted through the
premodern periods in China, Korea, and Japan. The commentaries by
Daguan Tanying, Mu'an Shanqing, and Juefang Huigong, even if they
disagree with each other, undoubtedly contributed to the increasing
appreciation of the poems.

Shanqing's commentary, which now follows, first discusses the problem
of the variant titles for the verses. He emphasizes the coherence of the
set, points out the fact that some grammatically irregular expressions
in the poems must be explained by the constraints imposed by the rules
of poetry, and then goes on to clarify individual concepts that come
up in the poems. His interest lays primarily in the first five "doctrinal
verses." He devotes only a single bit of commentary to the "practical
verses." The most remarkable thing about these comments may be that

they reveal that even nearly contemporary readers needed considerable help in understanding the terms used in the poems. Even for Song period students and scholars of Chan, they were not an "easy read."

Furthermore, Shanqing clearly points out the references to Huayan doctrine in the poems. He also links Changcha's poems to Faxiang and Tiantai teachings and to more secular encyclopedic knowledge. This indicates a general attitude of Buddhist monks and scholars of the time, including Changcha in the original text, who were less concerned with doctrinal or sectarian purity, but eclectically used teachings of varied provenance as ready resources for their own discourse. The main difference between Changcha and Shanqing is that Changcha refers to Huayan and Tiantai terms and concepts only to eventually reject them. The rejection is downplayed, or perhaps not fully realized, by the scholarly Shanqing. Shanqing seems to be especially interested in the ideas of stages toward buddhahood, and the idea of a quasi-historical maturation of Buddhist teaching during the Buddha's lifetime, which Changcha attributed to successive generations of buddhas.

CHRESTOMATHY FROM THE ANCESTORS' HALL,
VOL. 8 (1098–1110) Mu'an Shanqing

The *Ten Verses of Unfathomable Depth* that circulate in Buddhist temples all have no preface. Some time ago I traveled to Mt. Lu and obtained the preface from the memorial hall of Tong'an temple. I render it here:

> These Verses of Unfathomable Depth are marvelous. They far surpass the three vehicles. No longer are they entangled in origination through circumstance, nor are they independent.
>
> When put into practice they resemble the bright moon and illuminate the sky. But if times change and the opportunity is lost, they resemble a bright jewel hidden in the depths of the sea.
>
> Moreover, while students of the Way have different levels of ability, the wondrous truth is infinite. Very few have reached it and many are confused about its source.

These verses are an exceptionally bright light on all phenomena and things. This means that both principles and phenomena recede with them, and names and words are defeated. Thus, they kindheartedly point at the moon, without missing the tiniest things.

If you don't get lost searching for the needle in the water, the treasure already held in your fist waiting to be opened will be bestowed on you.

I have given these small words, in brief, as a preface to demonstrate the gist of the poems.

When I humbly look at the titles of the *Ten Verses of Unfathomable Depth*, they don't lack deep meaning. But later, some people deleted and changed them at their convenience. They did not understand the original motivation for giving these titles and wrongly set up their own interpretations. This is truly deplorable.

Furthermore, two poems—"The Mind of the Enlightened Ones" and "Changing Ranks"—were deleted in the *Jingde Era Record of the Transmission of the Lamp*. Fortunately, the other poems did not lose their old order.

If you are not clear about the Mind of the Enlightened Ones (verse 2), how could you be able to bring about the Unfathomable Function (verse 3)? If you have not really accomplished the Revolving Function (verse 8), how could you Change Ranks (verse 9)? This is an error [introduced] by the Transmission of the Lamp, which also has new titles that don't match at all the meaning of the poems. Students should check them well themselves.

The titles are "The Mind Seal," "The Mind of the Enlightened Ones," "The Unfathomable Function," "The Transcendent within Dust and Dirt," "The Buddhist Teaching," "The Song of Returning Home," "The Song of Not Returning Home," "The Revolving Function," "Changing Ranks and Returning," and "Before the Rank of the Absolute."

The Mind Seal

Dharma coming from the West. Not relying on the written word. Transmission of the Mind Seal in a single line. Directly point at the mind, see one's nature, and realize buddhahood.

The "three stages of wisdom" and the ten ranks of sagehood[123]

The Flower Garland Sutra clarifies that the ten ranks of security,[124] the ten ranks of practice, and the ten ranks of merit transfer[125] make up the three stages of wisdom. The ten ranks of sustainment are the sages, and the stage of wonderful enlightenment designates a Buddha. The ten ranks of sagehood therefore directly correspond to the sages of the ten ranks of sustainment. These are: (1) Joy, (2) Separation from Defilement, (3) Emanation of Light, (4) Flame of Wisdom, (5) Hard to Surpass, (6) Before the Eyes, (7) Going Far, (8) Being Unmoved, (9) Good Wisdom, and (10) Cloud of Dharma. The Nirvana Sutra says that even bodhisattvas of the ten ranks of sustainment cannot be acknowledged to have seen buddha nature yet. So how could followers of the Vehicle of the Listeners or of the Vehicle of the Solitary Enlightened Ones ever get to see it? One can compare it to a drunkard who wants to go a long way. Their view of the way is obscured. The bodhisattvas of the ten ranks of sustainment have a smaller wisdom than the tathagathas, so this is again the same.

Not yet... how can they?

In the discussions in the Chan monasteries, it is regularly claimed that errors have been circulated and that the words [of these verses] have been turned upside down. But people don't realize that in making verses, tone and rhyme must be observed, and that the meaning can therefore not always be straightforwardly expressed. I can quote, as an example of this, the line that says, "Don't ask about the coming from the West, nor about the East."[126]

I myself was unsure about this in my own reading until coming upon [the Ten Verses]. At that time, I visited the capital and obtained an old Chan record from the library of the Liu clan, who are Buddhist patrons. The *Ten Verses of Unfathomable Depth* were at the end of the book, but I did not see the preface. The second verse says that the three stages of wisdom have not yet acquired the gist [of the Dharma], and that the ten stages of sainthood have not yet reached its essence. When I comprehended this phrase, all my doubts melted away, and I knew on the spot the mistake of those concerned only with the quality of the copying.

The Three Vehicles
[These are those] of the Listeners, of the Solitary Enlightened Ones, and of the Bodhisattvas.

Spoke... one after another
The Buddha was the first to complete the Way. For thirty-seven days he just thought, before he went to the hermit park and places where people lived. For twelve years he expounded the Dharma of arising through circumstances and no-self, but it was still as if he had not yet spoken. In this way, the principle of no-self is called the first Buddhist teaching and it makes up the scriptures of Small Vehicle Buddhism.[127]

Then, since all people mistakenly viewed things as existent, he taught that all dharmas are empty. But he had not spoken yet about the dependent and perfect nature of things. This is called the "teaching of emptiness."

Then he expounded the "Great Vehicle of the Characteristics of All Things." Phenomena are empty, but the mind is not empty. This is called the "Middle Way Doctrine." The Saṃdhinirmocana Sūtra belongs to this.

Lastly, he revealed the view that all beings have buddha nature. He united the three vehicles into one vehicle. He united the temporary and returned to the real. That is called the "Common Objective Teaching." The Lotus Sutra belongs to this.

At the time when he was going to pass away, he entered nirvana. He taught that everyone, including even the *icchantika*,[128] had buddha nature. Everybody can become a Buddha without fail and enjoy permanence, bliss, personality, and purity[129] if they have the right mind. This is called the "Teaching of Permanence." The Nirvana Sutra belongs to this.

The Dragon Palace
According to the *Huayan Commentary*,[130] six hundred years after the Buddha passed away, the Bodhisattva Nāgārjuna entered the palace of the Dragon King and found the Flower Garland Sutra. Altogether, there were three volumes. The first two volumes could not be carried with ordinary powers, but he managed to take out the third volume, which spread in India. Fifty fascicles were translated in China during the Jin

Dynasties of this country. Eighty fascicles were translated during the Tang dynasty. But only thirty-nine of the forty-eight chapters of the third volume have reached China; the other nine have not.

Full characters

In Sanskrit texts there are "half" and "full" characters. When the word meaning is not sufficient, then you get half characters. It is like the Chinese character for moon lacking its other half. If the logic is exhaustive, then the word meaning is complete. Thus, the Chinese character for sun is a full character and the meaning is real within itself. The half characters [in Sanskrit] have bad meanings, as for example "affliction." The full characters have good meanings, as for example "permanence." Further, the half characters have a form like the Chinese character for "speech" 言, and the full characters have a form like the Chinese character for "word" 語. If you combine two together, they are an example for a full character. If you have the "speech" character alone, you get a half character. The half character is a simple unit, but it makes up the basis for the full character. Exactly because it is a half character, it can become the base to make up a full character. You can compare it with an ordinary person, who can attain perpetual abode exactly because he is ignorant. The character produces the meaning. All characters are like this.

The crane tree

When the World-Honored One was about to enter *nirvana*, the *sāl* trees covering the place where he lay down turned white out of grief. This resembled a white crane. That is why we call them crane trees.

The last sermon

At the time of nirvana he collected the still unresolved questions [of his disciples] and made it into the rear guard among the sutras. Therefore, we call [the Nirvana Sutra] the last sermon.

The blue lotus flower

This is a name for dark blue flowers, and also for the blue lotus flower. Its petals and leaves resemble the pear. Its fruit resembles very much a fist. Its taste is sweet. It bears fruit without blossoming. But if it has a flower, then it is priceless. Therefore, in the sutras we use it to metaphorically express something very rare.

The next commentary comes from a record that is from about the same time as Shanqing's Chrestomathy and has been regarded as a basic classic within the Chan/Zen tradition. It is called the *Record from the [Chan] Groves*.

Its author, Huigong, has two main concerns. First and foremost is his appraisal of Changcha's poem. Huigong appraises the poem by demonstrating the interconnectedness of Changcha's ten verses, especially by showing how they form a logical linear progression, with the contents of one poem leading to the next. His other main concern is a critique of the commentary on the poem by Daguan found in the *Lineages of the Five Houses*. This was the major extant commentary available during Huigong's time. Although Daguan's book is unfortunately lost, it seems to have been provocative in nature and to have challenged orthodox lineage claims and other more prominent points.[131]

For one thing, Huigong takes issue with the assignment of Changcha to a different lineage. Note that Daguan's view would in this case not have had any significant impact on the overall picture of Caotong/ Sōtō lineage, since both lineages associated with Yunju and Changcha were not major lineages and died out almost immediately. Furthermore, Huigong seems to criticize Daguan's allegedly biased interpretation of the poem in terms of the absolute. Despite these disagreements, the quality of the poem seems to have been beyond dispute between the authors.

RECORD FROM THE CHAN GROVES, VOL. 2 (1107)
Juefan Huigong

Master Tong'an Changcha wrote the *Ten Verses of Unfathomable Depth* and through them spread a wonderful and subtle message. His words are subtle and beautiful and illuminate the Chan temples. However, since many years have passed much of their true meaning has been lost.

Now the titles of the verses in the *[Jingde Era Record of the] Transmission of the Lamp* are not the same anymore. Only the *Lineages of the Five Houses* by Daguan has discussed this in considerable detail. The older book[132] that I had once obtained was slightly different from what was written in the *Lineages of the Five Houses*. In the Transmission of the Lamp, they classify Master [Changcha] as a disciple of Master Jiufeng. But Daguan tags him as a disciple of Yunju. I don't know where Daguan got this from.

But Fayan of Qingliang wrote an appraisal shortly after the master died, which is as it is found in the Transmission of the Lamp. Accordingly, the claim in the Five Schools must be doubted.

As for the order of the ten verses, you have to look at the titles. They are all connected. The first five poems show the theory, and the latter five ones show how it is put into practice. Moreover, the titles of eight poems are composed of two characters. They are all interconnected, forming layers and cross-referring to each other.

The first verse is called "the Mind Seal." At the end of the poem it is said that a free and empty mind is still separated from it by a great barrier. Therefore [Changcha] composed "The Mind of the Enlightened Ones." In the first line it says, "How could the unfathomable function ever degenerate to being the result of achievement?" Therefore, he composed the poem about the True Function where, in the beginning, he asks, "Why would you tie yourself down to tainted worldliness?" Therefore he wrote a poem about the Transcendent within Dust and Dirt and stated there that "The Three Vehicles split up and assumed only provisional names." Consequently, he composed the [poem about] the order of the vehicles. This is the outline [of Chan teaching] that he showed.

Now we come to the sixth verse, called "The Song of Returning Home." At its end he asks, "How will you sing the song of returning home?" Therefore he composed a poem about Returning Home. At its end, he says, "I had nothing to offer my parents." If somebody thinks that this [stage of emptiness] is the rank of the absolute and sits on it, then this is not the wonderful and subtle [truth]. Therefore he composed the poem of the Revolving Function. If you are smart and understand everything, you lose the essence. You still have your ego views. That is called great sickness. Therefore he composed the poem of Changing Ranks. Changing ranks is the so-called going to the realms of other beings. This is totally the world of the relative. But you must return to the absolute so as not to let the blood lineage[133] cease. Therefore he composed the poem "After Passing the Absolute."[134]

These [five] verses are then those of putting [the theory] into practice. The *Lineages of the Five Houses* focuses on the last verse about the absolute. But the Transcendent within Dust and Dirt means that enlightened already exists within the deluded, and that is already it.

TABLE 1: LIST OF PERSONAL NAMES

Transliteration of names are given first for pronunciation in their native language (Sanskrit, Chinese, or Japanese).

PERSONAL NAMES	CHINESE	DATES
Avalokiteśvara Bodhisattva; Guanshiyin Pusa; Kanzeon Bosatsu	観世音菩薩	mythological bodhisattva of compassion
Baizhang Huaihuai; Hyakujō Ekai	百丈懐海	749–814
Kṣitigarbha Bodhisattva; Dicang Pusa; Jizō Bosatsu	地蔵菩薩	mythological bodhisattva who saves suffering beings in hell and other evil realms
Mañjuśrī Bodhisattva; Wenshu Pusa; Monju Bosatsu	文殊菩薩	mythological bodhisattva of wisdom
Caoshan Benji; Sōzan Honjaku	曹山本寂	840–901
Changsha Jingcen; Chōsha Keishin	長沙景岑	d. 868
Chengguan; Chōkan	澄観	738–839
Ciming = Shishuan Chuyuan; Sekisō Soen = Jimyō	石霜楚円 ＝ 慈明	986–1039
Daguan Tanying; Takkan Don'ei	達観曇穎	989–1060
Dahui Zonggao; Dai'e Sōkō	大慧宗杲	1089–1163
Daitō Kokushi = Shūhō Myōchō	大燈国師=宗峰妙超	1282–1337
Dajian Huineng; Daikan Enō	大鑑慧能	638–713

Personal Names	Chinese	Dates
Daman Hongren; Daiman Dōnin	大満弘忍	601–674
Datong Shenxiu; Daitsū Jinshū	大通神秀	d. 706
Deshan Xuanjian; Tokusan Senkan	德山宣鑑	780–865
Dōkyō Etan = Shōju Rōjin	道鏡慧端=正受老人	1642–1721
Dongshan Lianjie; Tōzan Ryōkai	洞山良价	807–869
Eihei Dōgen	永平道元	1200–1253
Emperor Wu of Liang; Ryō no Butei	梁武帝	Reign: 502–549
Fayan Wenyi; Hōgen Mon'eki	法眼文益	885–958
Guifeng Zongmi; Keihō Shūmitsu	圭峰宗密	780–841
Guishan Lingyou; Izan Reiyū	潙山霊祐	771–853
Guling Shenzan; Korei Shinsan	古靈神贊	750–820
Hakuin Ekaku	白隠慧鶴	1685–1768
Huangbo Xiyuan; Ōbaku Kiun	黄檗希運	d. 850
Huike; Eka	慧可	487–593
Huiran; Eran	慧然	unknown
Juzhi = Judi (in Koan); Gutei	俱胝	unknown
Kanzan Egen = Musō Daishi = Hon'yū Enjō Kokushi	関山慧玄 = 無相大師 = 本有円成国師	1277–1360
Keizan Jōkin	瑩山紹瑾	1268–1325
Kuya Yuanwu; Kogai Engo	枯崖円悟	ca. 13th century
Lianggong; Ryōkyō	良供	unknown
Lingyun; Reiun Chigon	霊雲志勤	unknown
Linji Yixuan; Rinzai Gigen	臨済義玄	d. 867
Mazu Daoyi; Baso Dōitsu	馬祖道一	709–788
Miyin Anmin; Mitsuin Anmin	密印安民	unknown

Personal Names	Chinese	Dates
Mu'an Shanqing; Boku'an Zenkyō	睦庵善卿	unknown
Nāgārjuna; Ryūju	龍樹	ca. 2nd–3rd century
Nanquan Puyuan; Nansen Fugan	南泉普願	748–835
Nanyang Huizhong; Nan'yō Echū	南陽慧忠	d. 775
Nanyue Huairang; Nangaku Ejō	南嶽懷讓	677–744
Qingyuan Xingsi; Seigen Gyōshi	青原行思	660–740
Sansheng Huiran; Sanshō E'nen	三聖慧然	unknown
Shigong Huicang; Sekkyō Ezō	石鞏慧藏	unknown
Su Tongpo; So Tōba	蘇東坡	1036–1101
Takamori Saigō	西鄉隆盛	1828–1877
Tengan Sogyō	天巖祖曉	1667–1731
Tiantong Rujing; Tendō Nyojō	天童如淨	1163–1228
Tong'an Changcha; Dōan Jōsatsu	同安常察	unknown
Tong'an Daopi; Dōan Dōhi	同安道丕	d. 905
Utpalavarnā; Rengeshiki Bikuni	蓮華色比丘尼	mythological Sister Blue Lotus Color
Wumen Huikai; Mumon Ekai	無門慧開	1183–1260
Xiangyan; Kyōgen Chikan	香嚴智閑	d. 898
Xuansha Shibei; Gensha Shibi	玄沙師備	835–908
Xuefeng Yicun; Seppō Gison	雪峰義存	822–908
Yangshan Huiji; Gyōzan Ejaku	仰山慧寂	804–890
Ying'an Daoyuan; Ei'an Dōgen	永安道原	unknown
Yongming Yanshou; Eimei Enju	永明延壽	904–975
Yuanwu Keqin; Engo Kokugon	圜悟克勤	1063–1135

Personal Names	Chinese	Dates
Yunju Daoying; Ungo Dōyō	雲居道膺	d. 902
Yunmen Wenyan; Unmon Bun'en	雲門文偃	864–949
Zhaozhou Congshen; Jōshū Jūshin	趙州從諗	778–897

TABLE 2: LIST OF TEXTS CITED

TRANSLATED TITLE AND DATE OF COMPOSITION	CHINESE/JAPANESE TITLE	AUTHOR/ EDITOR	
Anecdotes from (a Hermitage) Resting on the Clouds	雲臥紀談	Yunwo Jitan	Xiaoying Zhongwen
Assembled Essentials of the Five [Records of the] Lamp (1252)	五燈會元	Wudeng Huiyuan; Gotō Egen	Dachuan Puji
Blue Cliff Record (1125)	碧巖録/碧巖集	Biyanlu/ Biyanji; Hekiganroku/ Hekiganshū	Yuanwu Keqin
Chrestomathy from the Ancestors' Hall (1108)	祖庭事苑	Zuting Shiyuan; Sotei Ji'en	Mu'an Shanqing
Clarification of the Five Ranks (1260)	五位顕訣	Wuwei Xianjue; Goi Kenketsu	Caoshan Benji
Collection from the Ancestors' Hall (952)	祖堂集	Zutangji; Sodōshū	Jing, Jun
Collection of Texts for Ceremonial Purposes in Zen (14th century)	禅儀外文集	Zengi Gemonshū	Kokan Shiren
Comments on the Clarification of the Five Ranks (1793)	五位顕訣元字脚	Goi Kenketsu Ganjikyaku	Zenmyō Gettan
Daodejing (3rd–2nd century BCE)	道徳経	Daodejing; Dōtokukyō	Laozi and others
Dhāraṇī of the Great Protectress, Queen of Mantras (Mahāpratisarā-Dhāraṇī) (date unknown)	大隨求陀羅尼	Dasuiqiu Tuoluoni; Daizuigu Darani	unknown

Translated Title and Date of Composition	Chinese/Japanese Title	Author/Editor
Diamond Sutra (Vajracchedikā-prajñāpāramitā-Sūtra) (2nd–4th century)	金剛般若経	Jingang Bore-jing; Kongō Hannyakyō	unknown
Eight Poems by Chan Master Tong'an (10th century)	詩八首　同安禪師	Shi bashou Tongan Chanshi; Shi Hasshu Dōan Zenji	Tong'an Changcha
Empty Hall Anthology (1295)	·堂集	Xutangji; Kyodōshū	Linquan Conglun
Essentials of the United [Records of the Transmission of the] Lamps of Our School (1183)	宗門聯燈會要	Zongmen Liandeng Huiyao; Shūmon Rentō Kaiyō	Huiweng Wuming
Eye and Treasury of the True Dharma (1231–1254)	正法眼藏	Shōbōgenzō	Dōgen
Flower Garland Sutra (Avataṃsaka-Sūtra) (3rd–4th century)	華厳経	Huayan-jing; Kegonkyō	unknown (multiple)
Gateless Barrier (13th century)	無門関	Wumenguan; Mumonkan	Wumen Huikai
General Discussions from the Chan Monasteries (1189)	叢林公論	Conglin Gonglun; Sōrin Kōron	Zhean Huibin
Glorious Matters from the Chan Monasteries (1197)	叢林盛事	Conglin Chengshi; Sōrin Seiji	Guyue Daorong
Huayan Commentary (9th century)	華厳経疏鈔	Huayan-jing Shuchao; Kegonkyō Shoshō	Chengguan

Translated Title and Date of Composition	Chinese/Japanese Title	Author/ Editor
Jianzhong Jingguo Era Continued Record of the [Transmission of the] Lamp (1101)	建中靖國續燈 •	Jianzhong Jingguo Xudenglu; Kenchū Seikoku Zokutōroku	Foguo Weibai
Jiatai Era Comprehensive Record of [the Transmission of] the Lamp (1204)	嘉泰普燈 •	Jiatai Pudenglu; Katai Futōroku	Leian Zhengshou
Jingde Era Record of the Transmission of the Lamp (1004)	景徳傳燈録	Jingde Chuandenglu; Keitoku Dentōroku	Ying'an Daoyuan
Lancet of Zazen (1242)	坐禅箴	Zazenshin	Dōgen
Letters of Master Dahui Pujue (1166)	大慧普覚禅師書	Dahui Pujue Chanshi shu; Dai'e Fukaku Zenjisho (Dai'esho)	Huiran, Huang Wenchang
Lineages of the Five Houses (1050s)	五家宗派	Wujia Zongpai; Goke Shūha	Daguan Tanying
Master Dahui Pujue's Chan Arsenal (1186)	大慧普覚禅師宗門武庫	Dahui Pujue Chanshi Zongmen Wuku; Dai'e Fukaku Zenji Shūmon Buko (Dai'e Buko)	Daoqian
Miscellaneous Records by Master Kuya (1263)	枯崖漫録	Kuya Manlu; Kogai Manroku	Kuya Yuanwu
Mixed Records from the Mountain Hermitage (1375)	山庵雑録	Shan'an Zalu; San'an Zatsuroku	Shuzhong Wuyun
Nirvana Sutra (Mahāparinirvāna-Sūtra) (4th century)	大般涅槃経	Daban Niepan-jing; Daihatsu Nehan-kyō	unknown

Translated Title and Date of Composition	Chinese/Japanese Title	Author/Editor
Poem Collection of all Schools of Zen (1288)	江湖風月集	Jianghu Fengyueji; Gōko Fūgetsushū — Songpo Zongqi
Points to Watch in Studying the Way (1234)	学道用心集	Gakudō Yōjinshū — Dōgen
Precious Flowers of the Lamp Transmission (1034)	傳燈玉英集	Chuandeng Yuying-ji; Dentō Gyokuei-shū — Chengxiang Wangsui
Record from the (Chan) Groves (1107)	林間録	Linjianlu; Rinkanroku — Juefan Huihong
Record of Anecdotes from Lake Luo (1160)	羅湖野録	Luohuyelu; Rago Yaroku — Xiaoying Zhongwen
Record of Equanimity (1223)	從容録	Congronglu; Shōyōroku — Hongzhi Zhengjue
Record of the Correct Lineage of the Dharma Transmission (1061)	傳法正宗記	Chuanfa Zhengzongji; Denpō Seishūki — Fori Qisong
Records of Master Linji (1120)	臨済録	Linjilu; Rinzairoku — Sansheng Huiran
Records of Master Xutang (1269)	虚堂和尚語録	Xutang Heshang Yulu; Kidōroku/Kidō Oshō Goroku — Miaoyuan
Records of the Masters Sōzan und Tōzan (1741)	曹洞二師録	Sōtō Nishiroku — Gimoku Genkai
Shōbōgenzō (Written in Chinese) (1235)	真字正法眼藏	Shinji Shōbōgenzō — Dōgen
Song of Realization (late 7th century)	證道歌	Zhengdaoge; Shōdōka — Yongjia Yuanxue
Song of the Jewel Mirror Samadhi (9th century)	宝鏡三昧	Baojin Sanmei; Hōkyō Zanmai — Dongshan Lianjie
Song of Zazen (1720s)	坐禅和讃	Zazen Wasan — Hakuin

Translated Title and Date of Composition	Chinese/Japanese Title	Author/Editor
Sutra of the Three Thousand Names of the Buddhas of the Three Ages (unknown)	三劫三千諸佛名經	Sangō Sanzen Shobutsumei-kyō	unknown
Ten Normative Treatises on the Chan School (10th century)	宗門十規論	Zongmen Shigui-lun; Shūmon Jukki-ron	Fayan Wenyi
Ten Verses of Unfathomable Depth = Ten Poems by Chan Master Tong'an (Chang)cha (10th century)	十玄談 = 同安察禪師詩十首	Shixuantan = Tongan Cha chanshi shi shishou; Jūgendan = Dōan Satsu Zenji Shi Jisshu	Tong'an Changcha
The Eye of Humans and Gods (1188)	人天眼目	Rentian Yanmu; Ninden Ganmoku	Huiyan Zhizhao
The Merging of Difference and Sameness (8th century)	參同契	Cantongqi; Sandōkai	Shitou Xiqian
Transmission of the Treasure Grove (801)	寶林傳	Baolinzhuan; Hōrinden	Zhiju

Notes

1. 不立文字 Source unknown, first recorded in the ninth century.
2. For more on this point, see Harada Sensei's comments on the third of the Ten Verses.
3. Yoshio Nishiguchi, "Tōzenji-han Keitoku Dentōroku Kaidai" [Commentary on the Dongchan-si edition of the *Jingde Era Record of the Transmission of the Lamp*], in *Keitoku Dentōroku (Fushū Tōzenji-ban)*, ed. Zen Bunka Kenkyūsho, 3–11.
4. See Seizan Yanagida, "Daizōkyō to zenroku no nyūzō" [The Tripitaka and the inclusion of Chan records in the canon], in *Sōhan, Kōrai-bon Keitoku Dentōroku*, ed. Yanagida Seizan (Kyoto: Chūbun Shuppansha, 1976), 724–31; Albert Welter, "Mahākāśyapa's Smile: Silent Transmission and the Kung-an (Kōan) Tradition," in *The Kōan: Texts and Contexts in Zen Buddhism*, eds. Steve Heine and Dale S. Wright (Oxford: Oxford University Press, 2000), 92; Morten Schlütter, *How Zen Became Zen: The Dispute over Enlightenment and the Formation of Chan Buddhism in Song-Dynasty China* (Honolulu: University of Hawai'i Press, 2008), 22.
5. Beong-geun Yu, "*Jūgendan* o meguru mondai: *Jūgendan* no seiritsu ni tsuite" [A Problem Concerning the *Shixuantan*: The formation of the *Shixuantan*], in *Indogaku Bukkyogaku Kenkyū* 51, 2 (2003): 605–7.
6. For a detailed discussion, see Seizan Yanagida, "Kaisetsu [commentary]," in *Sodōshū (Daijō Butten 13)*, ed. Seizan Yanagida (Tokyo: Chūō Kōron-sha, 1990) 461–82.
7 家風 (jiafeng; kafū) A style of Chan/Zen that depends on the individuality of the particular master or lineage.
8. An allusion to the second of the Ten Verses.
9. An allusion to the ninth of the Ten Verses.
10. An allusion to the sixth of the Ten Verses.
11. An allusion to the fourth of the Ten Verses.
12. An allusion to the third of the Ten Verses.
13. An allusion to the eighth of the Ten Verses.
14. An allusion to the second of the Ten Verses.
15. An allusion to the second of the Ten Verses.
16. An allusion to the seventh and tenth of the Ten Verses.
17. An allusion to the sixth and seventh of the Ten Verses.
18. An allusion to the ninth of the Ten Verses.
19. An allusion to the third, fourth, and fifth of the Ten Verses.
20. An allusion to the fifth of the Ten Verses.
21. The source text, the Essentials, has a different ending for this dialogue, which goes as follows:

The master replied, "You are so smart, and I am so ignorant. Try to speak to the assembly."

The monk said, "What do you blame me for?"

The master said, "You only look at the sharpness of the gimlet and fail to see the squareness of the chisel."

22. An allusion to the seventh of the Ten Verses.

23. A great Chinese military strategist of the fourth century BCE.

24. In other words, the disciples were completely unable to understand his strategies.

25. An allusion to the fifth of the Ten Verses.

26. That is, being careful and kind.

27. Both the magpie and the juniper tree were auspicious symbols in ancient China.

28. An allusion to the first of the Ten Verses.

29. That is, although they drank milk on the advice of the doctors, they didn't appreciate the good advice.

30. A reference to the Buddha.

31. That is, he is like a newborn baby.

32. Yi-Hsun Huang, "Huayan Thought in Yanshou's *Guanxin Xuanshu*: Six Characteristics and Ten Profound Gates," in *Reflecting Mirrors: Perspectives on Huayan Buddhism*, ed. Imre Hamar (Wiesbaden: Harrassowitz, 2007), 241–59.

33. Matthias Obert, *Sinndeutung und Zeitlichkeit: Zur Hermeneutik des Huayan-Buddhismus* (Hamburg: Felix Meiner Verlag, 2000), 65–69.

34. Translation from Burton Watson's *Lao-tzu: Tao Te Ching* (Indianapolis: Hackett, 1993).

35. Wai-Lim Yip, *Chinese Poetry: An Anthology of Major Modes and Genres* (Durham: Duke University Press, 1997), 172–73.

36. Leslie Kawamura, "Bodhisattva(s)," in *Encyclopedia of Buddhism*, ed. Robert E. Buswell, Jr. (New York: Macmillan, 2004), 58–63.

37. Mario Poceski, *Ordinary Mind as the Way: The Hongzhou School and the Growth of Chan Buddhism* (Oxford: Oxford University Press, 2007), chapter 6.

38. The Chrestomathy gives the title "Before Stopping Ranks," but there the Chinese character for "stopping" (止) is apparently a corruption of the character for "absolute" (正).

39. *Shinpan Zengaku Daijiten* [Great Dictionary of Zen Studies], new ed., ed. Komazawa Daigakunai Zengaku Daijiten Henbōsho (Tokyo: Taishūkan, 1985), 252.

40. 印可証明

41. 以心傳心 This phrase appears in volume six of *Collection from the Ancestors' Hall*, but may be even earlier.

42. 一器水瀉一器 This line appears in *Shōbōgenzō, Gyōji*.

43. 平常心是道 This line appears in the tenth volume of *Transmission of the Lamp*, as case #19 in the *Gateless Barrier*, and in the *Records of Master Xutang*. It is attributed to Nanquan Puyuan.

44. 動静一如大衆、抜群無益 Found in *Pure Standards* and *Bendōhō*. Attributed to Dōgen.

45. 本證妙修 This line was coined in the Sōtō sect based on a passage from *Shōbōgenzō, Bendōwa*.

46. 教外別傳 This phrase appears in volume six of *Collection from the Ancestors' Hall*.

47. 玄之又玄 / 衆妙之門 This is from the opening verse of the *Daodejing*.

48. 古松談般若 遊鳥弄真如 From *The Eye of Humans and Gods*.

49. 逢茶喫茶。逢飯喫飯 From *Shogaku Kaisan Niso Zenji Gyōroku*.

50. 無所得無所悟 From *Shōbōgenzō, Zuimonki*, by Dōgen.

51. These words are from the Śuraṅgama-sūtra.

52. 天台 (Tiantai) East Asian Mahāyāna Buddhist school that venerates the Lotus Sutra.

53. 父母未生以前の面目 From *Shōbōgenzō, Keisei Sanshoku*.

54. 法戦式 (fazhanshi; hossenshiki) This is a "graduation" ceremony for a head monk.

55. 五葉 (wuye; goyō) The five petals can refer either to the five Chinese ancestors following Bodhidharma (that is, the second to sixth Chinese ancestors), or the five Chan sects that started to flourish in China thereafter.

56. Attributed to Onkō Jiun.

57. 人人具足箇箇円成 This line appears in *Dōgen's Extensive Record* and as case #62 in *Blue Cliff Record*.

58. 毫厘有差天地懸隔 From *Faith in Mind Inscription*, attributed to Jiangzhi Sengcan.

59. 去亦不變異 This line appears in the seventeenth volume of the *Jingde Era Record of the Transmission of the Lamp* and as case #30 in the *Shinji Shōbōgenzō*. It is attributed to Caoshan Benji.

60. 動中の禅は静中の禅に勝ること百千万倍 From *Wild Ivy* by Hakuin.

61. 冷暖自知 From the Platform Sutra of the Sixth Patriarch; the saying is attributed to Daoming (Huiming).

62. From *Under the Umbrella Pine*.

63. From the *Records of Master Gappa*.

64. 供養十方諸仏不如供養一個無心道人 This line appears in *Essential Dharma of the Transmission of the Mind*.

65. Translated by Mu Soeng in *The Diamond Sutra: Transforming the Way We Perceive the World* (Boston: Wisdom Publications, 2000), 155.

66. 魚行似魚 鳥飛如鳥 From the *Lancet of Zazen* by Dōgen.

67. 可以隨處作主遇縁即宗。 This line appears in case #47 of the *Gateless Barrier* by Wumen Huikai.

68. 三賢 (sanxian; sanken) The 1st to 30th (11th to 40th) rank (stage) on the 42(52)-stage bodhisattva path.

69. 十行 (shixing; jūgyō) The 11th to 20th (21st to 30th) rank (stage) on the 42(52)-stage bodhisattva path.

70. These are the "Five Houses of Chan" that developed during the Tang and Song dynasties. The Sōtō Sect 曹洞 (Caodong), going back to Dongshan Lianjie and Caoshan Benji, and the Rinzai Sect 臨済 (Linji), going back to

the figure of Linji Yixuan, have survived until the present. The Unmon Sect 雲門 (Yunmen), which goes back to Yunmen Wenyan, the Igyō Sect 潙仰 (Weiyang), which goes back to Guishan Lingyou and his disciple Yangshan Huiji, and the Hōgen Sect 法眼 (Fayan), which goes back to Fayan Wenyi, have all now been absorbed into the present day Rinzai Sect.

71. 佛道を習うというは自己を習うなり　自己を習うというは自己を忘るるなり From *Shōbōgenzō, Genjō Kōan.*

72. 端坐思実相。衆罪如霜露慧日能消除 This is from the Sutra of Contemplation of the Dharma Practice of Universal Sage Bodhisattva, a part of the three-fold Lotus Sutra.

73. この法は人人の分上にゆたかにそなはれりといへども、いまだ修せざるにはあらはれず、證せざるにはうることなし From *Shōbōgenzō, Bendōwa.*

74. 萬法歸一一歸何處。 This line appears in the tenth volume of the *Jingde Era Record of the Transmission of the Lamp.*

75. 習学 (xixue; shūgaku) A pejorative term for gradual meditation practice.

76. 修證不二 This line was coined in the Sōtō sect based on a passage from *Shōbōgenzō, Bendōwa.*

77. This formula is found in volume five of *Jingde Era Record of the Transmission of the Lamp* and in *Notes on What to be Aware of in Zazen* by Keizan Jōkin.

78. 此のものなくんば彼のものなし、此のものあるが故に彼のものあり The precise source of this line is unknown to the author, but something similar to it appears in the second chapter of *Zhuangzi.*

79. 本有圓成仏 何故為迷倒衆生。From *Crazy Cloud Anthology,* #550, by Kanzan Egen.

80. 實相無相 From the Lotus Sutra, this line also appears in the *Gateless Barrier.*

81. 通身心 Appears in Devarāja Pravara Prajñāpāramitā Sūtra and *Shōbōgenzō, Butsudō, Kattō.*

82. 無位眞人 面門出入 From the *Records of Master Linji.*

83. 眼横鼻直 From the Manzanji edition of *Dōgen's Extensive Record.*

84. From the *Bendōhō* 辨道法 chapter in Eihei Dōgen's *Pure Standards* (Shingi 清規).

85. 只須らく、十二時中、無理會の處にむかって、究め来たり、究め去るべし From the *Posthumous Admonitions of Kōzen Daitō Kokushi.*

86. 山下作一頭水牯牛去 This line appears in volume sixteen of *Collection from the Ancestors' Hall* and in volumes eight and nine of *Jingde Era Record of the Transmission of the Lamp.*

87. 臘八摂心 (laba shexin) Sesshin traditionally held in Zen monasteries at the beginning of the twelfth month in commemoration of the Buddha's enlightenment.

88. 本来無一物何処惹塵埃 From the *Platform Sutra of the Sixth Patriarch Dajian Huineng.*

89. 是法住法位。From the "Skillful Means" chapter of the Lotus Sutra.

90. 草木國土悉皆成佛 The source of this line is unknown, but it is primarily used by the Tendai, Shingon, and Kegon sects of Buddhism.

91. From *Taiheiki* by Keishō Ungaku.
92. 爲勇猛衆生成佛在於一念。爲懈怠者得果須滿三祇。This line is drawn from *Mirror of the Mind* by Yongmin Yanshou.
93. This poem appears in volume ten of *Jingde Era Record of the Transmission from the Lamp*, and as case #12 in *Gateless Barrier*. It is attributed to Changsha Jingcen.
94. 三界 (sangai) These are the realm of sensual desires (kāma-dhātu), the realm of form (rūpa-dhātu), and the formless, purely spiritual realm (arūpa-dhātu). The two higher realms are reserved for gods of higher achievement.
95. なんぢ、経にまどふ、経、なんぢをまよはさず。From *Shōbōgenzō, Bukkyō*.
96. 從聞思修入三摩地 This phrase appears in the Śūraṇgama Sutra.
97. 世界非世界是名世界
98. 扶律顯常 The precise source of this phrase is unknown, but it is a Tiantai/Tendai sect saying.
99. 語默動靜體安然 From *Song of Realization* by Yongjia Yuanxue.
100. 肯心自許 From *Song of the Jewel Mirror Samadhi*.
101. 大悟十八回、小悟その数を知らず From *Jottings at the Bamboo Window* (Yunqi Zhuhong), *The Tale of My Childhood*, and elsewhere. It is attributed to Hakuin.
102. This poem is from *Recorded Sayings of Chan Master Dahui Pujue* and is attributed to Dahui Zonggao.
103. 見有佛處急走過 無佛處不得住 Case #282 in the *Recorded Sayings of Master Zhaozhou*.
104. "The rank of absolute faith" commonly refers to enlightenment, and "the rank of saving people" commonly refers to post-enlightenment activities.
105. 禅は、佛法の総府なり This line is attributed to Minnan Eisai.
106. 身心脱落脱落身心 This line appears in *Shōbōgenzō*, where it is attributed to Tiantong Rujing.
107. 自己を忘るるといふは、万法に証せらるるなり 万法に証せらるるといふは、自己の心身および他己の心身をして脱落せしむなり From *Shōbōgenzō, Genjō Kōan*.
108. 觸處生涯隨分足 This is case #4 in *Record of Equanimity* by Tiantong Hongzhi.
109. 娑婆界 (suopojie; shaba-kai) The world of impurity and suffering, that is, the world in which we live.
110. 応無所住而生其心
111. 毫釐有差天地懸隔 This line appears in *Faith in Mind Inscription*, case #17 of *Record of Equanimity*, and as case #127 of *Fukan Zazengi*. It is attributed to Jiangzhi Sengcan.
112. 木人方歌 石女起舞 From *Song of the Jewel Mirror Samadhi* by Dongshan Liangjie.
113. 潛行密用 如愚如魯 只能相續 名主中主 From the *Song of the Jewel Mirror Samadhi*.
114. 五位 (wuwei; goi) The five ranks describe the relationship (harmonizing) between absolute and relative.
115. 汝被十二時使。老僧使得十二時 This is case #28 of the *Recorded Sayings of Master Zhaozhou*.

116. 劍樹 刀山 (jianshu daoshan; kenju tōsen) "Forest of swords and mountains of daggers" refer to a hell in Buddhism with trees whose leaves were actually blades. As soon as the person would enter the hell, a strong wind would blow, causing a whirlwind of sharp blades. Also refers to a death penalty in ancient China, where delinquents had to walk barefoot on swords and daggers that were set sharp side up.

117. 黙照枯坐 (mozhao kuzuo; mokushō koza) This is a pejorative term for Sōtō Zen practice from a Rinzai perspective. However, the term "silent illumination" was coined within the Sōtō tradition itself, by Hongzhi Zhenjue.

118. 佛道を修行する者は、先ず須く佛道を信ずべし…

119. 直指人心 見性成佛 This line is attributed to Bodhidharma, but first recorded by Yongmin Yanshou in the tenth century.

120. 頭上安頭 This line is found in volume sixteen of *Jingde Era Record of the Transmission of the Lamp*, case #34 of *Blue Cliff Record*, case #41 of *Record of Equanimity*, and in *Shōbōgenzō*.

121. This song is from Edo period Japan.

122. 坐禅は坐禅なり From *Shōbōgenzō* and *Lancet of Zazen* by Dōgen.

123. 十聖 (shisheng; jisshō) The 31st to 40th (41st to 50th) rank (stage) on the 42(52)-stage bodhisattva path.

124. 十住 (shizhu; jūjū) The 1st to 10th (11th to 20th) rank (stage) on the 42(52)-stage bodhisattva path.

125. 十廻向 (shihuixiang; jūekō) Ranks from the 21st to the 30th (31st to 40th) rank (stage) on the 42(52)-stage bodhisattva path.

126. The Chinese sentence in the poem contains two words for "and" following each other, which is clearly grammatically odd.

127. Mu'an Shanqing explicates the idea that the various Buddhist teachings as known in Tang period China are the product of different phases or periods in the historical Buddha's teaching during his lifetime. This idea was first developed in the Tang period Faxiang school, who posited three periods, and later developed especially in Tientai and Huayan Buddhism, who posited four or five periods.

128. 一闡提 In Mahāyāna Buddhism, icchantikas are the most base and deluded human beings, who indulge in an immoral lifestyle and despise Buddhist teachings.

129. The "four pāramitās of knowledge" taught in the Nirvana Sutra, which according to the Mahāyāna tradition can be enjoyed in nirvana.

130. This probably refers to the *Huayan-jing Shuchao*, a commentary on the Flower Garland Sutra by Chengguan.

131. cf. Schlutter 2008: 141–42.

132. An edition of the *Jingde Era Record of the Transmission of the Lamp*.

133. The lineage of Dharma transmission.

134. Literally, "After Passing One Color."

References

Addiss, Stephen. 2008. *Zen Sourcebook*. Edited with Stanley Lombardo and Judith Roitman. Indianapolis: Hackett.

Baroni, Helen J. 2000. *Obaku Zen: The Emergence of the Third Sect of Zen in Tokugawa Japan*. Honolulu: University of Hawai'i Press.

———— 2002. *The Illustrated Encyclopedia of Zen Buddhism*. New York: Rosen.

Blofeld, John. 1958. *The Zen Teaching of Huang Po on the Transmission of Mind*. New York: Grove Press.

Bodiford, William M. 1993. *Sōtō Zen in Medieval Japan*. Honolulu: University of Hawai'i Press.

Broughton, Jeffrey L. 1999. *The Bodhidharma Anthology: The Earliest Records of Zen*. Berkeley: University of California Press.

———— 2004. Fazang. In Buswell, Robert E. Jr. (ed.), 284.

Buswell, Robert E. Jr. (ed.). 2004. *Encyclopedia of Buddhism*. New York: Macmillan.

———— 2004. Icchantika. In Buswell, Robert E. Jr. (ed.), 351.

Cuevas, Bryan J. 2004. Rebirth. In Buswell, Robert E. Jr. (ed.), 712–14.

DuBois, Thomas. 2004. Millenarianism and millenarian movements. In Buswell, Robert E. Jr. (ed.), 527–30.

Dumoulin, Heinrich. 1988. *Zen Buddhism: A History, vol. 1. India and China*. Translated by James W. Heisig and Paul Knitter. New York: Macmillan.

———— 1990. *Zen Buddhism: A History, vol. 2. Japan*. Translated by James W. Heisig and Paul Knitter. New York: Macmillan.

Faure, Bernard. 2000. Quand l'habit fait le moine: the symbolism of the kasyapa in Sōtō Zen. In Faure, Bernard (ed.), *Chan Buddhism in a Ritual Context*, 211–49. London: Routledge Curzon.

Gethin, Rupert. 2004. Cosmology. In Buswell, Robert E. Jr. (ed.), 183–87.

Getz, Daniel A. 2004. Sentient beings. In Buswell, Robert E. Jr. (ed.), 760–61.

Graham, A. C. 1981. *Chuang-tzŭ: The Seven Inner Chapters and other writings from the book Chuang-tzŭ*. London: George Allan.

Green, James. 1998. *The Recorded Sayings of Zen Master Joshu*. Boston: Shambhala.

Hamar, Imre. 2007. A Huayan paradigm for the classification of Mahāyāna teachings: the origin and meaning of Faxiangzong and Faxingzong. In Hamar, Imre (ed.), *Reflecting Mirrors: Perspectives on Huayan Buddhism*, 195–220. Wiesbaden: Harrassowitz.

Harada, Sekkei. 1996. *Sandōkai Fusetsu* [Lectures on the *Cantongqing*]. Tōkyō: Penhouse.

———— 2008. *The Essence of Zen*. Boston: Wisdom Publications.

Hori, Victor Sōgen. 2005. Kōan and Kenshō in the Rinzai Zen curriculum. In Heine, Steven, and Dale S. Wright (eds.), *The Koan: Texts and Contexts in Zen Buddhism*, 280–315. Oxford: Oxford University Press.

Huang, Yi-Hsun. 2001. A Study of Yongming Yanshou's *The Profound Pivot of Contemplation of Mind*. PhD dissertation. University of Virginia.

———— 2007. Huayan thought in Yanshou's *Guanxin Xuanshu*: six characteristics and ten profound gates. In Hamar, Imre (ed.), *Reflecting Mirrors: Perspectives on Huayan Buddhism*, 241–59. Wiesbaden: Harrassowitz.

Jaffe, Richard M. 2004. Meiji Buddhist reform. In Buswell, Robert E. Jr. (ed.), 530–31.

Jōban, Yoshinobu. 2005. Hisamatsu-sensei no iwayuru Yuimakyō kyōjō kōan [The Vimalakirti Sutra teaching and vehicle kōan according to Hisamatsu]. *Fūshin 52*.

Jorgensen, John. 2005. *Inventing Hui-Neng, the Sixth Patriarch: Hagiography and Biography in Early Ch'an*. Leiden: Brill.

Kagamishima, Genryū. 1988. Kaidai [Interpretation]. In *Dōgen Zenji Zenshū* 4: *Eihei Kōroku*, 299–329. Tokyo: Shunjūsha.

Kawamura, Leslie. 2004. Bodhisattva(s). In Buswell, Robert E. Jr. (ed.), 58–63.

Kinami, Takuichi. 1976. *Jiun Sonja Wakashū* [Collection of Japanese Poems by Jiun Sonja]. Kyoto: Sanmitsudō.

Kraft, Kenneth. 1992. *Eloquent Zen. Daitō and Early Japanese Zen*. Honolulu: University of Hawai'i Press.

Leighton, Taigen D., and Shohaku Okumura. 1996. *Dōgen's Pure Standards for the Zen Community*. New York: State University of New York Press.

———— 2004. *Dōgen's Extensive Record: A Translation of the Eihei Kōroku*. Boston: Wisdom Publications.

McRae, John R. 2000. *The Platform Sutra of the Sixth Patriarch: Translated from the Chinese of Zongbao*. Berkeley: Numata Center for Buddhist Translation and Research.

———— 2003. *Seeing Through Zen: Encounter, Transformation, and Genealogy in Chinese Chan Buddhism*. Berkeley: UC Press.

Morohashi, Tetsuji. 1984–1986. *Dai-Kanwa Jiten* [Great Chinese-Japanese Dictionary]. Tokyo: Taishūkan Shoten.

Morrison, Elizabeth. 2010. *The Power of Patriarchs: Qisong and Lineage in Chinese Buddhism*. Leiden: Brill.

Muller, Charles E. 2009. *The Diamond Sūtra* (translation). Nantou: Chung Tai Translation Committee.

Nakamura, Hajime. 1981. *Bukkyōgo Daijiten* [Great Dictionary of Buddhist Terms]. Tokyo: Tokyo Shoseki.

Nishiguchi, Yoshio. 1990. Tōzenji-han *Keitoku Dentōroku* kaidai [Commentary on the Dongchan-si edition of the *Jingde Era Record of the Transmission of the Lamp*]. In Zen Bunka Kenkyūsho (ed.), *Keitoku Dentōroku (Fushū Tōzenji-ban)*, 3–11.

Nishiyama, Kōsen, and John Stevens. 1975–1983. *A Complete English Translation of Dōgen Zenji's Shōbōgenzō The Eye and Treasury of the True Law)*. 3 vols. Tokyo: Daihokkaikaku.

Obert, Matthias. 2000. *Sinndeutung und Zeitlichkeit: Zur Hermeneutik des Huayan-Buddhismus*. Hamburg: Felix Meiner Verlag.

Ogata, Sohaku. 1990. *The Transmission of the Lamp: Early Masters*. Wolfeboro: Longwood Academic.

Ōtake, Susumu. 2007. On the Origin and Early Development of the *Buddhā-vatamsaka-sutra*. In Hamar, Imre (ed.), *Reflecting Mirrors: Perspectives on Huayan Buddhism*, 87–107. Wiesbaden: Harrassowitz.

Poceski, 2004. Huayan school. In Buswell, Robert E. Jr. (ed.), 341–47.

—— 2007. *Ordinary Mind as the Way. The Hongzhou School and the Growth of Chan Buddhism*. Oxford: Oxford University Press.

Power, John. 2004. Hermeneutics. In Buswell, Robert E. Jr. (ed.), 320–21.

Sasaki, Ruth Fuller. 2009. *The Record of Linji*. Edited by Thomas Yūhō Kirchner. Honolulu: University of Hawai'i Press.

Schopen, Gregory. 2004. Diamond Sūtra. In Buswell, Robert E. Jr. (ed.), 58–60.

Schlütter, Morten. 2008. *How Zen Became Zen: The Dispute over Enlightenment and the Formation of Chan Buddhism in Song-Dynasty China*. Honolulu: University of Hawai'i Press.

Shibayama, Zenkei. 2000. *The Gateless Barrier: Zen Comments on the Mumonkan*. Boston: Shambhala.

Shih, Heng-ching. 1992. *The Syncretism of Ch'an and Pure Land Buddhism*. New York: Peter Lang.

Sim, Kyung-ho. 2009. 17-seiki ikō no nihon kangaku to chōsen kangaku no rekishiteki setten ni tsuite [On the historical relationship between Japanese and Korean Chinese Studies from the 17th century on]. *Meiji University Ancient Studies of Japan* 1: 13–23.

Stone, Jacqueline I. 2004. Lotus Sūtra. In Buswell, Robert E. Jr. (ed.), 471–77.

Waddell, Norman. 1999. *Wild Ivy: The Spiritual Autobiography of Zen Master Hakuin*. Boston: Shambhala.

—— 2009. *Hakuin's Precious Mirror Cave*. Berkeley: Counterpoint.

Watson, Burton. 1993. *Lao-tzu: Tao Te Ching*. Indianapolis: Hackett.

Welter, Albert. 2000. Mahākāśyapa's smile: Silent transmission and the kung-an (kōan) tradition. In Heine, Steve, and Dale S. Wright (eds.), *The Kōan: Texts and Contexts in Zen Buddhism*, 75–109. Oxford: Oxford University Press.

—— 2004. Lineage. In Buswell, Robert E. Jr. (ed.), 461–65.

—— 2008. *The* Linji lu *and the Creation of Chan Orthodoxy: The Development of Chan's Records of Sayings Literature*. Oxford: Oxford Unversity Press.

—— 2011. *Yongming Yanshou's Conception of Chan in the* Zongjing Lu. A Special Transmission within the Scriptures. Oxford: Oxford University Press.

Williams, Paul. 2004. Nāgārjuna. In Buswell, Robert E. Jr. (ed.), 581–82.

Yampolsky, Philipp. 1967. *The Platform Sutra of the Sixth Patriarch. The Text of the Tun-Huang Manuscript*. New York: Columbia University Press.

—— 1971. *The Zen Master Hakuin: Selected Writings*. New York: Columbia Press.

Yanagida, Seizan. 1976. Daizōkyō to zenroku no nyūzō [The Tripitaka and the inclusion of Chan records in the canon]. In Yanagida Seizan: *Sōhan, Kōrai-bon Keitoku Dentōroku*, 724–31. Kyoto: Chūbun Shuppansha.

———— 1990. Kaisetsu [commentary]. In Yanagida, Seizan, *Sodōshū (Daijō Butten* 13), 461–82. Tokyo: Chūō Kōronsha.

Yip, Wai-Lim. 1997. *Chinese Poetry: An Anthology of Major Modes and Genres.* Durham: Duke University Press.

Yoshisawa, Shōkō. 2002. Zazen Wasan. In Yoshisawa, Shōkō (ed.), *Kohiki-uta; Zazen Wasan, Chobokure* (Hakuin Zenji Hōgo Zenshū 13), 256–68. Tōkyō: Zen Bunka Kenkyūjo.

Yoshizu, Yoshihide. 1985. *Kegon Zen no Shisōshiteki Kenkyū* [Studies on the Historical Thought of Huayan Chan]. Tokyo: Daitō Shuppansha.

Yu, Beong-geun. 2003. *Jūgendan* o meguru mondai: *Jūgendan* no seiritsu ni tsuite [A problem concerning the *Shixuantan*: The formation of the *Shixuantan*]. *Indogaku Bukkyogaku Kenkyū* 51/2, 605–7.

ZGD = Komazawa Daigakunai Zengaku Daijiten Henbōsho (ed). 1985. *Shinpan Zengaku Daijiten* [Great Dictionary of Zen Studies]. New edition. Tokyo: Taishūkan.

Index

About the Author and Translators

 Sekkei Harada is the abbot of Hosshinji, a Sōtō Zen training monastery and temple, in Fukui Prefecture, near the coast of central Japan. He was born in 1926 in Okazaki, near Nagoya, and was ordained at Hosshinji in 1951. In 1953, he went to Hamamatsu to practice under Zen Master Gien Inoue and received *inkashomei* (certification of realization) in 1957. In 1974 he was installed as resident priest and abbot of Hosshinji and was formally recognized by the Sōtō Zen sect as a certified Zen master (*shike*) in 1976. Since 1982 Harada has traveled abroad frequently, teaching in such countries as Germany, France, the United States, and India. From 2003 to 2005 he was director of the Soto Zen Buddhism Europe Office located in Milan. He currently resides at Hosshinji Monastery. He's the author of *The Essence of Zen*.

Daigaku Rummé was born in 1950 in Mason City, Iowa. In 1976 he entered Hosshinji Monastery as a layman, where Harada Roshi ordained him in 1978. He lived and practiced at Hosshinji until 2003. On several occasions he accompanied Harada as his interpreter on visits to Europe, India, and the United States. Rummé is the head priest of Zenshuji Soto Temple in Los Angeles and director of the Association of Soto Zen Buddhists.

Heiko Narrog was born in 1965 in Karlsruhe, Germany. He has a PhD in Japanese Studies from Ruhr University, Bochum, and a PhD in linguistics from Tokyo University. He has practiced at Hosshinji with Harada Roshi since 1986 and is currently associate professor at Tohoku University in Sendai, Japan.

About Wisdom Publications

WISDOM PUBLICATIONS is the leading publisher of classic and contemporary Buddhist books and practical works on mindfulness. Publishing books from all major Buddhist traditions, Wisdom is a nonprofit charitable organization dedicated to cultivating Buddhist voices the world over, advancing critical scholarship, and preserving and sharing Buddhist literary culture.

To learn more about us or to explore our other books, please visit our website at www.wisdompubs.org. You can subscribe to our eNewsletter, request a print catalog, and find out how you can help support Wisdom's mission either online or by writing to:

Wisdom Publications
199 Elm Street
Somerville, Massachusetts 02144 USA

You can also contact us at 617-776-7416 or info@wisdompubs.org.

Wisdom is a 501(c)(3) organization, and donations in support of our mission are tax deductible.

Wisdom Publications is affiliated with the Foundation for the Preservation of the Mahayana Tradition (FPMT).

Also Available from Wisdom Publications

The Essence of Zen
The Teachings of Sekkei Harada
Sekkei Harada
Translated and edited by Daigaku Rummé
176 pages, $15.95, ebook $11.62

"A book that deserves to be read and reread."—Zen Master Dae Gak

The Zen Teaching of Homeless Kodo
Kosho Uchiyama Roshi and Shohaku Okumura
Edited by Jokei Molly Delight Whitehead
232 pages, $17.95, ebook $11.99

"Kodo Sawaki was straight-to-the-point, irreverent, and deeply insightful—and one of the most influential Zen teachers for us in the West. I'm very happy to see this book."—Brad Warner, author of *Hardcore Zen*

The Hidden Lamp
Stories from Twenty-Five Centuries of Awakened Women

Edited by Zenshin Florence Caplow and Reigetsu Susan Moon
Foreword by Zoketsu Norman Fischer
440 pages, $18.95, ebook $13.81

"An amazing collection. This book gives the wonderful feel of the sincerity, the great range, and the nobility of the spiritual work that women are doing and have been doing, unacknowledged, for a very long time. An essential and delightful book."—John Tarrant, author of *Bring Me The Rhinoceros: And Other Zen Koans That Will Save Your Life*

Dongshan's Five Ranks
Keys to Enlightenment
Ross Bolleter
320 pages, $18.95, ebook $11.99

"Very well done."—Robert Aitken, author of *Taking the Path of Zen*

DŌGEN'S EXTENSIVE RECORD
A Translation of the Eihei Kōroku
Translated by Taigen Dan Leighton and Shohaku Okumura
824 pages, $26.95, ebook $19.63

"A labor of love and a generous offering to those who choose to wander beyond the beaten path."—*Inquiring Mind*

EIHEI DŌGEN
Mystical Realist
Hee-Jin Kim
368 pages, $19.95, ebook $14.53

"A essential volume in any Dōgen library."—Zoketsu Norman Fischer

THE BOOK OF MU
Essential Writings on Zen's Most Important Koan
Edited by James Ishmael Ford and Melissa Myozen Blacker
Foreword by John Tarrant
352 pages, $17.95, ebook $13.08

"The most important of all koans finally gets the attention it deserves. A very valuable book."—David R. Loy, author of *Money, Sex, War, Karma*

ON ZEN PRACTICE
Body, Breath, and Mind
Taizan Maezumi Roshi and Bernard Tetsugen Glassman
Foreword by Robert Aitken
208 pages, $14.95, ebook $10.89

"I recommend it to beginners and advanced Zen practitioners. It is challenging, wise, and encouraging."—Roshi Pat Enkyo O'Hara, abbot of the Village Zendo (NYC)